Dragonfly Dreams

Dragonflies
Blue and green armored
There's something about dragonflies
something quite ancient

*Bunny ~ Watson
and
Tim Veryzer
august 2, 2018*

TIM VERYZER

PAGE PUBLISHING, INC.
New York, NY

First originally published by Page Publishing, Inc. 2018

ISBN 978-1-64138-774-3 (Paperback)
ISBN 978-1-64138-776-7 (Digital)

Printed in the United States of America

'Dragonfly Dreams' is dedicated
to my beloved Watson and Bunny

Contents

Green Fire

An immaculate wolf looks out over the swamp
where the universe ends
in its eyes green fire
The stars shine from indigo skies
clouds drift over frogs slumbering in mud blankets
their countless eyes are
green fire
Green fire in the sky
green fire in the cave
green fire in the wild dogs eyes
way back in the deep woods swamp
Floating in winter air
above shadow pines
a ball of green fire
A catamount awakens and looks out over
whispering brown cattails
with eyes of

green fire
Shimmering up through the ice
of a bottomless swamp woods pond
green fire
The ancient creature awakens in its deadfall cave
it has lived for eons
its timeless eyes are
green fire
A coyote stalks its prey
in sub-zero winter
its eyes glow
green fire
A majestic owl calls out to the woods in darkness
a gentle tan rabbit crawls into its hutch
to sleep the night away
it closes its eyes
they are green fire

The Amazon

Inside a gray driftwood box, this much-weathered journal was discovered by one J. Handicott Jebson, a midshipman aboard the clipper ship *Carfax*. The box was tangled in some seaweed that was part of a vast seaweed island in which many rotting wooden sailing ships were entrapped. The mysterious island was floating somewhere in the Sargasso Sea area of the uncharted mid-Atlantic. Jebson said he and other crewmen saw giant squids, jellyfishes the size of whales, and glowing giant red fireworms crawling in and out of the fetid weed. The stench from the drifting island of flotsam and ghost ships caused Jebson's eyes to water. The *Carfax* did not stay long at the forlorn island of writhing monsters and decaying weed. These pages are taken from the journal of Sarah Briggs, and they tell an amazing story.

The Journal of Sarah Briggs

Friday, November 24, 1872

> Weather, clear. Strong winds from northwest. Latitude, 38°. Longitude, 17°40'14" west.
> And I looked, and, behold, a whirlwind came out of the north, a great cloud, and a fire infolding itself, and a brightness was about it, and out of the midst thereof as the color of gleaming bronze, out of the midst of the fire."
> —Ezekiel 1:4

Benjamin woke me at three bells to come on deck and see an amazing light. I gathered little Sophie up in her new red Christmas blanket with snowmen, stars, and green pine trees upon it, which I had just finished, followed by our liver and white English springer spaniel Royal, we scrambled up onto the deck of the brigantine.

Benjamin was commissioned by the owner of the *Marie Celeste*, a Mr. Mycroft Watson, because he had experience during the Great War as the captain of a navy vessel that carried munitions at all times. We sailed out of New York Harbor on the sixteenth of November bound for the African coast. The cargo aboard this voyage is 1,700 barrels of pure alcohol, a highly volatile chemical.

I never leave Sophie on this ship, this ship that was once named the *Amazon*. After she rammed and sank the freighter ship *Hiedelberg* and her captain died of a mysterious illness, the *Amazon* was considered a cursed vessel. When her name was changed to the *Marie Celeste*, most sailors would not set foot on the decks of the ship. I am uneasy sailing on this vessel in which I am not welcome on as the crew looks upon a woman aboard as a Jonah, a thing of ill omen. Further, I fear the ship herself. She has an evil aura. When she passes, she leaves a sickly-yellow tinge upon the firmament.

Benjamin has told me that the night watch woke him. Upon going on deck, we witnessed a very strange sight. The sky was a blanket of dark blue, the stars shimmered, and in the western sky, a brilliant green light in the shape of a giant elongated orb, floated slowly to our west was showing. Thinking it a star or planet or comet, I sighed in astonishment. Royal Flying jib, sat staring at the mysterious glowing object.

Several of the men made ominous mutterings and pointed at the thing. My captain looked at it through his spyglass. Suddenly, the greenish shape, as it was shaped like a gigantic walnut, moved straight up and stopped, hovering like a massive cloud forty times as big as our ship. After some minutes, the light moved a great distance to the east of our position. It moved so fast that we saw only a blue-green streak as evidence of its movement.

I recalled that Captain Colombus and his crew witnessed strange green Saint Elmo's firelights. The highly credible reverend Cotton

Mather wrote a long account of his viewing of moving lights in the night sky. Many conquistadors wrote of seeing unearthly glowing objects. Captain Megellen and his men also saw green-blue lights. I believe these lights were seen in the skies and below the seas.

A runic inscription found in the province of Hälsingland, Sweden, tells of a voyage by Vidor Viking in the eleventh century. The runes tell of strange green and yellow lights seen in the skies as the Vikings crossed the Atlantic to Vineland (*Viking* for America) on their way to mine copper in Michigan's Upper Peninsula. An ancient circle of mammoth stones similar to the ones found at Stonehenge, having a circled cross and an ancient ship carved on two of the stones, was found atop Mount Huron in the Upper Peninsula by the Vikings. The runes say the altar marked a valued spot from which to view the mysterious lights.

Suddenly, the edges of the light turned yellow, and the craft was upon us! It was, perhaps, twenty leagues off our port side. The thing appeared as a great yellow-green moon that had the general shape of a giant walnut. It was as wide as if forty of our brigantines were placed end to end in an arc. The curious object changed from the yellow-ish color back to the green-blue color. I felt becalmed, as if bathed in soothing tropical twilight. The craft from beyond, for surely this glowing thing was not a natural occurrence, now hovered not sixty yards from the gunwales of our north, facing the port side. The orb then shot up into the darkness at unknown speeds and appreared to wink out, disappearing.

I know not what this thing is. I, being one who can sense ghosts, although Benjamin forbids me to speak of this, sense no ghostly pres-ence about the light. Somehow, however, I sense that it is not of the Lord. Yet I feel no evil emanating from it.

SB, Saturday, November 25, 1872

Nine bells, morning. Terrible thunderstorms.

Our voyage has been uneventful, save for the venting of noxious fumes and smoke from the storage holds four days ago. The damaged kegs that caused the loss of our longboat, leaving only a yal in case of disaster, caused the deadly, flammable fumes. We were lucky young John Martian (Little John), the blind cabin boy, went below to practice his flute as it was he who discovered the fumes.

The giant orb has returned! Royal lay on the deck unafraid as she watched it carefully. We have all, all except perhaps the unusual Indian, Nicomus, come to realize, after observing this astonishing light, what dire straits we may be in.

The blue-green walnut-shaped thing has, except for vanishing straight up in a flash, only to return, changed by having a glowing ring of yellow sunshine surrounding it and radiating from the craft, as we now call the flying, hovering form. The seamen say it must be controlled by some beings or force as no comet could do what they have witnessed the gigantic craft do with their own eyes. After hovering off our port bow for the entire day, the craft returned to its blue-green, aqua coloration and abruptly dove beneath the gray waves like some great leviathan, making not a sound or causing any commotion of the surface of the sea as it vanished.

The craft returned and lay below our ship for the night. For some reason of unnatural form, the *Marie Celeste* will not move from the spot we have been in since we encountered the glowing thing. Seamen brothers Big John and Chris Martian, who served under Benjamin aboard an iron clad ship during the War of the Great Rebellion, took the yal to ascertain why the ship is suspended so. At about six hundred yards, the yal struck an invisible wall. As the pair were rowing fast, the hull cracked, sending the small boat below rapidly. The sailors swam back to the ship unharmed. The sea surrounding us is calm, as if we are encircled by a clear wall.

The deck has been bright at night, interrupting the natural sleeping routines of the sailors. The whole crew is half-crazed with fear. I am glad there are no cannons, guns, or strong drinks aboard as these men, although good-natured, could become violent, except for the odd Indian, Nicomus. I do not feel even cannonballs could damage this craft of green light. By acting negatively toward the ship of light, we might, in fact, anger whatever force or beings are associated with it. The craft that now resembles a gigantic deep sea behemoth like the one written about in Job 40:15–24, 41:1–34.

Regarding the mysterious Mascouten Indian, Nicomus, well, the kindhearted Benjamin adopted him. He had lived in a swamp-cave not far from our large log cabin back in Northern Michigan. The land surrounding our cabin is called the Dead-Stream Swamp, or the Long Crossing Swamp. To the Mascoutens, this country of mist and marsh was very sacred. The Indian legends speak of bottomless pools and bogs that are guarded by balls of red or green fire. They sometimes spoke in hushed tones about the great water spirit that guarded the swamp-woods. It appeared as a giant ball of green light that resembled a small moon. Hovering above certain obscure ponds, the green moon spirit drank by drawing water up into itself. To the Mascoutens, it looked as if the great water spirit was making tornadoes of water as it drank. The whirlpools left behind often stayed for weeks. The swamp forest consists of vast stretches of cattail marsh, streams, quicksand, and islands that form around ancient gigantic pines.

Nicomus was of the great wolf clan. His facial features are Nordic. Ancient tales tell of the first Mascouten chief. They say that he came from across the sea in a big canoe that had the head of a serpent carved into its bow. Many children of the tribe were born with light-brown or blond hair and blue eyes. I do not know how old he is. Maybe forty or fifty, I would guess. His skin is like brown leather. Wabby his coyote-like dog with gold-coin eyes and zebra stripes never leaves his side. The two seem to talk to each other with their eyes. He moves like a wolf and has piercing green eyes that seem to see into one's soul. He had been the medicine man of his tribe. He was said to also be a bearwalker, an immortal being who can change into a ball of green light or become a bear at will. His Indian name is Wab-Wak-Ashaw, which means Little White Fox. According to Nicomus, his people were slaughtered by the Potawatomis tribe that lived to the northeast because the Mascouten tribe knew where the fountain of youth was. The conquistadors had been wrong. According to stories passed down from the Mascouten tribal elders, the legendary fountain lay not in Florida but in the territory of Michigan. The old medicine man had been horribly tortured by the Potawatomis, who did not kill him because they feared he would return as a bear or a fireball and destroy them.

SB, Sunday, November 26, 1872,

Nine bells, night. Weather, clear. Wind, six knots from northwest.

I watched the shimmering blue-green craft burst from the waves, so smooth, not like a whale, which causes a great frothy commotion among the waves but with not even a ripple or small wave. It now hovers in its original position just to the northeast of us. Oddly, around the same time as the appearance of the starlike thing Sophie's illness vanished. Her blue eyes have cleared, and the deep cough and lung fever that caused us so much concern are also gone. This is a great burden removed from us as we feared the yellow fever or consumption was upon our dear one.

An amazing thing transpired before our eyes this night, for the bright walnut-shaped thing suddenly changed from being blue green in the star-filled indigo sky to a bright yellow-orange color. It suddenly became day aboard the *Marie Celeste*!

"Look there, off our port side," Chris Martian called from behind the ship's wheel.

Looking, we all saw a thing, a creature, emerging from the sea. A creature like none have ever seen before. It was the size of a barn standing on the end. It glowed pale pink, the color of salmon fish flesh. Vertical lines having cilia ran the length of its barrel-shaped, bulbous body. Three massive tentacles extended from its middle, writhing and lashing out at the ether. Long cilia undulated from the barrel-like top and bottom of the beast. This grotesque creature did not swim but hovered above the sea, somehow suspended on a cushion of air. Oddly, Royal followed this barrel thing with her eyes. As it drifted over the dark waters toward us, the crewmen began to display signs of panic. There was nothing they could do. We have no guns as after Benjamin's war experiences, he didn't allow any guns or strong drinks aboard. We only have knives and Benjamin's old broken sword, which is used to stir paint.

SB, Monday, November 27, 1872, Sophie's Sixth Finger

Four bells, morning. Weather, clear, calm.

I awoke to some wonderful, although unexplainable, discoveries! First, I was awakened by my dear Benjamin, who kissed me very passionately. He said, "Sophie is awake and has climbed out of her cradle. How, I don't know, but she has climbed out." He is now on deck, surveying the strange craft.

Next, to my amazement, Sophie, who is two and had not walked as yet, had somehow been up in the night for her cradle was empty, as Benjamin said. I found her sitting on the floor, playing with her doll and her wooden blocks. I was astonished to notice that during the night, Sophie had developed the nub of a sixth finger just below the knuckles of each of her baby fingers!

After Sophie ate much hash and bread and butter, for which I also had a hearty appetite, I took her on deck. Or should I say she took me, for she now suddenly had much strength and almost pulled me up the steps! On deck, Sophie, who screamed and cried when she first viewed the blue-green oddity, giggled (which she had never done, being melancholic to the point that our doctor proclaimed she had Usher's sickness). Sophie sat down calmly on a coiled rope and watched as thousands of orange monarch butterflies swirled in the sky.

The otherworldly creature that appeared yesterday had eventually floated up onto the deck. Benjamin ordered that no one interfere with it as it floated over the planks, which was good as several of the men had drawn their knives or reached for belaying pins. The obtuse creature then released from its underside a duplicate of itself not much more than the size of a wooden barrel. It floated below the decks to explore. After some twenty or so minutes, the smaller barrel octopus ascended to the deck. Our faithful Royal followed the bizarre beast wagging her long tail gently. To my horror, it went over to Sophie, whose hand I tightly grasped, and lightly brushed her cheek with a purplish tentacle. Oddly, rather than fear and terror, I felt warmth, as if I had eaten much chocolate. The thing then floated over to the larger barrel creature and vanished up under it. The barn-sized sea behemoth glided out over the waves and gently floated up into the glowing craft.

Then an even stranger phenomenon occurred. The walnut craft transformed back to its soothing blue-green color. As it was silhouetted by the red sky of morning, a million, billion butterflies appeared. Not just monarchs but all types and colors of the species—tiger swallowtails of yellow and black, orange and brown buckeyes, and great purple hairstreaks. Giant green darner dragonflies, armored in shimmering green and blue hovered and flew about as well. They were able to go through the invisible wall, and some landed on us at times. Sophie laughed and giggled. She struggled to have me lose her tiny hand; this I would not do.

When midday arrived, I helped Chris make a large lunch for all: sweet corn, country ham, honey wheat biscuits, and wooden mugs of chocolate cocoa and milk from the cow aboard, Anna Bell Lee. We all ate topside, using planks for a table. We ate as one big family. Even the one who had no tongue, Nicomus, shared our table. I thought I spied a small smile upon his lips as he munched the buttery corn, which he much oversalted.

SB, Tuesday, November 28, 1872,

Eight bells, morning. Weather, stormy. Wind, northwest, four knots.

The seas have become mountains of dark-blue rock with frothy caps. Benjamin fears we are in for a gale as the morning sky is pink. When I awoke at four bells, Sophie was already up and out of her crib. Although it was dark in our cabin last night, I find she has made a strange design on the floor with assorted objects, a top, spools of colored thread, and so forth. The large figure, as it is about ten feet by six, appears to be of an immense dragonfly. What metamorphosis is transforming my beautiful child, O Lord! What will she become? I can't help but to weep with fear and confusion.

After a fine breakfast of crispy bacon, wheat cakes, eggs, and the juice of apples, we went on deck to see an amazing sight. The strange craft had now transformed so that purple hues highlighted its form. It resembled a gigantic salamander with a massive triangular head, a behemoth sea monster from the deepest depths. Its purple outline glowed against a sky the color of storm as it ascended.

The storm that moved us not. The storm, somehow, was kept at bay. The clear wall had expanded. Within this gigantic sphere of clear protection, somehow, have begun to come again dragonflies! Not just any dragonflies for some measured sixty feet or so across the wings. Many glowed with colors out of space, shiny oranges, green, and purples unknown to us. How can such things be? Among them were green darners adorned in shimmering green and blue armor, violet tails, red skimmers, and monarch butterflies the size of kites. As they moved and hovered above and around us, we stared in astonishment.

SB, Wednesday, November 29, 1872

Four bells, morning.

I awoke to find that I had a strange tingling in both of my feet and ankles. Upon lifting the comforter, I was shocked to see a green light, a Saint Elmo's Fire, dancing around them! As I cried out and reached for Benjamin, I felt that he was gone. I saw that his leather-bound gold leaf copy of Mr. Charles Dickens's *A Christmas Carol* lay open to stave 3, in which the second spirit comes to Ebenezer Scrooge from the stars too aid in his reclamation.

From my melodeon came the softest, most soothing music that I have ever heard. Upon rising and lighting the lamp, I saw that it was our beloved Sophie using twelve fingers to play the sweet tune, Royal lay nearby mesmerized. I am amazed at the metamorphosis of our daughter! I realized as I looked to my feet that the green glow had vanished and that the horrible pains I had from a fall off a cliff when I was seven were no more!

Sophie, Royal and I went up on deck at around six bells. Upon arriving, I noticed that the ship was free and rolled with the waves. I observed these few miraculous changes: Nicomus, who's tongue had been cut out, spoke; Chris Martin, who was lame from a war wound, could walk; Royal (Flying jib) our aging English Sprinyer Spanial was restored to youth and ran about the deck happily after Little John, who shrieked and giggled with excitement as he saw things for the first time, for the lad was no longer blind!

The shimmering craft floated along with us off our starboard side. Its color was the light green of the underside of a fern leaf. The brig sailed along briskly in the winds, which were coming from the northeast. The topgallant, four masts, and jib sail were all fully billowed out. Benjamin was at the wheel. The glowing large green craft hovered about sixty yards off our port bow. It stood out majestically against the sky of purple twilight.

As we sat nearby the strange Indian, Nicomus and his dog walked slowly over to us. I was shocked as he spoke using very good King's English.

"We are the guardians of the water of life everlasting. My coywolf and I were hunting a giant boar ten thousand years ago. The boar gored my upper left thigh. My coywolf killed the beast. She was also badly injured. When two sabertooth tigers came in, having smelled the fresh blood, we took cover under a large deadfall of trees. The massive cats kept us under the rotting trees and stumps for weeks. We ate moss and bark. We drank from a pond hidden under the fallen trees. Our wounds quickly healed, and we both grew strong.

"Soon after we crawled out into the sun, a large green orb of fire appeared. A voice told us many strange and wonderful things. The voice asked if we would guard the pond. We, of course, said yes." Nicomus paused. "Captain Briggs, how would you and your kind wife and Sophie like to go to a place covered with shallow tranquil aqua, Permian seas, and green islands with pine trees three miles high? A world with no cruelty, evil, or death, only constant winds and gentle giant blue and orange beetles?"

Nicomus took a deep breath and finished by saying, "If you wish you may travel with Wabby and I to a tranquil planet that has endless giant flowers of the most fantastic and pleasing colors and fragrances, and giant fruits and vegetables. There are oranges and green caterpillars as long as the necks of three giraffes. We will soar over tranquil light blue lakes and vast swamp lands riding blue and green armored dragonflies. Do you wish to come with us?"

"Of course!" I replied, smiling first at Benjamin then at Sophie.

Here, the journal abruptly ends.

*   *   *

The brigantine *Marie Celeste* was found at four in the afternoon of November 29, 1872, in the Azores, six miles north of the island of Santa Maria, by the merchant ship *Dae Gartia*. Captain Dalton stated that the remnants of a magnificent feast sat upon the galley table. Rain slickers were about, and tobacco and pipes lay ready on tables. Warm mugs of coffee and cocoa yet remained as well. The broken sword of Captain Briggs was discovered, stained red. Originally, it was thought to have been used in foul play. It was later found to have only red paint on the blade. Captain Dalton, an able and intelligent seaman, noted that her longboat and smaller yal were both missing and is of the opinion that the *Marie Celeste* may have been abandoned a considerable distance from the spot at which she was picked up, since powerful current runs up in that latitude from the African coast. He confesses his inability, however, to advance any hypothesis which can reconcile all the facts of the case. In the utter absence of a clue or grain of evidence, it is to be feared that the fate of the crew of the *Marie Celeste* will be added to those numerous mysteries of the deep that will never be solved until the great day when the sea shall give up its dead.

The Griffin

A much-weathered and decomposing journal was recovered from a remote, ancient log cabin located on Michigan's Upper Peninsula, near a river that empties into Lake Michigan. Some Indians had spoken with the hermit who had dwelt there. They said he was a man skilled at making things out of wood. He made a canoe that he used on the river. He sometimes made fine canoes for them and traded with them. The Indians seldom traveled to his cabin as it lay in sacred grounds, the land of the spirit trees and the spirits who guarded them. The stranger was said to have come to that land around the same time that some Indians had seen a great canoe that had been built by the white men. The following is from the journal of the man the Indians called the canoe maker.

September 15, 1679

My name is Sven Seabold. I have been enlisted as ship's carpenter on the newly built cargo ship of Commander LaSalle, the *Griffin*. She is sixty foot long and forty-five tons burden. On her deck are two three-pound cannons and four swivel guns. She has proven herself seaworthy, having weathered a storm off Thunder Bay in Lake Huron. We set sail in three days, if the weather be favorable, for Washington Island. We are bound for Niagara. The *Griffin* has just taken on a cargo of excellent furs. Our captain is a salty dog.

There is a crew of fourteen hands aboard, as well as six passengers, a cabin boy, and a ship's doctor. I am fortunate enough to have a cabin, which I share with my English springer spaniel Jib and one crewman, Nicomus, and his odd coyote like dog with zebra stripes and eyes that glow like green fire in the dark. He is called Two-Hats as he possesses the habit of wearing two hats in colder weather. Two-Hats is a mascouten Indian, and although given some ship's duties, he also acts as a guide and interpreter. He has lived all his life in these lands and so is familiar with both the terrain and its peoples.

September 18

Set sail today with a light and favorable west wind. All passengers and hands aboard. Spirits high on this sunny morning. The oranges, reds, and yellows of the vast tree lands are magnificent. Even the captain seems cheerful.

September 20

Had dinner at the captain's table last night. A most excellent meal of roast turkey, potatoes, exceptional sweat corn, and more. Cheerful company of mostly passengers. One man voiced his views on our journey. He is a good friend and confident of Commander LaSalle, being employed as a chart and mapmaker. It is Mr. Oliver's opinion that although the ship's main mission is to deliver its cargo to Niagara, as well as for the passengers to gain safe harbor, we also have a commitment to exploration.

Jamie, a young lad and the son of the only married couple aboard, asked Mr. Oliver if he'd ever seen any monsters or sea serpents on his explorations. Mr. Oliver had previously explored parts of the remote Congo as well as the extreme wilds of Northern Canada.

"Laddy, I've seen giant squid so large they can capsize a ship with their tentacles. I've seen horned lizard dragons. And in both the Congo and in the dense forests of Canada, I've encountered tall hairy manlike creatures having great strength, perhaps the strength of twenty men" was Mr. Oliver's reply.

"Do you think we'll see any monsters on this voyage, sir?" asked the youth.

"One never knows, my boy. Anything is possible in unknown territory, lad," answered Mr. Oliver.

September 22

Put in at a small bay. A company was sent ashore to hunt for game. Although we have more than ample supplies, it is always good to set fresh meat upon the table. Two-Hats went along. I, meantime, surveyed the ship's hull from inside and out. Finding two slightly loosened spots, I proceeded in these repairs, using calking.

Shore company returned in longboat with two deer, five turkeys, and several rabbit. We had heard shots, so figured as much. We shall eat well on our travel!

Two-Hats expressed some concern over some signs and tracks that he had seen ashore. It is his belief that we are being watched by some evil tribesmen, possibly of the Huron tribe. Two-Hats fears they may try to come aboard using canoes or ambush a hunting party in the future. I told him to be at ease. I assured him I would speak to the captain regarding this matter and that I would encourage the captain to put an additional man on night watch as well as to ensure that all shore parties are heavily armed and aware of the possible dangers.

September 23

Dined on venison, which I in no way favor, and turkey. Talk turned to the ship. How fine the ship's company thinks she looks, all polished teakwood and oak. With her three fine masts and her aft banner, having a green background with a bright-orange griffin adorning the center. What a sight she must be to the savages, as Dr. Jepson, of Cambridge, calls them. Spoke of the weather, how fair it's been, hoping for continuance. Mr. Oliver commented on the fine map work he has completed.

The lad, Jamie, asked of Dr. Jepson, he being a man of the sea, having served as a ship's doctor on some six ships, if he had ever seen any sea monsters.

"I've spied many strange things at sea, lad. Once hauled up in a fishing net was a half-human, half-fish creature, much decomposed. Upon my examination, I determined it to be something of what seamen commonly call a mermaid, although I was unable to determine the gender of the ghastly thing. I've examined rotting remains of cuttlefish measuring 120 or more feet in length. Once on the great lake Superior and then again on lake Charlavoix, I saw what looked like rogue waves. Upon closer inspection using the spyglass, heads and undulating serpentine bodies and fins could plainly be seen. Others aboard the ships I've sailed on also took up the glass and would testify as to seeing what I had seen."

"Once while aboard the *Exetter*, we came upon giant jellyfish that were easily eighty feet across. I've seen box jellies that can hardly be seen and have a sting so deadly that it will kill a healthy man in minutes. There where those pink barrel things with tentacles coming out of their middles I saw deep in a swamp, but oh well, I'd best not speak further of such things. Aye, laddy, there be more things in the world than we of mankind can think possible. I for one can swear to that, and my eyes be true as any man's," concluded Dr. Jepson.

"Oh, Mommy, oh, Daddy, I want a spyglass. Please could you get me one, oh please!" the young lad cried out.

The captain requested of me this day to make cabinets for his cabin and also a wooden sea chest.

September 24

Little Jamie Stievenson has his spyglass. The captain, who seems quite a crusty old chap, has shown a kind side, for he has retrieved an old, scratched, and extremely weathered ship's watch glass and gave it to the child. The captian has awarded me a raise. More savings for the future home that I will construct in New Holland.

September 25

Weather is still fair. The winds are out of the southwest. The voyage is purposefully slow as there is no specified due date and no danger of our goods spoiling. The captain much respects the wishes of LaSalle that although the ship is built as a cargo ship, her main mission is to explore and chart the lands and seas of this vast wilderness world. I plan to go, for some relief from the ship, on the next hunting expedition.

September 26, 27, 28

All the ship's company are in good spirits. Many joke and kid little Jamie Stievenson about the strange creatures he claims to see with his spyglass in his constant and vigilant search for dangerous savages and sea monsters.

"The kid's seen the bloomin hairy man, he has," remarked Finius, a topgallant and mizzen sailor and an excellent sailmaker as well.

"He's seen another sea serpent again this day. Keen eye, this lad," commented Mr. Oliver in jest.

Weather is fair. We pause often to take depth readings and view the shoreline for maps. The woods have taken on a feeling of loneliness. One feels small in comparison.

September 29

Sky is ash gray. Winds are from the south southwest. Going ashore with the hunting party. Asked Two-Hats to stay close as I'm unfamiliar with these lands and only some part a woodsman. We lie somewhere in the northern Bay de Noc.

September 30

Astounded by the supreme unknowness of the vast expanse of shoreline. One enters a world of never-ending pines, oaks, cedars, birches, and more. The canopy over some areas are so dense, making light scarce, particularly beneath the somber and majestic great pines. Looking up the thick trunks of these giants, one sees immense branches reaching and intertwining with one another, creating their own sky of darkness.

Upon rendezvous with the others as evening approached, we discovered they had met some friendly Indians who were camped in the area for hunting and fishing. They call themselves Potawatomi. They have much corn and some furs, along with a large complement of game and fish. They seem very anxious to engage in trade. The Potawatomi have invited us to camp with them. They express a wish to meet the great chief of the giant canoe, as they call the captain. We will return to the ship with their message. Rutlage, a sailor, has assured me that aboard are several chests of trinkets and goods—such as mirrors, hatchets, knives, fishhooks, and beads—reserved for trade with Indians.

Seven Bells, Evening

Captain, after speaking with Mr. Oliver, is very pleased for the opportunity to meet Indians. He feels they can be a great help with information about the coast and interior of the territory ahead of us.

October 1

Went this afternoon to shore with the captain. My Jib wagged her tail and chased squirrels about tall oaks and pines. Little Jamie begged to go but was forbidden.

Some hunting. Mainly sat near the campfire of the Potawatomis. Four braves, very fit and muscled. Wearing buckskin breeches and bone breastplates. Their faces are colored with paint of their warrior color, blue. They have bows, arrows, small hatchets with sharp-worked stone blades. The natives are equipped with knives, these also of stone—flint, I think. These are very sharp and efficient in the skinning of game.

The captain traded for several bushels of corn. He also obtained a number of good-quality fur hides, black bear, beaver, and deer. The Indians were mainly interested in the metal knives, hatchets, and glass beads. They were both curious about and frightened by the mirrors.

After an excellent meal of turkey, duck, corn, and apples, we sat, smoking tobacco and telling tales of sea travels, which greatly interested our hosts. Two-Hats spoke their language well and so related our words. Forlorn wolves howled as darkness settled in around us. The braves spoke in turn, each telling of themselves and their crowning achievements, like slaying a giant grizzly that was carrying people off from their village. They also shared some of their legends. One legend was of hair-covered giant bearlike men, who roamed the sacred lands north of here. These bear-men were ferocious, and were called Kosh-na-na. They smelled of fetid fish and rotting eggs. No Indians would venture into the vast wilderness where these creatures lived. Warriors and others who had gone into these forbidden lands seldom returned.

Another brave, sharp-nosed, his red clay face glowing in the orange light, spoke of great sea creatures that could shatter a canoe with a flick of their massive fishlike fins. They are called *Antuat*, meaning "giant teeth." These lake monsters are said to become very vicious and hungry just before and after wintertime. Like bears, they seem to become daring and risk danger to feed before and after a time of rest or when food becomes scarce. Many braves have been eaten by these predators. Those who have lived to tell of attacks say the things have great scales and are as long as ten canoes.

An older brave told of a great mountain lion, bigger than the biggest grizzly. He said it is tan-red in color with black stripes and two long fangs. The Indians claimed that it is a night hunter mostly, but that even by day, it cannot be seen because it can change its colors to become invisible. This tigerlike cat is called *Solom-Wazzi*, meaning "two fangs." It is known to take people from villages at night and to slay and carry off even the fiercest of hunters. Remains of its kills have been found.

The last brave told of wild boars weighing six hundred pounds or more. These animals could cut ten men to pieces using their razor-sharp, curved tusks. They were known to consume fields of crops planted near villages. If one saw two red eyes staring out at them from the darkness of trees or brush, they should climb as high into a tree as they can, for they will never defeat or outrun these *Kai-Jib-Na*, or "razor tusks." He spoke in hushed tones of bottomless bogs. As smoke drifted into the damp night air, a lone owl cried out. We moved off to our sleeping places, these tales dancing in our heads. Tomorrow we go back aboard the Griffin.

October 2

Oppressive dark clouds have blown in, making the looming wilderness appear menacing to our west. We have plenty of fresh game and stories to help pass the time, as it looks like a storm is soon to be upon us.

October 3

Rained all night, with dense fog this morn. I shall take several men ashore to cut and secure wood for the cabinets and sea chest.

Five Bells, Evening

The Potawatomis have gone. No trace of camp, probably because they want no enemies to know of them.

October 4

Rain continues among foreboding gray clouds. An odd incident has occurred. It seems that yesterday, young Jamie was active on deck with his new prize, the spyglass. All at once, he cried out that he saw a sea monster.

One seaman, Midshipman Pierre Foote, asked, "What do ya see, lad?"

To which Jamie replied, "It's out there, a great beast as long as any dinosaur! Here, see for yourself." Jamie handed the glass to Foote.

Upon looking in the direction indicated by the boy, Foote stood frozen, paralyzed, gazing out over the brownish water. In a minute or so, the seaman handed the glass back to Jamie. After which, a glazed and confused look upon his person, Foote retired to his berth, saying that he had suddenly fallen ill. The sailors who saw him said that he shook and trembled, as well as had the appearance of a whitened ghost. Foote does not speak of this matter. Although he seems somewhat less ill, he still projects a lethargic and distressed humor.

At dinner, the boy was queried as to this occurrence. He states that he saw a large, scaly, finned monster resembling some of the sea dinosaurs he had seen renderings of. He said that it was still at first, and he thought it to be a large tree or trunk of a tree moving in the waves. He swears that he saw a large fin come up out of the water, become clearly visible for an instant, then splash the surface as it disappeared. He could see no head, per say, yet he claims to have seen one plate-sized greenish eye with a small red center. Most believe that the boy's imagination has gotten the best of him. However, several sailors have stopped making jest about the boy's story, choosing instead to avoid the matter. Mr. and Mrs. Stievenson have scolded young Jamie and warned him against making up tales.

I shall begin my cabinet work on the morrow, having gathered some fine oak and cedar.

October 5

Rain all day. Worked below, sawing and smoothing boards for cabinets.

October 6

Rain. Wind.

October 7

Captain's anxious for us to get underway again. He has sent some men ashore to look out from high mountain-like coast. Rain has let up to a hazy sprinkle. Thick fog has moved in. The oppressive atmosphere carried in by the fog weighs on one and soaks into the clothes and body. Can only see ten or twenty yards from ship. Must wait for fog to lift before making sail.

Three Bells, Afternoon

Yelling, splintering of wood commotion, and much splashing were heard from the port side of the ship. Two men were hauled from the water. Sailor LaWibble was greatly injured, with deep cuts to his right arm, legs, and forehead. He has lost much blood and is with the ship's doctor. The other seaman, a Mr. Matese, gave a disjointed and terrifying account of the events.

As the shore party was returning to the ship, something bumped the boat. The next thing remembered by Matese is being thrown into the water as the rowboat was smashed to pieces. There was much yelling and confusion. Matese, seeing the helplessness of the situation, swam for the ship. He swam directly into Mr. LaWibble and, seeing his state, proceeded to his aid in coming to and aboard the ship. As to the fate of the other two sailors, the second rowboat was dispatched to search. The heavily armed men found nothing of their lost shipmates. They saw many pieces of the destroyed boat floating on the surface. The search party saw no sign of any creature or thing that could have caused such damage. All aboard concerned about the badly injured Mr. LaWibble.

The captain has lit torches positioned in the ship's railings. He has also had the two cannon aboard made ready. The swivel guns have been loaded and primed as well. The watch is to be doubled. The good captain is not taking the loss of two men lightly. I quite agree with these measures. Some of the crew want to be allowed to stalk this demon in the thick fog. This disastrous occurrence paints young Jamie's story in a darker color. Much talk and jitters among both crew and passengers.

October 8

Still to foggy to depart as many treacherous rocks are about this area. All quiet. The captain walks around the deck every two hours at least. Nothing more to note to chronicle.

October 9

Woke with a vague feeling of oppression and misfortune. There is a pervasive atmosphere of fear and isolation permeating the *Griffin*. I, like the other men, do not go above deck unarmed. I have a firing piece, on half cock, in my belt at all times.

Although the water is calm, the sailors on watch and others report hearing splashing sounds, like something big is circling out there. All aboard are anxious to depart. If only this accursed fog would lift.

October 10, 11, 12

No change. Sailors murmur of a jinx or that we are in haunted waters. By the accounts of the Indians we had met, we did lie in sacred territory, being off the coast of wilderness that they termed sacred or guarded by great spirits.

The talk at the captain's table has turned gradually more gloomy and foreboding.

October 13

Fog swept away by winds coming from southwest.

We shall sail today. Spirits of all aboard are lifted as all wish to be rid of this place.

October 14

Have cut across so as to head out from the bay. As gales and storms are much a threat in November, being called by sailors the witches of November, the captain will have us make haste along the coastline until we have reached a safe point, where from we may proceed to our final destination of Niagara.

October 15

Reached the main lake this morn. Southwest wind continues. Upon trying to take depth readings, sailor Jean LaMete notes that he is unable to make bottom. As the depthing rope is one hundred fathoms, this means the bottom exceeds six hundred feet. All aboard are amazed by this, mainly the captain, who believed that these fetid little ponds could never reach such depths.

I am near completing the cabinets for the captain's cabin. Although green, the woods that were gathered have proved reliable.

October 16

Wind has shifted, now coming out of west.

October 17

Approaching Manistique River area. Captain is debating on sending men to hunt. Many large slablike rock formations in the bay, particularly near the shore. Captain will not risk our remaining rowboat.

The coastline appears singularly desolate and menacing as it now often looms above the sea like tree-covered dragons and giants waiting to descend upon our small ship.

October 18

The two men who were on the midnight watch spoke to the captain about hearing sloshing and splashing sounds in the wee hours. Say they are reminded of the sounds whales or great white sharks make when swimming near a ship. Although the captain plays these observations down, for the morale of all aboard, there is much speculation and whispering among the crew. Their talk has now turned to speculation that a or some bull sharks are stalking the ship, having tasted the flesh of man. Some of the crew still believe we are being hunted by some kind of supernatural beast. One can sense fear on the men.

October 19

Have finished and made fast the cabinets in the captain's quarters. He appears quite pleased.

Still a somber shuffling of fear and anticipation among the crew. Didn't help when at dinner, little Jamie Stievenson said excitedly, "He's still out there. The sea monster is following us!" Of course, what is said at the captain's table trickles down quickly to the sailors. It's hard to keep anything from others on a ship.

October 20

Weather clouding up. Winds have shifted out of north northwest.

Night watch observed strange green ball-like lights. Northern lights? Swamp wisps? I shall try to see them tonight.

October 21

Winds greatly increased.

Did go on deck at three of this morn. Amazingly saw at around 4:00 a.m. a strange greenish glowing orb-like thing moving out over the sea and up in the night sky. Captain Columbus and his crew saw unearthly green lights in 1492. Mood aboard is fearful, apprehensive.

October 22

Much rain and ten foot waves. Wind is fiercely blowing from northwest and east.

We are caught in between winds. Sailors speak of a Jonah aboard who is causing the previous deaths and our bad weather.

October 23

We are overtaken by an uncommon storm. Winds are from northwest, east, and at times, the south. The captain says he has not seen a storm quite like this in his twenty-three years at sea. He has had the sails brought in and secured, fearing they will be torn to ribbons.

Five Bells, Evening

One sailor, a seaman, Quail, has been washed overboard in the waves.

October 24

Much water below deck. About three bells in the morning, we were hit by waves of enormous sizes. Many were lost or injured. I have received a bad cut to my forehead as well as my right shoulder, which feels crippled. My left knee is no better.

Water is three feet deep below deck. Alas, poor little Jamie drowned! May his soul rest in peace.

October 25

Sudden calm at two bells in the morn. All is frighteningly still. Can see only black night and countless stars. All masts sheered off to stumps. We are doomed to do naught but try to steer, if rudder be whole. The seven who now survive are the captain, the doctor, Mr. And Mrs. Stievenson, my shipmate Two-Hats, and crewman Rutlage. We talk of a survival plan.

Nine Bells, Morn

Crewman Rutlage reports the rudder has been torn off below the waterline. He claims he saw a gigantic shape undulate in the murky water. He refuses to return to the water for attempt at fixing the rudder.

The rowboat is gone.

October 26

During midnight watch, Stievenson and Rutlage report hearing noise as if some creature was circling ship.

Six Bells, Morn

As daylight breaks, we can see the unforgiving harshness of the coastline. Darkness peers out from autumn trees. Using a cracked watch glass, I see that we're lying out at a distance of one mile from the mouth of a river clogged with massive tree trunks and windfall trees. The area of this obstruction is that of a small island. The current or light winds carry us to it. We must prepare on how to go ashore if cast onto this island of dead trees.

It is upon us! As the captain began to summon us forward, it came, a blackened-brown thing. It is of bone-like plates and slashing, sharp spiked fins. It splinters the wood of our craft with each pass. The primeval stench of the beast reeks of rotting seaweed and death, stinging the eyes to blindness. The thing circles the ship as would a great shark then turns and rams full boar into her, staving in the sides. It rams us repeatedly, causing a rumbling and heavy splintering of her main timbers. We who are left grab and lash ourselves to anything sound.

I have roped myself to the main mast's stump. In the strangeness of dawn, I can see the thing methodically circling the ship. It has large green eyes with smaller orange centers the size of dinner plates.

The length of it is seventy feet or more. It looks like a monstrous, primeval sturgeon fish. And now the ancient behemoth comes in for the kill. A massive sea-grime tail smashes the beloved *Griffin*. It crushes her to finish us with its killer whale mouth of ghastly needle teeth, from which blood now drips. The leviathan has won. Save our souls! The last thing I remember is my beloved Jib gripping my shirt collar with her teeth and frantically dog paddling in the direction of the island of tangled deadfall trees.

Markel's Savior

Crisp brown leaves brushed across the earth, tumbling and crackling on their cartwheel journeys. The sun, going behind green horizon, shoots its last orange shafts into the sky. A damp, cold sea wind blew, bending green pines and birches back and forth frantically. In a clearing full of long yellow grasses, a lone girl crouches, setting down a large bundle of crooked twigs. Markel's long black cape flowed in the wind like ocean waves. Long sandy hair streamed about her head, getting in her mouth. She brushed it back with both hands.

Suddenly, a voice came to her from the dark emptiness between strange ancient bark faced trees. "Girl, are ye lost?"

Startled, lifting her head, her large brown eyes dilated with animal terror. She answered, fingers quivering at her pink lips, "Who's there? Why are ye hiding? Please show thyself, sir. Ye scare me!" Markels black and light tan wolf like dog Jonathan remained calm and stared, with brown eyes, in the direction of the voice.

"And come out, I shall. I fear your people and must be cautious. I mean no harm," a voice answered.

"I'm gathering wood for the hearth and mean no wrong, but I wonder what manner of strange man are ye?" Markel said as she scurried forward. Orange and brown leaves crunched under her feet as she reached for her bundle on the ground. She got up to go. Suddenly, there was movement, rustling, and soft steps. She shivered with fright. He was emerging.

"If ye come closer, I'll cry out for man and musket, sir."

"I'll not harm ye. I wish only company in the forest. Come feast on sweetmeats, fresh bee's honey, and apple juice. Come take my hand."

Markel, frail and fawn-like, turned her head. She was scared—although curious. He stood bathed in clear blue moon rays. A red-brown cloak of maple leaves and oak leaves rustled about his straight shoulders. He was small in stature and moved with grace and flowing balance. The boyish face gazed at Markel with gentle green eyes, deep set with wisdom. A large gray squirrel ran figure eights around his hide-clad feet and legs. The glowing round squirrel eyes focused directly on Markel's pale face. The furry creature chirped as if to greet her. Markel could tell they meant no harm. She saw their fear, their slight trembling. Her fear was fading now—the fast-pumping heart slowed in her chest. Jonathan's calmness helped to calm her. The stranger seemed timid, like a small rabbit sniffing the air to sense danger. They looked at each other clearly for an instant. Markel and Jonathan moved away.

"I go now woodsman. Stay ye away from log villages and men in tall black hats. These men fear that which is different and would burn ye as a witch or devil. Ye are kind and gentle, I can see. But take heed. I say this only because I am different from most."

The gray squirrel chirped loudly as the leafy cloaked figure twirled and faded into his shadowy woods realm. The fingerlike ferns brushed her legs as she walked the thin path back toward Roanoke, her home in the new world. Markel's small rough-barked cabin stood in a clearing about a mile from the main village. She preferred it this way. Having been a serf to pay her way from England, she had grown to dislike the staunch Puritan folk. The men who preached righteousness in their dark cloaks scared her. Some had looked at her with lust in their eyes aboard the ship. The smug, sharp-nosed, white-bonneted shrewish women, bending pious ears close to condemn poor misfits who were in some way different terrified her. Markel pulled the large oak hewn door shut and dropped her now cumbersome bundle. She placed three newfound small logs on the fire and sat, thinking as her dinner of potato and carrot stew began to boil.

That night, as she lay bundled and warm by the fireside, Markel's thoughts drifted. She pictured the kind stranger. She hoped to see him again. The thought that she someday might sent a warm glow through her body.

The children laughed and spoke with malice of Markel as they joked under shaggy sod roofs or as they ran back to the village on the path leading past the only cabin set apart from the village.

"I saw her just look up at the sky for hours once," said Bray Catcher, a pumpkin-headed lad with powder white skin.

"She was near naked, spinning and dancing in the woods around her cabin. Her evil dog danced also," reported Sara Livesogg.

"She's teched or has demons in her," concluded Cultrop, the town blacksmith's son.

That winter, the stonefaced men and women of Roanoke grew restless. Odd bits of gossip about a dark man, said to be the devil himself, were passed in low, serious tones. It was said that he could throw fire. If one's animals looked at him, they would wither and die. The wood-chiseled men of the village feared him deeply. They blamed him, as did the Croaton Indians who lived in the area, for the scarcity of game. It was said that the dark one caused weird disappearances about the land. Edward Mather's prized hog had been taken from a log-fenced pen. The hog weighed close to three hundred pounds, yet the fence was unbroken. They blamed this on devilry. People spoke of demons that snatched souls from the dying at the instant they left their bodies. The black-hatted men said that whip-poor-wills or crows were sometimes demons seeking souls to eat. The villagers sat in the common cabin, listening to such talk most winter evenings while pale-faced men exhaled gray-blue smoke from thin long bone-white pipes up into the pine beams above. The wicked prudish women of the village had conjured an evil brew, one aimed at Markel. They all feared her for she was alone and pretty—a temptation for their men. Stories began of the most vicious nature.

"Markel has been seen running, dancing, and singing at night, under the moon, in the forest," one hag would say.

"She sees and speaks with the evil one. Her bewitched dog is her familiar," echoed another false witness.

And so it went, rolling like a snowball, gathering momentum as winter passed. They had been lying in wait for deer or any game when he came to drink at the crystal river not far from the settlement. The forest man knelt cupping his slender hands. Water dripped from them as he lifted it to his mouth. Droplets splashed back into the water. The birds all became silent at once.

Crack! A shot rang out. The leafy cloak jerked as small black projectiles hissed in the air around it. The gentle green eyes raged as they looked to where the hunters stood. A large man shook big boned hands, fumbling with musket and powder horn. The other, rat faced under black brim, held a smoking blunderbuss, frozen. From the woodsman's eyes, hot spiraling fireballs flashed out at them. Orange-blue death coming at the hunters, who threw their iron burdens down into brown grass and fled shrieking. The fireballs made sounds like a cloth sail in fierce winds as they seared past the hunters' ears. He made his way toward his cave, knowing the mossy riverbank was unsafe. His back and side seared with molten rods of pain. His splendid leaf cloak ran with rivulets of blackish red. The squirrel ran with him, chirping in anger.

Loud shrill barks of hate alerted the forest creatures of danger. Two thick-furred brown grizzlies stood alert as they guarded their friend's cave, which was also one of their dwellings. Their eyes widened, their large toothed mouths opened slightly, as they spied him coming, crouching low and dripping crimson. He crossed the ancient opening, making a chirping sound to summon the bats to aid him. He made his way to a bed of dried grass. He laid down upon it. The cave was deep. Clear water flowed down the walls in places leaving mineral designs, ending in dim pools. A fire radiated yellow-orange warmth from the center of the cave. The bats came to him, black and brown alike. They tore away the cloak and, with their boney fingers, probed the speckling of small wounds.

After removing nails and lead from his back and side while he quivered, they cleaned the wounds with their flickering tongues. The woodsman thought briefly of the primitive and dangerous villagers before he drifted off to sleep. Flame-illuminated light danced about the stone walls as hundreds of dark shapes spiraled out of the cave's mouth and up into the night sky.

When the river ice melted, turning the waters black, they came. The tall men with brass buckles glinting on large brimmed hat and shoe. Jonathan sprang up and barked warning Markel of danger.

Markel ran and opened a rear window whispering, "Run Jonathan, hide!" her wolf like companion jumped out and vanished into dark ferns. They burst in the unbolted door, shouting "Witch! Witch!" and "Devil's friend!" as they grabbed her, thick woven quilt and all.

Markel was struck often as they carried her down the stoney path to Roanoke. They insulted her until they approached the dark clad crones who waited for the roast. Markel was bound tightly to a barkless pole. Bundles of twigs were piled high by jeering, sunken-eyed women in white bonnets. Suddenly, as a goat faced man put a black smoking torch to the twigs, its flame shrunk and vanished, yet there was no wind that clear morning.

Milos turned, wrinkling his deep brow. He looked in the direction of the crowd. He heard screams. People began reeling and convulsing. Dark yellow-brown bile spurted with force from their mouths. Their faces pulled tight in terror. White hands flailed about their heads as if they were trying to ward off invisible wasps. The black robed ones ran about the street like panicked chickens. Their feet began to glow phosphorescent blue. The eerie luminescence moved up their stockings and grew over their capes and heads. The villagers fell to the ground and writhed like wounded worms.

As they burst into blue-green flames and pinwheeled frantically about, loud shrieks of anguish burst upon the crisp air. Seconds later, the flames went out. The villagers lay motionless on the ground. He walked silently, buckskin soft, up to where Markel was. He slit her bonds with a small stone knife and took her soft arm. Hand in hand, they moved off into the deep woods.

The two walked through a cathedral of tall pines in the evening twilight. The pair had walked a great distance, out of nowhere Markel's beloved Jonathan appeared and joined them. They were now far from the settlement and its confusion. The tender brown needles were soft on their feet. Wind murmuring through high branches soothed them. In time, Markel and her rescuer reached a cave. A pair of amber eyes stood century at each side of the doorway. They entered. A warm fire sent shadows dancing on rock walls. The cave was dry and sandy. Yellow-brown grasses for sleeping nests lay invitingly near one wall.

"Are you hungry?" asked the stranger.

"No, thirsty, but not hungry. Most of all, I'm thankful, but I know not thy name. You saved my life," replied Markel.

"My name is Gowen."

"Thank ye, Gowen," Markel said as she tried to smile. "Gowen is old English for Gwain, like the Sir Gwain who was one of the round table knights loyal to King Arthur. Gwain means the green man of the forest, it fits you well! I must know the people of the village, the ones that were about to burn me, are they dead?"

"No, they will recover. They were just shaken and sickened by the rays of protection. Worry not about the unkind ones. You have been injured. Here, put some of this on your cuts and bruises. It will help the pain go. It will help healing," Gowen said, handing Markel a shiny, metallic blue jar with bluish cream in it. He then walked over to where a small stream flowed from the cave's wall and filled a wooden cup with water. He handed the cup to Markel.

"Drink and rest, my friend. Things will be better when light comes." With that, Gowen lay down on the straw-like grass and slept.

Back at the small settlement, people scrambled about like rats, gathering their things for the journey. The leaders had decided that the village was no longer safe. They had built and hidden two large log rafts just for such a time. They feared the powerful one who saved Markel, thinking him a warlock. The settlers also feared the Croaton Indians. They had wronged these people when they first arrived in this wilderness. The settlers killed one of their warriors. Feeling either the warlock would return or that the Indians might overrun them, they prepared to depart for an island called Croatoan. The settlers felt the island would be safer and more easily defended.

After hiding several wooden chests of books in underbrush and bushes, one of the Roanoke settlers had carved the word CROATOAN into a tree. They launched their overloaded rafts. The people of Roanoke looked back as the sun's first rays broke over the blue sea horizon. The staunch folk of the colony never came back to retrieve their books as planned. Later that day, a fierce storm came upon them, and large waves battered the rope and log rafts until they broke apart. The settlers were swallowed up by the sea.

Markel awoke to golden rays streaming into the warm cave. Jonathan lay calmly beside her. Gowen handed her a wooden bowl of steaming porridge. It tasted of honey and wheat. "I must leave. You may stay or go with me. If you choose to stay, I must use sleep to make you forget me. If you come with me, know that I go to other worlds. Worlds that lie far above in the stars," said Gowen.

"I have little here, only the woods and the kind creatures who dwell within them. I am misunderstood by my own kind. They do not know of the ways I use to heal or the herbs I use. The women are jealous and unkind. Even small children are taught to call me witch. Will these worlds be like this one?" replied Markel.

"Some will be like the earth. Others will be very strange and different. The world that I come from has two moons, green sky, and a blue sun. The beings of my world are friendly and live in caring ways with one another. Many of the natural ones are like your mammals, reptiles, birds, fish, and insects—very large insects. We have dogs with zebra stripes, and giant dinosaurs still live on my world. It is a world with warm and cold, ice and rain, and freshwater oceans. Lakes and rivers are everywhere, pure and clear. You and Jonathan would like my planet, I think, Markel. The people are unlike the harm doers of your old village," finished Gowen.

In the center of a grassy clearing not far from the cave sat the spacecraft. It was immaculate, a shimmering sphere made of maroon armor. Gowen turned as a circular opening appeared. The outworlder helped Markel and her companion enter. He turned, looking into the eyes of the grizzly bears that had guarded his cave so faithfully. They returned his look of thankfulness and moved off. In an instant, the great maroon orb shot up into the blue sky. The air made a rippling sound like cloth in violent winds. The orb vanished.

The Dog from the Stars

It was unearthly. I know not what it was that tread the snow the winter of 1907. I know not from whence it came. I only know that it was terrifying beyond belief. It began with the onset of odd killings of many of the area's livestock. The first incident occurred in December. A farmer named Hans P. Langstrom had three of his cows killed over a two-week stretch. The normal killers would be wolves or black bears. A bobcat or large coyote might also be able to kill an animal as large as a cow. The odd thing was the way in which the three animals were mutilated. The cuts were precise and jagged, like the shape of a cookie cutter. Some organs, like the hearts and livers, were removed. Eyes were missing. This was not how any predator known to roam the woody swamplands here about would have killed and devoured its prey.

Jeziah Hawker's horse, General Custer, was found torn up in obtuse ways. Some of Sven Lampsom's hogs were found horribly slaughtered. One of the hogs was not found. It had weighed three-hundred pounds. Dieter Croft, a chicken farmer, had scores of chickens vanish. He says he had heard or seen nothing. Mr. Croft and the others all spoke of finding paw prints in the snow, like those of a large cougar or mountain lion. It was when I began to hear my dogs bark that I became alerted to something lurking, usually late at night but not always, for I had returned from hikes to find my horse in a state of sheer terror. I began to take my bow when I went walking with my favorite dog, Deuter, short for Deuteronomy. She is a coyote like dog, that is reddish tan with black zebra stripes and a miniature lion's mane. On several occasions, Deuter stopped frozen into an on-point posture, the hair on her upper back standing up. This only happened when we were in the vicinity of bears.

It was March when that we headed out on one of our daily walks. We hiked all about the vast swamp-woodlands, which went for hundreds of square miles, surrounding the area of land where my sod-roofed cabin stood. A rare blizzard had blown in the day before. It left about six inches of snow on the recently clear ground. The unusual blizzard continued throwing fierce winds across the icy swamps. At times, the sun broke through as a soft white-blue orb. The snow made for good tracking. I was extra alert for those large tracks that others had seen over the winter. I also felt that since the water levels in the swamps and lakes was the highest I had seen it in the fourteen years that I had lived here, many creatures inhabiting the area had been forced to change their regular habits and territories. Waves battered the lakes shoreline back. The swamplands have filled up, and water is spreading out, making numerous new ponds and creeks. Many animals walked new paths. I know from hunting that cougars are very secretive and rarely seen by people. I had seen both bear and cougar tracks over the winter.

As Deuter and I approached an area in the snowy dirt road, she froze, the hair on her upper back standing up. As I looked in the direction she was looking in, I saw something shadowy and light orange to tan in color. It emerged from the dense brush, making sounds no more than whispers. It slowly, with deliberate catlike steps, crossed the road, stopping for an instant to turn its head slowly and glare at us with a color in its eyes that I've never seen before. The eyes were a strange almost green, but not green somehow. The pupils were orange, like luminous dots that seemed to pierce the air. I could not look at its eyes. I had to turn my head away, which felt very dangerous to me.

When I looked back, the cat creature was gone. I inspected the tracks. I had never seen any like them. They were like those of a large cougar or mountain lion. They were wide, where the pads and toes hit the ground. They showed claw marks, which is extremely odd as all cat species retract their claws, unlike wolves or bears. It was amazing, though, to me that they were so big. The tracks were the same size as those of a six-hundred-pound bear.

I had noticed several oddities aside from its intense eyes. The creature had two large canines protruding from the corners of its upper mouth, somewhat smaller than those of a prehistoric saber-toothed tiger. It had tufts of hair, like that of a bobcat or lynx, that jutted down into points on each side of its face. The jaw bone and surrounding area were very large, making for a bone-crushing bite. The shadow cat's legs were muscular and powerful in appearance. Its coat was darker orange tan radiating to lighter orange starting from the center of its back. Oddly the large cat had black stripes, tiger- or zebralike, that ran down its back. These stripes ran parallel to the ribs and came to points at the ends. I had heard about an animal called a catamount. I began to think this cat was such a creature.

Catamounts had somehow evolved into animals that could survive in the colder winter climates of Canada and the Northern United States. They have probably been around a long time. Perhaps much longer than anyone knows. This creature was gigantic. It must have weighted six-hundred pounds. Was it a relative of the *Smilodon*, a massive saber-toothed cat that had roamed North America ten thousand years ago? Could the catamount have roamed the earth when the saber-toothed tiger stalked its prey? I think so, as stranger things have occurred in nature. It seems that in the natural world, anything is possible, and if anything can happen, it generally does. Darwinism could, no doubt, explain this obscure creature.

I continued to track the creature that Deuter and I had happened across. I now kept my bow ready, with an arrow nocked. We went for miles back into the Dead-Stream Swamp area, north of Woughton Lake. We went through oak forests and winter swamp, where the new thin ice layer over the dark water cracked as we broke through. The catamount traveled by way of small cattail and pine islands that were plentiful throughout the marshlands. On one small islet, I discovered what resembled an ancient Indian totem pole. The totem had a bobcat-looking face carved into it. It also had a creature that looked like a barrel with tentacles coming out of its middle and one hideous eye. I thought maybe it had been made by Mascouten

Indians, who were said to have inhabited these lands before being wiped out. The Mascoutens believed that a great cougar or lion spirit guarded their swampy woodlands.

Just as I had decided to head back, the country opened up to a vast land of downed trees, stumps, and oppressive barrenness. I caught a last glimpse of something large and red tan disappearing among a large windfall of trees. I think it was the catamount. This country was called the Blasted Heath as long ago, something had fallen from the sky and changed the swamp forest into a charred landscape of gray and black. The object was described in Indian legend as having been a shooting star. It had appeared as a pointed dark shape. Surrounding it was a gaseous purple-blue cloud. Waves of heat, like those that vibrate just above hot sand, rippled around the thing from space. A trail of green tipped with orange arced, rainbowlike, from the back of the large comet. Just after it streaked by, a thunderous boom tumbled through the air like mighty thunder. The Indians said the earth trembled in fear of the thing from the great beyond of the stars.

We turned now and headed homeward. We could make it before dark even though the blizzard was still a torrent of whirling snow. It was Good Friday, with Easter to follow, and I had some things I wanted to do. I could not stop thinking about this creature, this thing called a catamount.

As Deuter and I trudged along, looking like a snowman and his dog, my mind raced. I think it was its eyes, its vulture eyes. Surely what we had seen was some kind of mutation. Some new form of a species of the animal kingdom. Or perhaps it could be a throwback, somehow coming to life again. Why didn't it attack us? One thing was certain: this catamount, this creature from the beyond, showed no fear of us.

I continued to focus on the creature as we reached our cabin, and as I hitched my sled dogs to the sled the next morning. The snow had slowed to light, hazy wetness. We headed into town. The dogs Nebular, Raven, Whiskers, Windy, Loner, and Blitzen pulled eagerly as Deuter scouted the trail ahead. I was happy about this because the dogs had been acting out of sorts and fearful ever since the catamount started lurking about. The wind-driven wet snow bent the pines and sent small tornadoes of snow whirling around us. This lulled the dogs into forgetfulness. When we arrived at the Woughton General Store, there was quite a crowd around the old Ben Franklin woodstove that sat in the center of the floor.

"Hey, how's things out there in that swamp of yours, Will?" asked Tom Jeffers, sipping from a blue mug.

"Yeah, Will, haven't seen you for a month of Sundays, seems like," said Zeke Bottoms, a heavyset, bearded farmer in blue dungarees.

"Here's some hot cocoa, Will, your usual. What will it be today, Will?" asked Sandy Wheatly, the store's owner.

"Oh, just came in to get some supplies and such. Let's see, some chocolate, please, Sandy. What's Easter without good old chocolate, ay? And some ham, a side should do, please. A sack of oats, flour, and a big hunk of beef too, please, Sandy. Whatever you pick out is fine. Let's see, oh, and a sack of beans, and I'd like this blue-and-green blanket here, please. It's for Deuter, but she doesn't know." At this Deuter, who was always at Will's side, perked up her ears and looked at Will quizzically.

"No surprise now, Will. You just gave it away. Deuter knows you'll be giving her that blanket now," said Sandy, looking affection-ately at Will.

"Well, I guess that's all. Thanks, Sandy."

"Hey, Will, you seen anything of this big cat or cougar that's been terrorizing half the countryside? We really need to pull together on this. Lots of folks have lost animals, and two nights ago, Maggie and Ed Tillson said it tried to drag their son Mark off. He's hurt real bad, but he'll live, I guess," said Joanh Chuchster.

"Yeah, Will, you seen him? We plan on starting a big hunt after Easter," interjected James Quillup, a hunter and trapper.

"Well, I'm on the lookout for the cat. It's got my dogs worried. So far, my horse and cow are okay," I answered.

"I heard from Old Pete, the Injun, that this ain't just a regular cougar or mountain lion. He says it's a giant cougar spirit that's been here since the beginning of time. He talks about an ancient Injun legend where this spirit guards the sacred forest and swamplands.

Old Pete claims this cougar can kill a grizzly and will kill humans to drive them out," said Mr. Quillup.

"Yeah, and I heard tell of an Indian legend about this spirit guard thing too. Some of the local Indians call it *Taus-nib-way*. They said it means 'two big fangs," added Zeke Bottoms.

"I heard about something one time," began Sandy. "They were diggin' a well, I think, over near Cougar Lake in Taymouth Township in Saginaw County. They came across some bones. It was an Indian burial. The bones were kids' bones. They had been dug up and broken. Then the bones were reburied, wrapped in a kind of ceremonial robe. The robe was made from cougar's hide and a cougar's skull. The folks from the university took the bones and robe. They said it had probably been used in ceremonies. They thought the children had been a chief's and the robe was put around their bones so that the cougar's spirit would protect them."

"The strange thing was that the professors believed the cougar bones were at least sixty-thousand years old, while the children's bones were only placed in the grave in about 1620. They were also baffled by the excellent condition of the cougar bones and confused as to how these bones, which resembled those of a prehistoric saber-toothed tiger, could be in no more a state of decay than the bones of the children. Anyway, that's how Cougar Lake got its name, I guess."

The clay men around the stove grumbled and fidgeted with their pipes as Sandy finished.

"We'll see you all later. Have a warm, happy Easter. I'll keep my eyes peeled for your cougar," said Will Evers. Then Deuter, Will, and his dogs were off into the snow-glazed winter landscape.

On the trail home, I thought about what was said at the town's store. One man, a Donald Grow, had told of something that happened in the Upper Peninsula back in 1903 in L'Anse. It seemed a woman, upon entering her sick husband's bedroom, saw the curtain next to the bed move. She could just make out, to her horror, a large clawed paw moving toward her husband's head. As she yelled and banged a chair on the floor, the thing took off. Looking out the window, she was just in time to spot a large cougar slinking off into the brush and pines near the house. Her slumbering husband was unharmed. He later said that he had a dream of an evil monstrous creature that tried to suck his breath away as he slept.

Most of the talk around the stove had been about how all these killings might be the work of more than one beast. When the word *catamount* was used, people's voice tones suddenly became more hushed and fearful. As I approached my cabin, an odd feeling of foreboding overcame me. Suddenly, Deuter stopped. She pointed at the barn. The hair on the nape of her neck stood up, as it did whenever we came across a bear. Then I heard my cow make an awful noise, as if death had just raked it with a clawed hand. I took my bow from the sled and readied an arrow. We headed forward.

When we were within fifty yards of the cabin, I saw the catamount. It moved slowly out of my small barn's doorway. Halting the sled, I loosed my arrow. My aim was true, and the arrow struck the large cat just behind the upper-right shoulder. The catamount paused, looked straight at me with haunting eyes, then turned its head away and vanished into the swamp-woods. As I entered the barn, I saw, to my horror, my beloved horse, Lenore, had been killed. Not just killed but torn asunder. Luckily, my treasured cow, Laural, was completely unharmed. Intending to keep her this way, I began planning how I would kill the beast. Tracking the wounded animal now was not the way. What if he led me astray then circled back to have another go at Laural? No, I would bide my time. Time is often one's best ally.

I had some satisfaction just knowing that my arrow, even now, was ripping at the flesh of the catamount. Maybe it would die. I would use my advantage of time. Only after a day or so would I venture forth to slay the sinister beast. I took Laural and my small pack of dogs to Sandy at the general store. She would care for them while Deuter and I were gone.

The next day, we set out. The sky was the color of a storm. Deuter, who was an excellent tracker, led the way. We moved over mud-grizzled trails. Much of our trail went through marshland. The icy tarn waters had thin ice on them from last night's cold. Deuter was able to follow a fresh sent through these stagnant watery places. How, I do not know. The direction we headed would take us to the area called the Blasted Heath once again. As we paused to rest on a small swamp island, we discovered something startling. Deuter, who had been very upset as we approached the islet, cautiously sniffed around some small pines and tall brown swamp grass. Suddenly, she gave out a single forlon howl of anguish. I had only heard her howl this way once before: this was when we discovered Lenore's body.

Looking behind the trees and brush, I saw the badly mauled body of a large black bear. The bear weighed about five-hundred pounds. Upon close examination of the corpse, I could see that this kind of damage could only have been done by wolves or another bear. And yet there was something strange and ominous about the wounds. They all had a jagged cookie-cutter slicing around the edges. What kind of creature could do this? None that I knew of. My horse's wounds had looked like this also. The other thing out of the ordinary about this kill site was the discovery of several large cougar-like tracks in patches of snow and mud around the body. These tracks were from the same animal that I had seen several days ago and that I had found around my cabin and barn the night of the attack on my horse. They were the tracks of the catamount.

The fresh condition of the bear's body and the newness of the tracks told me that this attack occurred last night. So if this was the same cat, and it surely was, my arrow must not have done much harm to it. Yet even if it were in perfect health, the catamount should not have been able to kill the large bear, unless maybe the bear was sick or injured. At least I had never heard of a catamount or cougar that had ever killed a large bear—cubs, yes, but a full-grown male, like this one, no. I felt I knew animal behavior and physiology quite well, having gone to veterinary school. I closed my office after the death of my wife. I never had it in my nature to put animals away. I moved to this fine swamp country to study its insect life. I still retained my knowledge of native species, and I am sure that whatever killed this bear acted alone and displayed strength beyond the normal strength of any known wildcat species.

Deuter and I moved off the islet and away from the gruesome site. We were within five miles of the area called the Blasted Heath. The prehistoric landscape, with all of its deadfall trees and dense brush made for difficult and slow traveling. As we reached the edge of the Blasted Heath, afternoon was fading, and a wind-ghosted snowstorm came upon us from the southeast. The ground was the color of an ancient wooden house. Among the ash-like soil were blackened stumps and windfall trees. I was just able to make out some catamount tracks where Deuter sniffed in the gray-black mud of this forsaken place. I did not like the thought of being out in the coming darkness with this monstrous thing. We needed to find a sheltered place and build a fire. I could come back to get some pine branches to build a shelter if we failed to find a large fallen tree or a group of them.

So far, the snow was coming down in small wet flakes. I could see quite a distance. Deuter and I began our search for a sheltered spot. Within an hour, the snow changed to big wet flakes. It fell in such large quantities that I could hardly see my hand at arm's length. I tried not to panic, knowing that staying calm in situations like this is the key to survival. The snow was so wet and easily packed together that if worse came to worse, I could quickly fashion a warm igloo-like structure. Fire was now the main problem, for I would not want us to be without a campfire in this unearthly realm of the catamount.

All at once, Deuter began to sniff the air and nudge me as if she wanted me to go in a certain direction. I took her leather leash from my pack and hooked her on to it. I would not risk us being separated in this soupy snow. Now I could follow along as a blind person follows their faithful guiding dog. We walked like this for what seemed hours. Darkness was closing upon us. As Deuter became excited and pulled harder and faster, I became aware of a strange and pungent odor that permeated the air. It was a marsh-woods scent that was completely unfamiliar to me. The scent was similar to that of raccoons or foxes. It was mossy, piney, and reeked of dead flowers baking in the hot sun. And yet there was something more sinister lurking beneath these smells. Something I had never encountered before. Something unearthly, like the smell of lightning.

After walking up a gradual assent, we came to a large hill. Deuter dug snow away from a spot on the hill. With a jerk, she pulled me into an opening in the side of the hill. It was small, and

I had to crouch down. I was startled by the darkness at first, but as my eyes adjusted, I began to see that we were in a large cave. There was an eerie greenish light illuminating the chamber. The light came from green emerald-like crystals that were embedded in the gray-blue cave walls. *Were they emeralds?* I wondered. These strange green stones, however, gave off light. As far as I had known, emeralds did not possess this quality. As I looked about the cave, I was delighted to see a large quantity of both dry and wet wood scattered about the sandy floor. Our fire problem was solved, and we had shelter as well. Thanks, Deuter! There was even a small pond near the back of the cave that was replenished by water flowing out of the cave's upper wall.

I remained apprehensive and on guard for even though our survival chances were greatly improved by Deuter's discovery of the cave, there were several dark tunnel openings toward the rear of the cave, and the odd stench that permeated the cave became much stronger there. I worried that we had taken shelter in a den occupied by other creatures. Seeing no distinct animal tracks within the cave, I decided we could stay here for at least tonight. I kept my bow ready at arm's length. Deuter, on the other hand, was already resting quietly in a little nest she had fashioned of swamp grasses. I took this to mean that she felt at ease in this unusual cave den. This in turn placed me in a relaxed and somewhat drowsy state of mind. Surely she would not be so at ease if the catamount or other creatures were near.

I busied myself by making a large fire near the cave's opening. As ancient flame shadow creatures danced about the gray walls and smoke began to lull me into twilight sleep, I shook myself back to alertness. There could be no sleep for me this night. Not with the dangerous cat lurking in the snowy darkness. I took some jerky and peanuts from my pack. I began chewing on the jerky while I sharpened some sturdy sticks into spikes. I would place these, angled outward, at the cave's opening. I also planned to make torches using sticks and dried swamp grass. I noticed that much of the grasses lying about the floor were what the Indians called sweet grass. It is often used in ceremonies. Sweet grass is said to purify and to keep evil spirits away.

Deuter awakened, and I gave her some peanuts and jerky. I finished the spikes and torches and made several spears as well. I then proceeded to convert some of my arrows into fire arrows. These would pack more punch than regular arrows. I carried no gun; I do not believe in these weapons. Besides which, some animals have such keen olfactory senses that they can smell gunpowder or gun oil a mile away. The catamount may well be among them. I knew that dogs can smell one-hundred times better than humans, blood-hounds one-thousand times better. Deuter hates guns; she had what appeared to be a long healed circular scar of a gunshot wound on her right rear hip. I believe that she had been shot sometime before I found her sick and starving in a remote area of the swamp-woods. This made sense as Deuter was very like a coyote both in appear-ance and nature. Deuter had saved my life several times since that November day I came upon her.

Both to keep awake and to satisfy my curiosity, I decided we would explore the strange and very uncommon swamp cave. As we headed into one of the openings at the back of the cave, Deuter's glowing amber eyes looked questioningly into mine. As we moved along the dark moss stone passageway, I marked the right wall with some blue trailblazing chalk. We were descending. Water dripped and ran in vein streams along the dank walls. At times, the spring-thaw water caused the ground to rumble and tremble. These rum-blings reverberated throughout the long tunnel. After a time, the passageway opened up into an immense cavern. The walls gave off the same greenish light as the first cave. A vast expanse of stalactites and stalagmites, cave tunnel openings, and a large clear cave lake stood before us.

Deuter began to head for the lake, which also had a stream running into it. We walked to where small waves washed onto the sand, and she began to drink deeply of the icy water. Giant seven- to twelve-foot-tall cattails, the color of the underside of leaves, grew in marshy patches. White frogs with glowing indigo eyes chirped somberly, deeply. Glowing purple fish and albino crayfish flittered and darted in the shallows. As Deuter waded into the water, I saw a dark shape darting toward her legs. I jumped. As I did so, she sensed the creature and sprang to shore. It was an abnormally large white pike like fish with spiky long jaws. It veered off and vanished into the depths.

Deuter and I headed away from the lake and back to the tunnel from which we had entered the cavern. We would spend the remainder of the night watching for the animal we came to slay. Something caught my eye as we passed close to the cavern's wall. It was a cave drawing colored in red, tan, and yellow ocher. It showed a sun and what looked to be a comet or shooting star. Below were many trees, mostly pines, that had been sheered off near their bases, and the singed trunks all lay flat. They lay in the same direction, radiating out from where the comet thing was shown to strike the ground. I wondered how old the cave painting was and who had painted it. Had this network of caves and the magnificent cavern been used by ancient cave dwellers? Did they record a meteor or comet hitting the earth in this area?

When we arrived back at the cave, the fire had burned down to embers. I quickly built it up again. I was stunned as I looked out beyond the cave's entrance to see two glowing green eyes dotted with orange centers about fifty yards away. I grabbed my bow and readied an arrow. I fired. The catamount's eyes vanished. I readied and lit a fire arrow. To the right, the eyes appeared again. I released the arrow at them. Again, the cat moved with lightning speed and evaded my shot. The arrow trailed off and landed in the darkness. I no longer saw the glowing eyes. I sat, straining my eyes to see into the inky night. Deuter sat near, her eyes fixed, her ears alert. I could take a torch and stalk the beast, but I thought that too risky. Again, we would use time and wait.

As we chewed beef jerky watchfully, my thoughts drifted to the cave painting. I recalled a tale told to me by an old Indian. He was a medicine man that I came across in the Upper Peninsula. He had spoken of an ancient legend that happened way back in time, just after the giant turtle spirit formed the land with its mossy-green shell. Some warriors out hunting saw a bright star. It streaked across the pastel-blue sky, trailing an orange-indigo tail. It was a hazy-green color. As it came near, the warriors heard it speaking in whispers and hisses. After it passed, it made a rumble like thunder, and the earth trembled. Fire and smoke-dust knocked the men down, killing one of them. They were badly burned. Soon after, a terrible thunderstorm reached across the swampwoods lands with blue-white crackling fingers.

Days later, some warriors from the hunting party and others from their village walked to where the star had fallen. Their eyes widened in awe and amazement as they looked upon blackened earth and fallen trees. The trees were singed and smoking. They walked a great distance until they reached a deep burning pit. The trees all bent to the ground in circles, radiating out from the pit. The Indians became frightened and ran as a deep-green glow came, fog-like, creeping over the rim of the dark hole. This thing was not often spoken of thereafter. Sometimes, in whispered tones, Indian mothers would warn their children not to go near this evil spirit ground. The mothers warned their children that ghost creatures, more horrible than they could imagine, would take their spirits and, after much torture, would eat them alive. The medicine man had told me, "Never go to the land of the green fire."

I continued to keep watch. I fed the fire. I became very drowsy now. I made pine needle tea. Morning could not be far off. It was then, out of the pitch-darkness, that I heard the cry of the catamount. The sound was unlike anything I'd ever heard. It was like a woman in anguish and a desperate coyote's howl. My blood turned cold. I shivered. Deuter looked at me, her eyes orbs of fear. She stood up. Peering into the darkness, I saw the two green eyes. They stayed stationary, as if the thing was just sitting, waiting. Then, to my horror, I watched as two more sets of eyes appeared, one set on each side of the first eyes. Now there were three ominous pairs of glowing green eyes. Had these other two catamounts been waiting on either side of the cave entrance? Could there be more than three of these beasts? These ferocious cats were very different. Cougars and mountain lions hunt alone. They are not like wolves, which usually hunt in packs.

I had no time to reason about my enemies. I readied my bow and lay my quiver close at hand. My spear, likewise, I set near the fire. I kept my pot on the flames, with boiling water in it. I lit several torches and stuck them in the cave floor nearby, as once things started, I would not have time to light them. Deuter, my faithful Deuter, stood at the ready. The hair on her upper back stood up. It was then that something out of the ordinary occurred.

Deuter, who seldom howled in the seven years we had been together, gave forth the most forlorn and ominous howling sound I had ever heard. It was both haunting and unearthly. Like the sound some swamp creatures boil up with when winter's first icy grip catches them off guard. And strangely, from the depths of this vast gloomy cave-labyrinth came a howlish cry of great similiarity. An answer? All I can say about this cry is that it was not of this earth. It was a high-pitched moan, like a wolf in pain. Then it changed to a long, low, mesmerizing, softer sound, almost like a sad woman singing in tones. It radiated off the distant cavern's walls and spiraled down the mossy corridors. Yet it also seemed to come from within my own head. For some reason, it caused a deep-seeded fear to rise within my very soul.

I shuddered. I had no time for pondering and consideration now of this mysterious howl, for as I looked out into the dark of the night, I saw three pairs of eyes moving in low and together toward the orange opening. It was then that the unbelievable thing, the thing that haunts and causes me to awaken at night because I have seen it again in my dreams, came forth from the depths of the cave. All at once, the smell of burnt oranges, wet sandstone, and ancient moss permeated the cave. At first, a luminous ball of eerie-green haze, like Saint Elmo's fire, flowed out of a dark passageway. As it emerged, it materialized into the huge form of a prehistoric Dire wolf like creature. There were three stripes that ran vertically down its sides. Each stripe came to a point at the end. Deuter has the same stripes, except hers are black. It was luminous, glowing blue indigo. It was ghostly transparent. The blue displayed its massive form-outline. The stripes in were an unfamiliar, luminous orange color. This walking ghost creature that is similar to a Dire wolf, with colors out of space, was no more of this earth than a comet.

My thoughts raced. The comet, the ancient thing of cosmic fires that had blasted through nebulous bleakness to get here, must have brought this creature from somewhere beyond space. It stood still.

Turning its long toothed head at us, it seemed to look into Deuter's eyes with eyes of green fire. In a silent flash, its gaze went in the direction of the three pairs of threatening eyes. With one giant leap, it was upon them. I could hear the catamounts growl and then cry out with the pain of a thousand claws raking across their flesh. A fierce struggle and the crashing of branches burst through the stillness. I heard the sound of bones cracking and breaking. Then silence. The night and the giant blue-orange lightning bug beast was all that was visible. The luminous spirit beast turned and walked slowly back toward us.

For some reason, I put the spear I held in my hand down. The glowing entity walked right up to Deuter. The creature and Deuter touched noses. An undescribable sound, like warm sun on a wheat field or amber honey dripping from a flower, came from both of them. Then the giant luminous creature became a ball of green haze and drifted slowly back down into the depths of the cave again. Deuter came over to me, and we curled up near the whispering fire and drifted into a somber-cave cricket-song sleep.

I told no one of this. I felt these events too out of the ordinary for people to believe. Who knows what they would think. I kept the cave's existence a secret. Not because of those green crystals. Nor because of the ancient cave painting. I guess because whatever the strange beast in the cave had been, it had saved Deuter and myself. It was just a feeling. Like the one I had when I saw the luminious saber-cat and Deuter touch noses. It was a feeling of goodness and warmth. Maybe this unearthly creature, this creature out of space, was good. Maybe it was its soul that I had sensed. And its soul was kind.

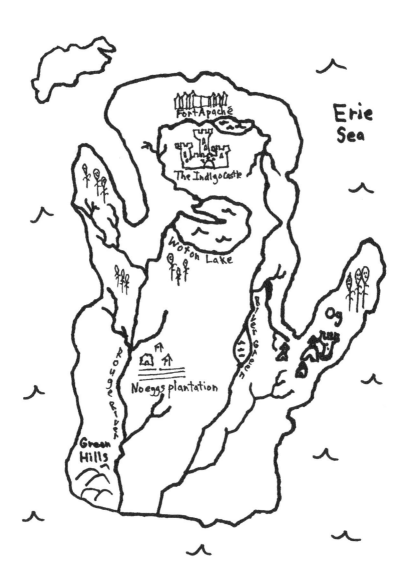

The Continent of M.U.R.

The Indigo Castle

Out of the sky and Into the Swamp Mud

It was late in the gold-green afternoon when the sky turned into gray-blue charcoal. The youth soared high above the continent of Mur. The continent that is about the same size and basic shape as the state of Michigan back on the planet Earth. That's when the mud began to fall. Chesh knew he would be a goner if he didn't land his cattail puff and find shelter. Now, red-ball lightning began to whiz about in the air around him like thousands of shooting stars. He began gliding down as quickly as he could while avoiding the mud flocks and whirling balls of fire. Fifty feet above the swampy surface, the tan-white puff that propelled him burst into orange flames. *Muggwomph!* was the last sound Chesh heard before he blacked out.

Opening his green eyes and feeling the warmth of the soft ooze around him, he realized he had landed in a yog-bog. It was dark, with billions of stars dotting the indigo sky. Realizing that he would slowly sink to a horrible death in the bottomless pit, he groped around for something to grasp and pull himself free. Ah, he was in luck. His right hand found a creeper vine, no doubt slithering in to feast upon him, having sensed the motion of his splat and, of course, smelling him. Chesh grasped the hungry vine with both hands, knowing they would be cut and torn by the carnivorous plant's spiky thorns, but he would be alive. Slowly, slowly, slowly, the cold vine arm drew Chesh out of the glowing yellow ichor encasing him. Relief pulsed through the youth's veins. He breathed deeply of the cool night air.

Just as he felt more solid ground touch his chest, he drew the cutlass knife from its sheath behind his neck and sliced the coarse, creeping death vine. It writhed like a worm cut in half. From the murky green darkness came an ear-piercing, inhuman shriek. It echoed about the pines and rotting tree falls surrounding him. The creeper vine was hurt, in pain. Chesh knew it would either send out many more tendrils, like creeping giant centipedes to seek and destroy him, or retreat into its dark lair to lick its wounds. He had to move out. Chesh touched his headlight on. He dragged his hook lines out of the murk. He wound the rope lines around his arm, cleaning the blackened remains of his puffball glider off.

He wasn't sure which way to head in the swamp-fogged soup. He chose to go in the direction opposite to the one that the creeper vine had come from. Chesh pushed a button on his sandals and mud paddles winged out on all four sides of them. He moved off into the marsh star night. After a time, he reached more solid ground. The dark summer over growth of the vast swamp country brushed his face. The youth sensed that he was moving gradually to higher ground. Sandy tan mud, cattails, and pines surrounded him. Not the giant sequoia-like cattails that shot up like mountains toward the planet's green sky. He was on a swamp island. Peering out, he could see the glowing green eyes of coyote-like animals that lived here. Silver-purple bats made whooshing, fluttering sounds as they hunted the air above. Plump June bugs were here early this year. Bat radar squeaks radiated through the morning's twilight.

Chesh retracted his mud paddles and trudged on. Feeling hunger pangs, he decided to seek a place to rest. As Meso's first green-gold rays burst through the fog, Chesh spotted a fallen tree. He made for it. He found the area dry. Plunking down near the soil-filled, uprooted base of the tree, the weary youth crossed his legs Indian style and ate some beef jerky and peanuts he had in his shoulder pack. He sipped icy water from a collar straw. Lastly, he savored a creamy chocolate bar, one of his favorite things of all the things in the endless universe. He felt better, less fatigued. Chesh's beetle-brown hair blew in the earthy-smelling air.

He touched his wrister to see if it still operated. The powerful microspeakers blared "*Twang twang twang*, we're goin' swamp ridin', giant cattail climbin'," a star country tune blasted out at his ears. The wrist communication device worked. It, however, was stuck on this station and was not able to send or receive audio-visual transmissions. *Oh well, I like classical and ambient music better, but I don't hate star country music. I'll survive,* he thought. The young planet pioneer knew he must begin the long trek back to the rubber tree plantation. He had taken a barring from the stars before when it was still dark. He had checked it with his compass. He would have to head north by northwest. It would be a long and treacherous journey through thick swamp pinewoods country.

Chesh slid his wasp pistol out of its belt clip. He aimed and fired at a rotting stump. An insect stream, an angry red beam, a shrill whine, and the stump turned into a melting mushroom candle. In an instant, the stump became brittle fall leaves, crumpling to dust in the wind. *Ka-thud.* Something struck him in the center of the forehead. Looking down, he saw a frantic June bug lying on its back, clawing the air. It was the size of a sparrow. It was tan with tiny rivers and streams of dark purple. The purple would glow in the dark. Most of the creatures and many of the plants on Myob glowed. It was the ones that didn't that you really had to watch out for. The colors white and black did not exist on this swamp planet unless they where brought from off world.

Chesh reached down and righted the struggling insect. He was famished now. He could have eaten the June bug, but Chesh didn't believe in killing things unless they were out to harm him. He took a peanut butter and jelly sandwich from the bright-blue pack and munched on it. *It will be afternoon soon, and Stesos will be comin' round the bend,* Chesh said to himself. Stesos was violet and made the temperature very, very hot. In the summer, anyway. Myob had winters too. Freezing green snow winters. A low rumbling echoed through the pines about Chesh. The cattails trembled. *Uh-oh,* he thought. He knew one of the large creatures that inhabited Myob was coming his way. He saved the rest of his sandwich and took cover in the dark water pooled at the base of the uprooted tree. The gargantuan footsteps rumbled closer and closer. He could hear trees being smashed aside. A twenty-foot pine fell at the clearing's edge. Cattails and brush parted.

The creature stepped into the open on giant beetle legs. It was a giant stego beetle. The massive legs had razor-sharp barbs running along their inner sides. It was the size of a one-story cottage. The gently curved body was tan. Three Earth-sky-blue scimitar-sword-blade swirling lines ran down each side of its body. They tapered to points at the lower ends. Chesh was in luck: stego beetles were herbivores. They are gentle swamp grazers that feast on swamp grasses and cattails. This beetle may have heard the wasp pistol or smelled his peanut butter and jelly sandwich and simply ambled over Chesh's way out of curiosity.

He didn't wish to anger the beetle. He knew they were gentle and intelligent, like horses. Stego beetles were used to haul the sap that they harvested from the giant rubber tree plants on the plantation. Chesh stepped out, walked slowly, lightly, up to the giant insect and extended his right arm, offering it the rest of his sandwich. The stego regarded the human with luminescent maroon eyes. It reached out slowly with a massive beetle arm-leg. As gently as a dragonfly landing on a leaf, the stego took the remnant of sandwich and ate it. Chesh noticed that a six-inch gash oozed green syrupy blood from near the end of the leg. Looking deeply into the enormous maroon orbs, he sensed the creature's pain. Chesh got some cool water from the brook and washed the wound. He then filled the opening with marsh mud and wrapped long swamp grasses around it and tied them fast. The stego beetle looked at Chesh, maroon fall leaf warmth shimmering from her eyes. She lumbered over to a reed pool and uprooted a bunch of cattails and dropped them at Chesh's feet. *Amazing,* thought the youth.

Chesh lounged about in the lush greenness next to a silvery gurgling brook, listening to the whispering winds of his sandhill refuge all day. The beetle stayed with him. *This beetle is very unusual and smart, a genius, I already realize this. It is just hard for me to think from its perspective. When I do, I am able to better see and understand the true unique wisdom of its genius,* thought Chesh as he looked at the tan-blue giant. *I already taught this beetle to sit when I hold up my index finger. I also say the word* sit. *If it—well, he or she—grasped this concept so quickly, who knows what is possible! Who can say where this gentle giant might lead? Surely it has evolved here for millions of years. The stego beetle's knowledge of this planet must be vast,* Chesh reasoned.

He was in no hurry to return to the settlement of dome houses and too-busy adults now. The youth's whole world seemed to stop like a bee sealed in amber. His view of the world around him seemed to have shifted, seemed off-kilter somehow. Chesh had never been very close to his father. He had never really forgiven him when his mom died in a freezing ice storm on a little-known world. His father had been away on a Zantarian planet, exploring giant glacial plates deep under red oceans. The plates contained many valuable minerals, tritium among them. Chesh had never really been on his own. Yeah, he had been on a few space-camping trips on various worlds. He had been in the Space Scouts on Roomerous-4 for two years. The scouts had used hovercrafts to go to a variety of interesting places and camped on planets, moons, asteroids, and the like.

But that was not the same as being on one's own. Without adults who always told and always knew. Who ordered and argued. Maybe it was because he was alone. Or maybe not having anyone know where he was had something to do with the good feeling deep within the chi of his stomach. Chesh only knew he felt very at ease in this vast, lush green swamp world. New feelings and thoughts welled up from within him. They grew along his tomato-vine soul. *I've never had any real adventures. I'm not much of an adventurer. More the stay-at-home, egghead type. Maybe it's time to try something new,* he thought.

"Well then, Mr. or Ms. Beetle, you'll need a name then. If or while were together, I'd like to call you something other than Mr. Beetle or Beetly. Let's see. Goliath, Talos, Qui-quag—no, I think not. Today is Tuesday, but no, I don't like that either. How about it, big guy or girl, what name do you want to be called, ay?"

Somehow as if by magic or telepathy or something, the name Peeny popped into Chesh's mind.

"Peeny? Did you say that? I've never heard the name Peeny before. Could I have spontaneously thought of it? Well, it is original. Peeny it is, then!" said Chesh. "Peeny sounds good! Peeny, I know your leg probably still hurts, but in not too long we are both going to get very hungry, and the peanuts, jerky, chocolate, and sandwiches in my pack will only go so far. We need to find food. I know cattail roots are edible. We have cattail root stew all the time at the plantation. I'll cook these and more for dinner. I'll see what else I can gather. After all, I am an expert on galactic mushrooms. I should be able to find some edible ones among the billions of mushrooms here on Myob."

Chesh hit the button on his wrister again. "I don't know who I'd been, a new metamorph gently rising. I see stars from here I know I've never seen. A thousand purple-orange monarchs swirl around me as I go swamp ridin', giant cattail climbin', all the while, *twang twang twang*." Chesh turned the wrister off.

"Must be a popular tune," he said.

Peeny looked at him and cocked her head, like a dog often does, as if to ask "What's that?" or "What are you doing?"

Chesh had decided Peeny was a female of the species. He could tell. Chesh had studied entomology extensively as he intended to become a universal entomologist. The dinosaur beetle lumbered over and began to eat some unshelled peanuts that Chesh had poured from his shoulder pack.

"Hey, we might need those. Stop, Peeny!" he exclaimed as he began scooping up the peanuts and putting them back into the pack. Peeny stepped over to a small reed pond and leaned down to chew on the tall green grasses around it. A giant Precambrian dragonfly hovered overhead. Its blue steel head and armor-green body were glinting and shimmering in the hue of purple light. It made several passes in straight lines then sped off toward the lush lowlands. Amber honey drops of benthum tree juice fell on Chesh's arms as he parted the vegetation and headed out on his quest for food. Peeny, to his surprise, followed him, her tan and blue dome shell towering above the thick sea of greenness.

They followed an ancient moss deer trail. Chesh saw mushrooms of many colors. Bright orange, pale blue, and brown with red dots. He picked some tan morels. They came upon a large area of raspberry vines. Peeny began feasting on the berries. Chesh ate handfuls as he harvested them. They gathered cattail roots, a green sweet grass, and a strange indigo blue husked corn. Chesh had never seen the corn before, but when he observed his beetle companion munching on some, he tried it, and finding it very much like sweet corn, he filled his pack with ears of it.

It grew warmer as the afternoon flowed on. Chesh began to feel tired and hungry. He wondered if the gentle beetle would let him ride atop her. He decided not to push the positive relationship the two had going. They headed back to camp. After a meal of cat-tail roots, roasted blue corn, and mushrooms, Chesh leaned back against the fallen tree and sipped pine needle tea. As the first stars of the Myobian night sky appeared, like millions of lightning bugs, the weary youth drifted off to sleep. His newfound friend lay, doglike, at his feet.

Life went on in this fashion for days. Yes, there were some new food discoveries. Cuca-pods, orange reed potatoes, and what Chesh called chicken plants because of their taste. And there was a vast menagerie of bizarre and unknown insects for study and obser-vation, both good and bad. The dragonflies were Chesh's favorites. They were mainly metallic shiny red or brilliant blue. These were the smaller ones. The prehistoric giants were metal green with sil-very blue heads. Whenever one of the smaller dragonflies landed on Chesh. Peeny made a happy humming sound. There were large bees also and abnormally big beetles of all kinds. Occasionally, a crow-sized wasp flew by menacingly. The mosquitoes were normal sized, at least the ones Chesh had run across so far. He found that since he had been eating the swamp's foods that he no longer needed his bug shield to repel either the mosquitoes or the biting flies. Even the fierce, tenacious moss deer flies avoided him.

I must discover what I am eating that causes this repulsive effect on these biting insects. I bet it could make a lot of people on a lot of worlds happy! he thought.

He didn't think of the riches a discovery could bring him. Chesh was not much on wealth. He was a rare type of person. One who had learned from an early age to value the here and now and what's in it. The kind of being who rescues hurt turtles, frogs, insects, and other creatures. He goes out of his way so as not to step on ants or their dwellings. "Ants live for seven years," he would always say to himself. Whenever an insect landed on him, Chesh felt special, honored. He looked at these visitations as omens of good fortune.

Chesh thought he had never enjoyed anything so much as this camping under the stars, in the swamp, with his newfound and most obtuse friend, the tan-and-blue beetle. He wished it would never end. *Why must it end?* he thought. But he realized his father would be worried sick about him. Surely people from the rubber plantation had been searching for him. Maybe they had found signs and traces of him back at the yog-bog, where he originally crashed. Maybe they thought him deceased. *Oh well*, thought Chesh, *a guy needs to be on his own, try out his wings. they'll be okay. After all, I cannot live all of my life sheltered and protected by my dad. Of course, I can't hurt him either.* Chesh knew he must ultimately return to the plantation. This would be hard for he was greatly enjoying this Robinson Crusoe–like life. The longer he stayed here, the harder it would be to go back. And what about Peeny? The two had grown very close even though their time together had been only about two weeks.

Peeny had let Chesh ride atop her. It was hard. Chesh used the sweaty stickiness of his legs to keep him on as there was nothing on the beetle's body for him to grasp. He had only fallen off a couple of times. Once when a twelve-foot-long centipede had reared up before them, and again when a red bristled thing the size of a barn and resembling an armadillo with the head of a rhinoceros beetle and the tail of an ankylosaurs sprang forth from some half-mile-high cattails. Peeny darted or lurched for the cover of a giant cattail or some dense underbrush. She used many techniques of ninja invisibility to elude aggressive creatures.

This reminded the young man of the times he had been forced into using his knowledge and skills in the martial arts of Tae Kwon Do, Judo, Isshin-ryu Karate, and Chinese Seven-Star Praying Mantis Kung Fu to elude or defend himself from bully deviates. The corridors, labyrinths, and rooms of school buildings became hiding places from the bullies of life. It was on the fields of battle that were the play or sports fields, where students pecked at one another like chickens in fenced pens or during gym classes that Chesh had chosen to defend himself. Chesh's dilemma had also become one of separation anxiety. Oddly enough, it was not separation from his father that bothered him so much. It was separation from his newfound beetle friend.

Chesh settled near the morning fire, his back against a log. He sipped his pine needle tea and gazed into the rising smoke and reflected. It was a murky day in the swamplands. The air was slow and thick. It had rained lightly in the night. The fern-covered green world wept. Chesh heard *"Slowly, slowly, slowly, said the slothos"* in his mind, as if telepathically.

Odd, does this beetle somehow project thoughts? he wondered. It was a different view of the land that Chesh now had riding atop Peeny. The giant beetle lifted her legs more slowly today, he noticed. *Maybe,* thought Chesh, *because there are more creepy crawlies about in this dampness. When I think about Peeny as a member of a species of giant beetle, relative to Darwinian evolutionism and Hodgkis's parallel planet hypothesis, she makes perfect sense. She had evolved to largeness in order to be better suited for survival. Being large allowed her to walk over many hazards, like red-death vines and spikers. It also made it possible for her to look out over vast expanses. This capability helped sustain the beetle's gleaning, grazing lifestyle, as well as alerting her to any threats or dangers.*

The gray cloud cover changed into fluffy giants tumbling in the green sky. The wind came, sweeping millions of multicolored moths in gusts. Chesh and his beetle steed moved slowly and quietly among the reeds. They paused, and Peeny knelt down to allow her rider to get off. The youth gathered morel mushrooms, blue corn, wild strawberries, and his favorite, chicken plant pods. The pods were shaped like large gourds. They were bright blue with thin orange stripes running lengthwise.

"I know you don't like them much, Peeny, but to me they taste like one of my favorite Earth foods, syntha chicken," Chesh said apologetically to his companion.

Suddenly the massive stego lifted its head skyward. She seemed to be sniffing the air. She looked at Chesh as if to beckon him aboard. Chesh had not seen this behavior before. He stuffed the last gord into the reed sack he had made and climbed up onto the beetle. Peeny took off at almost a gallop to the west. They skirted over pines and poplars. Through ponds, rivulets, and marl bogs. Finally, upon entering a valley-like area of larger trees and deep-green ferns and mosses, they came upon the thing that had called Peeny forth. Hanging suspended, caught in a rope net trap, was a humanlike creature. It neither struggled or cried out. *Perhaps it is dead*, thought Chesh.

Then the green-skinned creature moved. It made a kind of chirping sound that signaled distress. Peeny lowered her front spindly legs, signaling to Chesh "You should help," he guessed. The young man climbed down. He walked toward the net. Chesh saw that the creature entrapped was an Ogtavian. A Frogger, as the plantation workers called them. She, for the Ogtavian was a she, was very like a human. She had green skin, yes. And wore what to Chesh were odd garments, but she was quite humanlike. With the exception that her face had a subtle, unexplainable hint of froggishness about it. Maybe it was the somewhat wide and sensual lips. He could see her deep-indigo eyes looking pleadingly at him. Chesh took a small folding knife from one of his pockets. He carefully cut through the rope. After some strategic sawing, the creature was free.

She slid to the moss-sponge ground. She stood erect, and looking into the eyes of her rescuer, she said, "Thank you. My name is Deedo." She was beautiful. Almost oriental. The Ogtavian girl had high cheekbones, a turned-up nose, and streaming black hair. She was short, about four feet tall. She had a slender, well-proportioned body. She wore a one-piece oblique mist-blue shirtlike garment that displayed slender but muscular legs. About her neck, she wore an indigo-silver necklace with a crescent moon on it.

Chesh's eyes widened. "You speak English? I didn't know Ogtavians spoke our language! How did you learn it?"

"Yes, I can speak eighty-seven languages. Most of the languages are from planets far from Myob. Many of us have learned to speak languages by studying voice waves that come from outer space. Some languages have been brought back by our cosmic explorers of the long past. I must leave soon. As should you. The horned ones that set this trap will soon be back to check it. They may be near now," the beautiful young woman whose face possessed subtle frog-like features explained anxiously.

"The horned ones? You must mean the rustlers. The ugly, horned lizard-like things that come here to harvest minerals. I've heard that they capture creatures to sell on other worlds as slaves or work animals. I've only seen them once. One day about a year ago, some came to the plantation and argued with my father and some men. They wanted to drill for cobalisite on the plantation land. They left very angry and told my dad they'd be back," said Chesh.

"I must go quickly. Good-bye," said the Ogtavian.

"Please wait. I really am not sure where to go. You see, I'm kind of lost. I was floating on a cattail puff and got caught in a fireball storm. I guess I should head back to the plantation," Chesh explained.

"You know, I need to get back to Og. My father will be grateful. He will reward you, if you should choose to come with me. I'm sure we can get you safely back to your people once the danger has passed," said the Ogtavian anxiously.

"Traveling together would be safer. We have a saying on my native world, 'There is safety in numbers.' Yes, my friend and I will be glad to accompany you to the place you call Og," answered Chesh confidently. "And it just wouldn't do to have you become captured after just setting you free from a trap."

"My thank-yous be with you, in that case. What may I call you?" asked Deedo.

"Please call me Chesh." Chesh extended the index finger of his right hand. The patient stego beetle sat, lowering her rear so as to allow riders. The pair climbed aboard. Chesh had the Ogtavian girl hold onto his shoulders.

"I must ask, how did you ever befriend this myst beetle? They are very secretive creatures, rarely seen, let alone ridden, such as we are now doing. I am beyond belief! How?" The girl's eyes grew wide.

"She just wandered up out of the swamp where I stopped to rest after I walked away from the yog-bog that I crashed into. She was hurt. I gave her some food and bandaged her wounded leg. She just stayed around after. I don't know why. I call her Peeny. I don't know how rare these stegos are, though. We use them on the plantation to move things mostly. We treat them well. They just come in and work. We feed them mostly oats and wheat. They leave whenever they wish. Different beetles come at different times."

"We know. We watch. You see, those beetles that work for you are the norm of the stego beetle family. This stego that we are atop is called by my people a myst stego beetle. However, its stripes have a deeper, almost indigo color near the tips. This stego beetle's stripes end in back-facing curves. The regular stego's stripes' curved ends point forward. Your beetle is very different from any I have ever seen or heard of because she has no horns. The myst stegos are known to have special abilities and senses. They have been seen, rarely, using a deep-green ray that shoots forth from their eyes. Each time, the beetles used the ray to save their own lives.

"They are said to be telepathic, have precognition, and to see places from great distances by way of mental images. They can emit fog clouds of inky blueness that hide them or help them to elude predators. They can hear and smell over great distances, like whales of Earth. These elusive creatures are almost never seen. I find it difficult to grasp and fathom that I am traveling on one of these strange beetles," finished the Ogtavian.

"Incredible, simply incredible!" said Chesh, a look of sheer amazement displayed on his face.

They had traveled a great distance over sand reed hills and now into unending murk-water swamp. Peeny was striding at a fast pace and heading northeast when the rustlers came upon them. They emerged from a rambling wall of tall trees and giant cattails, three armored, horny-backed dark lizard men riding on the backs of giant snapping turtles the color of moss and slate. The dark riders came crashing and thundering across the open expanse of swampland. Large wooden swivel ballistae shot insect swarms over the beetle riders. And then the sticky giant spiderweb net closed over them.

Chesh and Deedo were now being held captive in a fenced large wooden enclosure. The crude roof of peat and the logs that formed it were all wrapped in thorny bramble vines. Six Ogtavians were being held also. Deedo and Chesh helped take care of the wounded. The stego beetle was chained some distance away. An armored ankylosaurs, a giant sloth bear, and a Pennsylvanian-period, monarch-like butterfly the size of a large tree were chained nearby.

The snapper-riding rustlers had descended upon them so quickly they had had no time to react. A large jagged harpoon arrow had grazed Peeny along the left side. It opened a slice wound, from which green liquid, which was the beetle's blood, had oozed. A vast web net enshrouded around them by jay wasps froze Chesh, Deedo, and Peeny in its sticky darkness. Chesh and Deedo were thrust into cages mounted on the snappers' backs. Peeny had been treated more cruelly. A manacle was locked around one of the wounded beetle's legs. She was dragged along, her wound bleeding into the swampy sands. They were being held, along with the other unfortunate captives, until dawn, when they would be taken to the lizard men's detention fort.

"I can tell you why the myst beetle did not fight. Myst beetles, as I said, are very extrasensory. They can read thoughts and feelings, we believe. Although we know little about these elusive creatures, we do know, from ancient Ogtavian mythology and some rare observation, that these complex creatures may well imitate the behaviors of their companions. Myst beetles are just so rare that we know little. Chesh, you did not really want to harm the rustlers, did you?" asked Deedo.

"Well, ah, well, I don't really know. I never thought about it," answered Chesh.

"You never fired your stinger weapon at them, did you?"

"Well, no, I never really had the time, though," said Chesh.

"Chesh, you never even drew it out!" Deedo prodded.

"Well, no, you're right. I never even reached for it. I don't know why."

"I do. It is not in your nature to kill, is it, Chesh?"

"I don't know. Well, I guess not," said Chesh.

Something opened up within the youth like a new blooming rose reaching moist petals to the sun, extending green thorns. Chesh thought of escape and survival. He sensed and felt the myst beetle's pain and anguish deep within the tendrils of his soul. He must save his companion. He did not care if he died doing it. Chesh could no longer watch as his friend Peeny suffered. Myob's green-purple dusk descended on millions of giant crickets's angry chirps. The three lizard men had started a large fire and sat around it, drinking from large tarnished mugs. They were roasting a maroon-and-blue creature that writhed and made piercing howl-shriek noises. It looked like a three-foot ant with the head of an anteater. A sweet, pungent odor permeated the air, along with billows of acrid, oily dark smoke.

Chesh watched the lizard things closely and hatefully as he sawed at the vines that held the large cage structure together, using the edge of a razor-sharp rock fragment. The lizard rustlers' camp was in a small clearing of reed grasses. The clearing was surrounded, overshadowed, by the towering sequoia cattails. They stretched a mile or more into the deep-blue depths of night. They were millions of years old. Wind echoed far above in their heights. Extremely large oaks and tall pines grew, with exposed root systems, in the tarn forest. The alien lizard men had chosen this spot wisely, for it was on higher ground, which afforded it an overview of the open swamplands. Being surrounded by the massive trees and the black tarn in which they grew made this location difficult to attack.

After their gruesome meal, one of the lizard men slither-climbed up one of the giant cattails to keep watch. The other two walked over to the cage enclosure. They were looking at Deedo with cruel, hungry reptilian eyes.

"For a frog, she's not too bad-a to gaze upon, aya, Rusug?" said the taller lizard rustler through curved fangs stained with deep-blue ichor.

"Not bad to look at-a, and what's that charm of metal-a she wears? I wonder if it beez worth-a any star marks or gems?" replied the other rustler.

"Here then, let's get-s the pretty out and have a look-a. Murdort will care little, lost in draughwine far, far, above-a. Yer, let's have a time!" said the taller lizard man, opening the door of the cage. He entered the cage and grabbed Deedo.

Chesh ran at him, slicing at his arm with the jagged rock. He was pushed away by a three-fingered clawed hand in his face. Chesh's head cracked into a cage log. He fell a crumpled husk. The youth shook his head. He was up. He did not think, only focused. He became an angry mantis. He sprang, reaching the cage door just as the lizard thing pulled it. Fiercely, he plowed into the large spiked creature. One lightning slice across the neck opened a wide gash in the leather flesh. A wave of brown blood surged from the wound.

The scaled lizard hand opened, freeing Deedo. Simultaneously, a loud roar shattered the air—an eerie giant beetle roar. It was Peeny. She jerked her leg. The giant snapper's yellow eyes spit fear as they ripped free of their shackles and bolted away from the enraged beetle. With a rhino's rage, Chesh charged the other lizard man as it drew a long dagger from its belt. Slash, chop, the scaled-lizard head looked up from gray mud, staring, blindly in search of its dismembered body. The leather-clad, spiky body jerked and convulsed in its violent death dance, spurting brown liquid into the night air. It fell to the ground twitching.

The third rustler began shooting orange-lightning firebolts directly at Chesh from partway down the giant cattail. Chesh sidestepped the firebolts and threw the razor stone using a windmill motion. The stone struck the rustler in the forehead, just above the nose. Brown blood gushed from the long vertical wound as the rustler dropped. Chesh, eyes aglow, then turned to the chained creatures. He gave out a cry that pierced the gray-purple air. The youth set his beetle friend free. He then set the other chained creatures free. The Myobian creatures looked at Peeny for an instant then turned and moved off to their realms. The six Ogtavians, clad in brown and green, moved toward their princess, Deedo. They looked up to the indigo tapestry of stars above. This is an Ogtavian gesture of thanks. Silently, they waited to follow.

The giant beetle turned, looked toward Chesh, and walked over to him. Peeny nudged Chesh and looked at him as if to say "Climb on. Let us be gone."

Chesh looked lovingly at the big beetle and said, "Thanks, friend, Peeny." He petted the beetle gently. As they rode toward the sand castle kingdom of Og, Deedo's home among cattail marsh pools, giant lily pads, and tens of thousands of shimmering dragonflies, the pair spoke.

"You, Chesh, will be well rewarded. Best to think of something worthy. I am an Ogtavian princess. My father is the king of our kind. His name is Monarch Wapiti. He does not hate your people. He simply seeks to know and understand you. We could have had our copper frogs vaporize all of your kind if we wished. We have had great difficulty using control in not destroying the lizard things. We never wish to kill. Those of Og only wish to live in harmony with the nature. Maybe by knowing me and my people better, you could help to achieve a better understanding between us. Maybe," spoke Deedo.

"A princess. I am honored. I feel humble. I feel happy. In this universe of infinity, where there are infinite possibilities and infinite diversity, I believe our peoples should and can coexist and, if wished, help one another toward harmonious cosmic unity. Thank you, Princess Deedo, for your honesty and compassion. On faithful steed, Peeny, to Og, good friend, please," said Chesh, smiling.

A blue-and-green dragonfly landed on Chesh's left shoulder. After several hours, the large myst beetle stopped abruptly. She went on point like a well-trained hunting dog. Peeny's head moved about, sniffing the air. She stopped pointing straight toward a clump of rustling cattail reeds. Chesh thought he heard the word *danger* reverberate inside the walls of his mind. He sniffed the air. It smelled of sulfurous, stagnant swamp water. Yet the scent was somehow sweetened. Like patulli tree oil with a hint of maple syrup. Chesh stared at the spot that his beetle friend was intent on.

"Oh, do not worry, Chesh. The myst beetle is only smelling the copper scent of our guardian frogs. We have reached the outer perimeter of Og. The guardian frogs will not harm us for they picked up my scent long ago, and recognizing it, they will not strike. The copper smell is no doubt unfamiliar to your friend as she may have never before ventured into this land. If you will allow me, I shall retrieve one of the copper frogs and hold it near to the beetle so that she may see that it is no threat. Or you may do this, if you wish," Deedo explained, her long-lashed large shimmering-blue eyes blinking happily.

"Will the guardian frogs harm me?" asked the youth.

"No, not as long as you are with me. Have no worries, Chesh," replied the princess of Og.

"I'll just watch, this time anyway, I think. Maybe if it's okay, I'll try it another time," said Chesh with a smile.

"As you wish," said Deedo.

She climbed down slowly and walked over to the small pond. A soft cheerful chirping came from the pond's reedy shoreline. Deedo reached down into the water. She lifted a leopard frog–sized shiny object into the air. Chesh could see the bright glinting rays of coppery sunlight reflect from the guardian frog. As Deedo came closer, Peeny sniffed uneasily. Chesh tried something. In his mind, he said the words "Easy, Peeny. Easy, my girl." The giant beetle seemed to give a relaxing shrug. She stared intently at the unknown thing with her glowing dinner-plate-sized maroon eyes.

"It's okay, Peeny. See, it is only a guardian frog that watches our territory. It means us no harm. It will only harm those it knows to be a threat to Og. See." With that, Deedo lifted the shiny frog close to Peeny's nostrils. The beetle sniffed cautiously at the unfamiliar creature. Upon closer viewing, Chesh could see the frog had glowing deep-blue eyes. It appeared to be made of copper metal, yet there were no seams. It was a thing of beauty.

"Do you wish to hold it, Chesh?" asked Deedo.

"Are you sure it won't harm me?"

"Yes, I am sure. Have trust in me, please."

Chesh reached out with his right hand, saying mentally, "It's okay, Peeny."

The frog was warm, not cold like metal. It did not move, simply gave out a chirp as if to say "He's okay." Chesh handed the frog back to Deedo. She gently returned it to its post among the whispering cattail reeds.

As they lumbered slowly onward, mugwumps and razorback beetles scurried among the weeds, and scadillions of dragonflies flittered about in the mossy air. The sky turned a deep-purple color as Myob's first sun began to disappear over the horizon. Chesh pushed the button on his wrister. "I dreamed I was a flyin', not in muck or marl lyin'. 'Cause I'll be swamp ridin', giant cattail climbin," it blared and twanged out.

Deedo froze. "What is that?" the Ogtavian asked in a soft, somewhat alarmed voice.

"Aw, it's just some song that they keep playing. It must be a hit or something," said Chesh.

"Hit," Deedo said questioningly.

"*Hit* just means a song that is popular."

"Oh, I see. However, *hit* defined by your *Webster's Dictionary* means 'to strike violently,' does it not?" asked Deedo.

"Yes, but in our language, it's possible for words to take on different meanings, especially when the words are used as slang," Chesh answered.

"Slang, oh, yes, language altered via enculturation to take on multiple meanings I understand."

A threatening howl-growl sound rang out from some giant cattails that were about three-hundred yards ahead of them. Peeny stopped and sniffed the air.

"That sounds like an animal in pain!" exclaimed Chesh.

"Yes, it is a giant slothos. They are no threat, harmless really, unless bothered," said Deedo.

"Should we try to help?" asked Chesh.

"Yes, of course we should. We must also think about making camp as it shall be dark soon."

"How much farther until we reach Og?" asked the youth.

"Not far now, about three days—three Myobian days, that is," answered the princess.

The six Ogtavians that had been following along silently all nodded their froggish heads. As if she had read their thoughts, the myst beetle slowly ambled in the direction of the anguished cries. In a short while, they reached a small clearing among the towering cattail trunks. On the marsh ground, near a partially nawed giant cattail, lay a massive creature. Light-blue liquid poured forth from a deep wound in one of its legs. The creature resembled a prehistoric tree slough—only it was six stories in height and had shiny long maroon fur.

Chesh and the Ogtavians all stared at the helpless creature as Peeny knelt down on her forelegs to let her riders down. A storm moved in, sending purple lightning bolts to peck at Myob-like giant storks. The ever-present winds began to blow harder, sending out ominous whistling and shrieking sounds among the ancient shadowy trunks. The slothos lay in a pool of its own blood, emitting the sound of labored breathing. Its amber-yellow eyes were trained on the strange group. It seemed to Chesh that the gargantuan creature was looking right into the eyes of his beetle companion. Pointy, rubbery-looking blue spikes protruded from the maroon fur. Its fore claws were each as big as a man. They were the color of blue coral.

"Can you help the creature?" Chesh asked.

"Me! You were the one who helped the myst beetle. Why would you not help this creature as well?" returned Deedo.

"I just figured, well, since it's your planet—" Chesh paused as he saw a look in the girl's eyes that almost said "Don't look at me" to him. "Okay, yeah, why not. I guess I don't have much to lose. Well, okay," Chesh said as he slid down the shiny beetle's back.

Deedo dismounted as well and followed closely behind the youth. As Chesh approached the slothos, it shifted in order to keep its eyes on him. He knelt down by the wounded leg of the beast. Slowly, slowly Chesh extended his hand down, softly touching the massive leg just below the gash. He left his hand there for a few seconds to see if the slothos would trust him. The slothos growled gutturally. A clawed paw rose high into the air. Chesh removed his hand slowly. He stood upright and tiptoed toward the head of the slothos. It displayed shiny long purple saber teeth.

When he got right in front of the slothos's face, Chesh reached into a large flapped pocket on his pants, where he had carried a stun beamer. Deedo had a look of fear in her eyes. The other Ogtavians looked on, frozen with fear, for they knew well the destructive power of one of these animals when angered, and this slothos was wounded as well. Chesh's hand came out in a slow draw. He bent toward the creature's mouth, getting dangerously close. The slothos wrinkled its nose slightly. Chesh reached down, opening the hand to reveal a small cluster of peanuts. He placed these on the ground gently. He then moved away. The slothos moved its head to sniff the peanuts. A gust of wind raced by Chesh's ears as the giant creature inhaled the peanuts into its mouth. It looked at the youth as if to say "You got any more?" Chesh's weapon had been taken by the lizard men when Deedo and he were captured.

Chesh went about gathering up swamp grasses, with which he would bind the wound. He again went over to the slothos slowly. He rinsed the wound that was about two feet long with water from his canteen. The creature moved not. He then filled the wound with swamp mud. Lastly, Chesh placed the swamp grass over the wound and secured it using twine that he always carried. Finished, he again walked to the creature's head and placed a bigger hand full of peanuts before it. The slothos looked at Chesh, blinking the huge train lanterns that were its eyes and made a long gentle purring sound. It did not inhale these peanuts, possibly choosing to save and savor them. The relieved slothos just looked at Chesh.

A soft wind-driven rain began to fall, making light pattering noises as it hit the giant cattails and mud ground. Lightning flashed, illuminating the amazed Ogtavians' light-blue eyes and faces with a purple glow.

On to Og

As they sat by the orange flames of a warm fire that night, suddenly out of nowhere, Chesh's wrister came on. It displayed a text message, as well as spoke it:

> Star-tran message. Attention, Uri Santory. Regrettably, my son, Chesh, has been lost. I must take a small party and search for him. There is little hope of finding him alive on this hostile planet. This will, of course, result in less man-power to run the plantation. Please advise me on this as soon as possible. If you will not allocate personnel to join the search, I shall go alone. Mathew Kaden.

Chesh's father's image flashed onto the small screen for an instant, and then it went blank. He had looked very perplexed to the lost teen. Chesh thought, *He looked real upset.* Glowing small yellow-green eyes gazed out from the swamp brush and fallen branches that surrounded the camp. Peeny slept not far from the fire. The rain continued, so Chesh constructed a complex lean-to–like structure to keep the light rain off. The Ogtavians did not utilize the shelter, preferring to sleep around the pine-sheltered campfire. Deedo had gone swimming in a nearby pond. Now she looked at the youth, seeming to sense his pain.

"Where did you live on your Earth, Chesh?" she asked.

"I lived next to the biggest inland lake in the state called Michigan. Woton Lake is a shallow lake similar to a prehistoric lake from the

Permian period. The lake is surrounded by swamp, miles and thousands of miles of swamp-woods. I grew to love the swamp and its mysterious, secretive creatures. Hidden things are astounding! Watson, my coyote-like dog, and I spent a lot of our time there," Chesh answered sullenly as he stirred the dying ambers with a stick and placed a log on the fire. The slothos slept peacefully where it had lain.

"Are you angry with your father, Chesh?" quarried Deedo.

"I've been angry with my father most of my life." The youth shifted his legs restlessly as he leaned back against a gray deadfall tree.

"I have difficulty understanding that as we of Og do not hold grudges." Deedo looked deeply into the orange-and-blue dancing flames.

Chesh said a polite "Good night" then drifted off to his lean-to for some rest.

Ten-thousand copper frogs began to chirp rhythmically. When he awoke, Chesh found himself covered in spiderwebs. "What the heckle! What are these? Hey, Deedo, what are these webs from?" he exclaimed, examining himself for bites.

"Do not worry, Chesh, they are only from dream spiders. They will not harm you. The spiders climbed their web strings and are high in their homes in the seed pods of the giant cattail trees by now." Deedo appeared in front of the lean-to, a froggish smile adorning her face. She too was coated with webbing.

"Well, why in the heckle do they weave their webs on us? I mean, what purpose does it serve them in the survival-food-chain, arachnid lifestyle they live?" Chesh looked confused.

"Remember, these are not Earth spiders, Chesh. The dream spiders weave the webs in exchange for our dreams. They have the power to see our dreams and, in a sense, become our sleeping selves. This gives them the pleasure of experiencing other creatures' lives in a way. In return, the host dreamer retains the highly prized and tasty web material to eat as a delicacy that brings both extremely robust health and immunity to venomous bites. Do you see, Chesh?"

"I think so. I dreamt of my swamp, the Long-Crossing Swamp, on Earth. I hope they enjoyed it. Can they be harmful?" asked Chesh.

"Only if harmed. If threatened with death, the dream spiders can blowgun spit a dart with venom so deadly that it can instantly drop a slothos like the one you helped. Sometimes in the swamp, the smallest things are the deadliest things. Let us be going. I have cooked Orang-ee roots, swamp beans, and tavlanga mushrooms for our morning meal. The mushrooms taste like your ham, I think." Deedo moved to the fire, where several leaf bowls simmered and smoked, sending pleasant, unknown food smells mixed with the scent of ham into Chesh's nostrils.

"Yeah, okay. Hang on a minute, please. I have to . . . ah . . ." Chesh searched for words that in Ogtavian meant go to the bathroom. Finding none better, he said, "Get rid of some unwanted stuff," and scurried into the swamp brush like a frightened rabbit.

When he returned, he ate heartily of the delicious fare while trying to remove some of the white webbing from himself. Chesh tasted some of the webbing. "Tastes like chocolate vaguely with an orangy flavor subtly mixed in."

"It is good that you seem to enjoy the webbing as we do. The more you consume, the stronger your body becomes. Do not worry about the webbing on your garments, for Myob's never-ceasing winds will whisk you clean of it in no time," Deedo advised as the wind picked up around them, causing the pine branches to wave excitedly.

The giant slothos had vanished in the night, leaving only a spot of indigo blood to attest to its past presence. Chesh walked over to Peeny, who was grazing gently on some yellow-tan grasses.

"Come on, Peeny, let's go, please," he said.

The stego did not move or even glance at him as she usually did.

"Come on now, Peeny. We must travel a long way today. Please, Peeny."

Still no movement from the beetle, just a look. The forlorn look of a dog whose treats had been given to another dog. Chesh took out a handful of peanuts and offered them to his friend. She sauntered over and gobbled them down in one quick gulp. Deedo poured water on the fire, and the small company departed.

Deedo made a kind of clearing-her-throat noise, like she wanted Chesh to listen. "Chesh, my people wish to become more proficient at your language, your English. It is my hope that you could teach them. I know my father, Monarch Wapiti, wishes it so. Would you do this, ah, please, Chesh?" Deedo looked at the youth, her eyebrows raised slightly.

"Hmmm, I don't know how long I'll be staying around. My dad's pretty upset. I don't want to stress the guy out too much." He banged his wrister with an index finger. It made a crackling noise then cut in with, "Don't know when I'll ever find time, 'cause I'm just now a dyin'. It's kind of a dark time, the autumn of my life's a shinin'. So I lay back on the soft earth, and I just think that I'll go swamp ridin', giant cattail climbin', all the while, *twang twang crackle crackle.*" The wrister went silent again.

"Darned thing," Chesh grumbled.

"That is the same song, is it not, Chesh?" asked Deedo, looking at Chesh.

"Yeah, it's some star country tune. It must be the current number one hit," answered Chesh.

Deedo had a very confused look on her greenish face. They rode on in silence. The swamp's water had deepened greatly due to the rain. Ghost winds of ancient Myob howled through the mile-high cattails. The water was three to five feet deep in places. Peeny had no difficulty traversing it and glided along at a good clip.

Chesh thought he could hear humming. *Of course, that couldn't be*, he thought.

The temperature gradually grew warmer under Myob's first green sunrays. White angels' hair webbing drifted everywhere. Chesh was soon covered again in dream spiders' webbing. He began to remove it from his eyes and mouth. He reached, backhanded, around into a pocket on the right side of his pack and pulled out a pair of protective goggles from it and put them on. Thinking he heard giggles from behind, he turned and looked at the Ogtavians hard. All seven sat motionless, perpetual half smiles upon their faces. As they moved on, Chesh quickly realized that the goggles made the web situation worse as he became blinded and had to use both hands to clean them off. He put the goggles back into his pack.

"Well, I've been thinking about how to teach your people English. It won't be easy because of the slang, and slang is always shifting like sands on a desert. Let's try, though! This will remove some of the boredom of the journey as well. Not that I'm bored. I could look every nanosecond upon the wonders of your world. I thought maybe you could be bored, seeing as you probably travel this area a lot," said Chesh.

"Board?" asked Deedo. "You mean like we turn into the material you call wood? The thing that your ancestors made their dwellings of?"

"No, not wooden boards. Bored as in you're tired of doing something. Bored like when there's nothing to do, nothing to watch on the viddy screen, nothing fun to occupy your time," Chesh explained.

"Oh, yes, I think I understand. There is more than one kind of bored. It would be like having no chores or activities for one to occupy one's time. Like if the wind died down and I could not go swamp riding on my hover disk, or there are no clouds to watch and no water to swim in," Deedo sighed.

"Well, yes, pretty much," said Chesh.

"Does not *pretty* mean "nice to look at"?" she asked.

"Well, ah, there's two kinds of pretty too," replied Chesh. "Let's try this. It's from one of my favorite old viddies of the Three Stooges. Repeat after me, Deedo." Chesh began to sing merrily, "A-a-say, a-a-say, a-i-bicky-by, a-i-bicky-by. Come on, join in if you want to learn!"

The regal princess began and was immediately followed by all six Ogtavians. "Now try B-a-b, b-a-b, b-i-bicky-by, b-i-bicky-by. C-a-c, c-a-c, c-i-sicky-si, c-i-sicky-si, c-a-c." The singing grew louder, and the smiles became wider. "D-a-d, d-a-d, d-i, dicky-di, d-i, dicky-di, d-a-d," Chesh and his Ogtavian students ambled cheerfully along.

By the time Myob's green sun had risen high, the group had sung through the twenty-six letters of the alphabet many times. By late afternoon, the purple lightning's thunder began to rumble and crackle. Peeny made for the highest ground she could find and hunkered down in an area sheltered by many giant cattail trees, giant Permian horsetails, and violet webcap mushrooms the size of houses. The terrain had changed some, and ferns as large as oaks grew everywhere. These ferns acted like huge umbrellas. They had silvery-purple bark on their trunks. The massive fern leaves were of a shimmering, radiant medium-blue color. Chesh and the weary Ogtavians set up camp on a sandy hill. Deedo and some of the others began preparing foods from roots, berries, wheat-like swamp grasses, and a few small yellowy fern plants called Segwa.

Chesh was busying himself by making a lean-to structure resembling a small hogan. Peeny lolled about, munching on swamp grasses that the Ogtavians had gathered.

"What the byamit is making my rear end itch so much?" Chesh grumbled in a low voice, scratching his rear end vigorously. It had been torturing him all day and now became unbearable.

"Are you experiencing some difficulty?" quarried Deedo.

"Yes, I'm having a problem. My hind end feels like a million fleas are biting it!" Chesh exclaimed with anger.

"Can I ask just one thing, Chesh, one thing that might rid you of your itching?" asked Deedo.

"Well, sure, sure, if you think it will help. I never mind you, or the others, for that matter, asking whatever they wish," answered Chesh.

"When you were in the brush this morning, did you touch anything with gray leaves?"

"Ah, well, ah, yes, I'm pretty sure I did. They were small plants with leaves kind of like maple trees'."

"That is the cause. Some of the gray-leaved plants are toxic, poisonous. You touched the gray-malkin plant's leaves. They are the cause of your itching. I will make a cream which you may rub on yourself to make the discomfort go away. I do not wish to discuss a subject that is delicate to many alien races, like the Krang warriors, for example. We do this type of business in the water and use no leaves. I suggest you do likewise, Chesh. I hope I have not offended you." The petite princess explained, her cheeks darkening with a blush.

Chesh stopped his hut building and walked over to the fire. "Thanks, Deedo. I appreciate your kindness."

"And you are kind as well," said Deedo.

She began gathering handfuls of a long red grass. She placed these in a leaf pot she quickly constructed of mud and placed it over the fire, adding water from a nearby rivulet. In a short time, the grasses had boiled. Chesh noticed a sweet-leaf-burning smell in the air. Deedo removed the leaf bowl, placing it near the fire. She removed a rock, as if by magic, from beneath her pale-green tunic. She used this stone tool to crush and pulverize the sweet grasses into a mushy reddish paste.

"Do you wish to apply the pitouch, or would you prefer to have one of my people do it?" Deedo asked.

Purple flashes began to rumble and illuminate wispy night clouds in the distance. The heavy winds of this morning howled like wild coyotes.

"That's okay. I'll put the stuff on. Thanks," said Chesh, scratching.

The princess handed him the leaf bowl, exhibiting a slight, shy smile. When Chesh returned, he sat down by the fire refreshed. The group sat around the glowing orange blaze in a triangular shape. Deedo was looking up at the twinkling stars and speaking. "That is Theeus," she said, pointing skyward. "It is the constellation closest to Ni, the green planet that leads us to Og. It is said that long, long ago, our ancestors were helped by the great warrior Theeus. He descended to them and showed them the ways of making arrow tips. These were used for hunting the Mammots and other beasts that attacked them. Theeus was a great warrior from above. There lies the Caston nebula. And there, Jemiflax, the spike-tailed reed cat. And there, the crafty trickster Coy-at. He watches in silence."

"Where is Jubilon, the sloth bear?" asked a younger Ogtavian named Zom.

"Jubilon guards the eastern sky in this time of our planet's turning. He has just awoken from his winter slumber and moves lazily and drowsily about near the entrance to his cave."

Chesh interrupted, "We have names for our stars, constellations, and nebulas too. Some of them are Leo, Casiopia, Virgo, and Hercules. Some Earthers believed that the stars controlled their destinies. My constellation is Leo the lion. He is a fierce creature of the jungle and savanna grasses. He is a large cat with a lot of fur around his neck. Leo was said to be brave yet to have a kind heart. There is an ancient story, or myth, about Leo. It was said that one day while out hunting, the great lion encountered a small deer fawn, or baby. The fawn was standing near its mother's lifeless body, mewing, crying out in anguish. The mighty lion from the night sky crept over slowly. Instead of swiping it with a massive clawed paw and satisfying its hunger, the lion chose to adopt and care for the small deer. Even now, the deer can be seen in the Earth's night sky, sitting at the feet of its savior."

The Ogtavians stared at the youth with glowing sapphire eyes.

"Our solar system, which we call Ni, after the smallest planet in it, is composed of two suns. The first sun to rise is called Mesos and is green. The after-midday sun that appears is purple and is named Stesos. Our planets rotate counterclockwise. Our solar system has six planets: Trigeon, Regolian, Myob, Ciaron, Kelsauros, and Ni. Myob has three moons, is the size of your gas giant, Jupiter, and has blue and orange rings similar to the rings of Saturn.".

"Long ago when science and technology ruled our lives, we ventured forth into the universe. We reached the end of the dark universe and explored the space that hovers outside the universe your people know. It is opaque yellow with light-blue– to indigo-colored planets and things like stars throughout. My Ogtavian ancestors also explored thousands of planets in what you call the known universe. We gained much knowledge." Deedo looked at the human to see how he reacted to her words.

Chesh looked amazed. *There is much more to these people than the primitives I took them to be,* he thought. Looking into the surrounding swamp-woods now, Chesh noticed hundreds of glowing yellowish eyes. He moved uneasily and looked to the frog princess.

"Have no fear, friend Chesh. Those are only the eyes of curious olasks. These night birds are like Earth owls, however most are dark purple with glowing orange eyes. They are neither good nor bad. They just like to observe. The olasks feed upon smaller things than us, things like vallas, mitoo-snakes, and grenus pods. We need not fear them," the princess said as thunder marched in and the faces around the campfire echoed back the lightning's purple glow.

"It's getting late. We yet have some ways to go. We shall rest now," said Deedo, lying down and closing her large Ogtavian eyes. The olasks began a chorus of a deep, gentle cricket song to lull the swamp creatures to sleep. Chesh retired to his lean-to.

When he awoke, he was again covered in white webbing. Peeny was asleep at his feet, or as close to his feet as she could get without destroying the rickety structure. Chesh yawned. He had lay awake last night, enjoying the gentle chirpping. He seemed to recall restless dreams where things with razor-sharp fangs came at him and strange, glowing reddish bats dove for his eyes. He shook his head. "Weird," he said.

Greenish rays began creeping over the horizon. Chesh walked wearily, stumbling often overexposed tree roots and sticks as he tried to navigate his way to the small rivulet beside their camp. Peeny looked after him. A soft splashing could later be heard. When he arrived at the flickering orange fire, a large bowl of bickel berries and cattail tops chuckled merrily.

"Good morning, Chesh," Deedo greeted him. "Did you sleep well?"

"Well, not exactly. Those olasks kept me up. I had some of the strangest dreams I've ever had. When that storm came in, the thunder made me toss and turn. I don't think Peeny likes storms. She was asleep at my feet, and she's never done that before. So to answer your question whether I slep well, no, I did not," Chesh finished.

"Did your itching cease?" Deedo asked.

"Oh, yes! Thank you so much! That red stuff sure does work. Thanks!" said Chesh.

"I have woven you a hat. It will protect you from the rays of both suns." She handed Chesh a hat made using cattail reeds. It was a sombrero as large as two sombreros.

"Hey, this is real comfortable. Thanks, Deedo. This will keep my bean cool!" Chesh exclaimed excitedly.

"Not if you get it too close to the fire, for I have yet to coat it with ro-coo oil and seal it with red wasp honey. Once I have done this, the hat will be fireproof, as well as more bug and water resistant." Deedo looked at Chesh, smiling broadly.

"Oh, yeah, okay," Chesh said, taking the hat off and placing it behind him.

"And what does this word *bean* mean? I thought *bean* in English meant something that one grows and eats. Am I incorrect?" Deedo asked.

"Well, this is where English gets really deceptive and tricky. *Bean* is a slang word that some cultures use to represent a human head. I guess because a bean is round like a head. Human heads have also been called knoggins, noodles, blocks, and other things. Terms like *knothead*, *meathead*, and *lunkhead* have also been used to refer to people's heads. You see, Deedo, language is like an ever-shifting current or a caterpillar transforming into a butterfly. Language is always changing, growing, evolving as the ones who use it change and evolve. Of course, the original and common meaning of the word *bean* is 'a legume or small round vegetable,'" Chesh explained.

"Oh, yes I see. Come on, lunk head. We must be on our way," said Deedo.

A stunned look came over the youth's face, then he smiled. "Yeah, you're really getting the hang of it now! Boy, are you a fast learner. This language teaching is going to be more complex than I thought."

"And would this be correct also, Chesh? We need to get moving, pea brain?"

"Yeah, ah, yeah you're really getting the idea now!" Chesh said, getting up. He thought he heard a whispering chuckle run through the usually stark Ogtavians as he rose.

Peeny lay munching on a pile of glistening reeds. The green sunrays danced across the fresh raindroplets, making them appear as ten billion emeralds. Thick air caressed Chesh's nostrils; it was the cleanness of the air that thrilled the young man. It seemed scented with patcholli tree oil, maple syrup, and mildewed leaves. Chesh remembered the way Earth smelled the last time he was there. He quickly flushed it out of his mind. The small company of travelers had taken on the appearance of a band of gypsy frog folk led by a cosmic cowboy. Of course, the myst beetle's size and tan highlighted by rich-blue swirls added greatly to the bizarre sight of these travelers through the skyscraper-like giant cattails and gigantic sky-blue ferns.

"Chesh, we will soon reach the city of Og. Do not touch or step on the purple grass with red tips. In fact, it is a good survival rule to avoid anything red as most red things on Myob are very poisonous. The grass of which I speak is Yijja-sap grass, and if a blade punctures your skin, you will die a frozen statue. The poison turns any creature's blood to stone," spoke the regal young lady.

"Thanks for the warning. I won't. I usually wear my mudders, though," replied Chesh.

"The grass is razor-sharp and will easily pierce your air sandals," she countered.

"Oh." Chesh looked at the terrain before them.

As they moved on, Peeny hummed to herself, emitting deep, soothing melodic tones. The country turned to a much sandier soil instead of the rich dark swamp dirt. Wheat-like-yellow grassy plains spotted with small ponds and veined with silver-green rivulet streams spanned out before them. The giant cattails grew in patches of two or three and were separated by at least half a mile. Spruce pines, birches, maples, and proud oaks grew on what the Ogtavians called tree islands. The six Ogtavians smiled broadly as they recognized their land.

Soon the purple sun of the afternoon reached the horizon, releasing trillions of blue-powder winged moths flittering up into the clear air of Myob. The group paused for lunch. They feasted upon leetus beans, bacon bark, and honeyed cattail stalk biscuits.

Chesh remarked, "This is delicious. I've never tasted anything so good. Better than real Earth bacon, made, unfortunately, by slaughtering defenseless animals. It would no doubt sell well on Earth."

They packed up and left after dowsing their fire. Chesh was very grateful for the hat, which he had grown used to. Despite its ridiculous size and floppiness, it served to protect him from the duel sunrays of the planet's afternoon. The temperature had reached 110 degrees. Steam wafted from ponds and dark bottomless marl bogs as they passed. Chesh felt moisture covering his skin.

The thick air was broken by a shrill whistling noise. Deedo grabbed Chesh's shoulders and yanked him backward. In an instant so fast that none saw what caused it, a blur cut through the ether. A chopping sound rang out like lobster claws clicking and cutting through branches. A purple octo-vine tentacle armed with large inward-curving claws dropped to the ground on the right side of the stego beetle. Simultaneously a parrot-sized dragonfly of incredible beauty alighted gently on Deedo's right shoulder. Its regal head a brilliant metallic blue, its body silvery green. Peeny did not even break stride.

"What the hecata! What was that thing!" Chesh cried, turning to look at Deedo.

"That was an octo-vine. They are somewhat akin to your octopuses, only much larger and more deadly. Octo-vines lurk and hang from giant plants, listening and sniffing for prey. You are lucky Duter saved you," Deedo replied.

"Who's Duter?" asked Chesh.

"Duter is my companion. He is a great monarch among the Oggadealions of dragonflies on Myob," she answered. "To tell the truth, I am overjoyed to see him as when I left, he was unable to be with me. Hello, my friend. Now I am at ease. How did you ever find me?"

Strangely, the youth heard these words in his mind: "You know, sweet Deedo, that I can always find you!"

"Did I just hear, somehow mentally, that dragonfly speak, or is the heat affecting my Earth brain?"

"That, Chesh, is difficult to answer. So that you will understand—" Deedo paused a moment. "You see, on our world, some, not many, but some very rare insects are capable of telepathic speech. Dragonflies can also enter our dreams. Surprised?" The princess stroked the dragonfly's shiny green body, gently using one of her webbed hands.

"Surprised, yeah, well of course I'm surprised. We don't have those on Earth!" Chesh turned to get a closer look at the amazing insect. The dragonfly's head was a blue chitinous knight's helmet affair that housed large pastel-purple eyes, two-thousand multicolored specks appearing in each fathomless eye. The main body was a shimmering bright green. Duter sported three wings per side. The two forewings were backed up by larger curved drive wings. Each drive wing had a dark-purple paisley eyelet on it. Duter had three formidable clawed legs on each side of his underbody. The two hindmost legs were much larger than the front legs. They were tipped with sharp crescent-moon scythes. Rather than fierce mandibles protruding from his mouth, the insect possessed an almost-human-looking mouth. This mouth now smiled, displaying razor-sharp, gleaming blue bat teeth.

"You should let me take your hat so I can coat it with wasp honey tonight. That way, it will have time to dry some before morning," Deedo said as Peeny pulled up onto a swamp islet to camp for the night. "Do not touch it!" exclaimed Deedo frantically as the teen reached for his hat.

He froze like an ice statue atop the colorful beetle. "Okay, I give up. why shouldn't I touch my hat?" he asked, perturbed.

"Because the fine red dust covering, it is from the spigitus ferns. It looks like harmless reddish dirt. However, if you were to get any on your delicate skin, it would eat away at it like acid or flesh-eating bacteria," declared Deedo.

"Oh," said Chesh, giving Deedo a horrified look.

"After I coat it with the honey juice, it will repel the troublesome dust. Your hat will also cause all biting flies, mostagoes, draller, and stinch alike to be repelled. Some of these, like the stinch bees, can take a chunk out of you the size of a marble, although they do make good soup." Deedo smiled broadly.

The thought of bee soup made Chesh queezy. "Please coat my wonderful hat with the sticky stuff, Deedo. I would appreciate it greatly. Thank you."

Chesh slid from Peeny's shell and hurried off into a thicket after the Ogtavians had dismounted and Deedo took his hat. Peeny lay down in a small pond to cool off, a regal beetle sphinx.

The space colonists named the giant rubber tree sap gathering land Noeggsplantation because chickens had long ago become extinct on Earth. Silver bubble domes glistened purple blue. They stood out from the long green myda grass surrounding them. Striped tan-blue stego beetles ambled and shuffled lazily among four-hundred-foot-tall rubber tree plants, pulling wooden carts loaded with barrels of rubber tree juice. Late afternoon rays of subdued green and somber purple danced among the thick orange leaves that hung high above, shuddering in the ever-present winds of Myob.

In a brightly lighted room, Chesh's father addressed a small group of men and women wearing light-blue jumpsuits. He pointed at a large map on a wall display. "None of you has to come. I don't mind going alone, I really don't. And I realize how dangerous this planet can be. I certainly don't expect those of you with children to accompany me on this dangerous search. I have, as yet, not heard anything from my son on any of the wrister's frequencies. I can only hope and pray that Chesh is still alive. I shall leave in one hour. If you will join me, be at the main gate and ready then, please. Thanks for listening, all of you." He looked at the small group, pausing for a moment as he gazed into each pair of eyes. He then turned and exited through an arched doorway.

The interstellar harvesters looked questioningly at one another and murmured as Chesh's father left. He waited at the massive wooden gate for fifteen minutes. One man showed up, an ex-planet crusader named Quintana. "I'm with ya, sir. We'll find the boy," he said. With a stout arm, he threw a large space bag into the back of the hovercraft and jumped into the seat next to his old commander. The shimmering powder-blue hovercraft lifted silently and wooshed off along a sandy road that led into the darkening Permian swamp forest. Giant redwood sized pines and cattails more than a mile high loomed in over the two men.

The Ort-ul, the invaders, had come to Myob from their planet Ort. It lay in a galaxy nine light-years away. Ort is a small dark planet that long ago had its natural resources used up. Ort-ulian spacecraft, shiny black alligato- skinned with Dimitron sail fins and sharp, curved barbs, had appeared in the Myobian skies five years ago. Each ship had the head of a dreaded universal beast at its front. They were the vikings of outer space, only much more vile and destructive.

Their first act upon landing had been to slay a great number of giant slothos and reed turtles and roast them for a feast. Teg, the Te-cheg or commander of Grunell, angerly stomped the stone floor of his command chamber, screaming obscenities in Ortus. "Key-jak, re-jak, voo-re-jak-ul. Kles des clearings appro kbs?" The lizard commander calmed himself. He sat down on a throne carved from a large boulder between two large viper hogs. He was now composed enough to speak English. Orange light from a large fire in a crater at the center of the chamber illuminated his sharp reptilian features.

"We cannot-a have escape! For the slayings of the three soldiers' death by a million bites and stings, I will-a select the insects to be used-a." His black eyes glowed reddish.

The Te-chang of his Re-jak enforcers stood before him adorned in dark leatherlike armor and wearing a commander's dagger. "At least we can tell-a of the clearings going well-a, my Te-cheg." The Te-chang shifted uneasily.

"Bra-dew-hoc!" stormed Teg. "Bredus Ketzek, berdus Ketzek!" he continued his tirade. In an instant, two guards appeared, holding a battered Ogtavian. His green blood dripped into rivulets on the gray stone floor.

"Ketzek, my once excellent scout, what has happened? How were my Re-jak killed? Remember, slaget, your kind are a delicacy to us, and I grow hungry," grumbled Teg.

The frog man's head flopped slowly from side to side as the guards shook him. Blood sloshed from his open mouth. He groaned then spoke, sending forth a shower of green specks. "My Teg, I serve you loyally. Did I not bring you the head of Grius, the admiral of the Ogtavian drifter ships? Have I not proved my loyalty a thousand times? I know not what transpired at the camp destroyed. I had been sent out in search of more captives. When I returned, I found the slaughter. I am lost to what occurred, my Teg," Ketzek finished.

"I believe you, Ketzek. You are spared for now." Teg gave a wave of his hand, and a third guard, which stood off to the side of the terrified Ogtavian, holding a wooden board with bullet ants, ring-wasps, viper bees, as well as many other red-marked motley insects, moved off slowly. Ketzek gave a long reptilian sigh of relief and passed out. He was dragged from the chamber.

"Elbus-ul, send three more tri snapper squads to the area of the escape. Pack them with-a viper bees, my good Re-jak. Find and smash or capture all Ogtavians within two-hundred kregets of the escape camp. Have fun-a with some of them to show-a their kind what we're about. Leave-a a trail of green blood-a!" The lizard commander paused. He gave out a gurgling, filthy throated laugh, displaying double rows of pike teeth, all yellowed and moss green. "Take-a that piece of bemus Ket-zek with you and see he does not return." He began to stroke one of the greasy viper-hogs with his three-clawed hand.

The Re-jak soldiers retreated quickly from the chamber.

Myob's green sun was already pasted in the sky when Chesh tried to open his eyes. He couldn't. He opened his mouth to yell, and mud poured down his throat. A muffled gurgling noise came out. Deedo, of course, hearing the sound with her enlarged ears, summoned the other members of the company, who were busy scraping mud from themselves. They rushed to her aid.

"Ah-too, ah-too, quickly now!" Deedo commanded.

The group began removing mud and the cluttered remains of Chesh's lean-to from atop him. They disregarded the myst beetle that lay sleeping beside the mess. In a minute, Chesh was pulled to his feet. Deedo and an Ogtavian named Vergus removed the mud first from his mouth and nostrils and then from the rest of his body. The youth coughed and spat mud. He rubbed at his eyes.

"No, no, do not do that! It will make it worse!" scolded Deedo.

"Yes, make it worse," added Vergus.

Coughing and blinking wildly, the disheveled youth said, "Holy cow, what the heckal! What in the cosmos happened? I almost died!" He looked at Peeny, who had some mud on her. He rushed to her side, kneeling down and touching her lion's main neck sensor hairs. Her maroon saucer eyes popped open. "She's okay," Chesh sighed. Chesh trudged through foot-deep mud to reach his backpack and the two large weaved saddlebags that had also been buried. He began to clean them.

Looking at the princess of Og, he asked, "Now, what the . . . I mean, what happened?" Chesh was trying to refrain from swearing as he did not want the Ogtavians to pick the habit up.

"It was a combination of things, I believe, Chesh. I was awakened by a flash of lightning. It was very distant, barely audible. That is when I saw your beetle move over to the shelter. Chesh, Peeny is afraid of thunderstorms! She moved to you for safety and security. At any measure, a storm soon moved in. Not a rainstorm. A mud-flock storm. They can be deadly."

The Ogtavians were busy making a fire and preparing some of the food stored in the giant saddlebags. Making a fire was quite a task after a mud storm.

"What's a mud-flock storm?" Chesh asked.

"It is just what it sounds like. Flocks of mud rain down upon Myob. At times, mainly in what you would call spring, they can be so fierce that they bury marlots and mammodons. Your shelter undoubtedly saved your life by fending off much of the choking mud," Deedo explained.

Pushing the button that activated his mud flaps, Chesh moved off to the creek to clean the remaining brownish glop from his clothing. "It's gonna be an interesting day. Very interesting!" grumbled Chesh.

The first Myobian sun, Mesos, had risen and traveled the pale-blue sky like a chariot of green fire.

"Come on, Peeny. Rise and shine. Think pos." Peeny opened one maroon platter eye. Chesh tried to explain what he meant by actually sitting on the squishy ground and rising. He laughed at the fresh mud on his pants and legs.

"Come forth, get up, riseth," he said somewhat sternly.

The myst beetle arose, mud slightly dripping from her under-belly. She lumbered behind as Chesh again went to the brook to rinse himself off.

"Having problems, Chesh?" Deedo asked.

"Oh no, no, everything's fine. We will be ready to leave after breakfast," replied Chesh.

The morning meal consisted of guanto grapes, which were shiny light-purple grapes the size of softballs, and tomats, a blue version of the tomato fruit but the size of watermelons and very sweet, along with a gruel made from a combination of beans and fruit, including potato-like botanos. After his respite in the creek, Chesh loaded the saddlebags onto Peeny's back. The small company of travelers again climbed onto the back of the myst beetle. The intrepid travelers appeared as gallant knights on an honorable quest. The day's journey was fairly uneventful, with the exception of the giant squid trees.

In the afternoon, when they were just leagues away from their goal, Peeny suddenly stopped. A large deep-red gelatinous mass was about three hundred leagues ahead. It was the size of ten elephants with thousands of glowing yellow eyes. The stench of rotting plant and animal matter wafted at the journeyers. All could see a brown-red haze looming about the blob thing, giving it a saturnine aura. Chesh somehow sensed then looked and noticed that the myst beetle's eyes had changed from maroon to bright green. Sensing the stego myst beetle, or its eyes, the swamp-jelly rolled away like lava. It disappeared into a swamp fissure, emitting repeated deep booming sounds on its descent into the vast network of mud caves below. Peeny continued onward over the sandy ground. When they reached the spot where the thing had been a steamy pile of tan and indigo, ichor remained. It gave off a retched odor.

"Stop, Chesh, please stop!" cried Deedo.

Chesh dug his heels lightly into the beetle's shell. She stopped. The Ogtavian princess slid down. She walked over to the fetid mass. She walked around it three times, knelt down, and removed a mushroom-hide herb bag from around her neck. Deedo took out some of the bag's contents and sprinkled it on the ground. Her oriental face glimmered jade in the sun's rays as she looked intently first to Mesos then to Stesos rising now from the west. The long lashes of her eyes closed and wisps of sparkling windswept snow issued forth from them in horizontal whirling minitornadoes. Softly, ever so softly, and as gentle as a summer cricket, she began to hum. The melody began to lull Chesh to sleep. He shook himself to keep from tumbling off his chitinous steed.

As they moved along, the youth asked, "What was that all about, I wonder, Deedo?"

"That was a pack of coy-ats. The crag-zunp-ul, or swamp jellyfish, as it better describes it, had just finished consuming them. Swamp coy-ats will all ban together and fight to the death even to save one of their kind. This is likely what occurred here. The beast moved slothfully. It was very full. I guess that is why it did not try for us. The coy-at is a very sacred animal to us. They are crafty watchers of the swamplands. I wished the pack a safe journey to their next way of being. I asked that they watch over the swamplands evermore."

The country had become very sandy. The sand changed from dirty brown to pure white. Just ahead were many spruce pines, birches, and maples. To the northeast, as Chesh reconnoitered, numerous ancient towering pines loomed above the horizon, swaying in the increasing winds. And above all, numerous giant cattails looked complacently down. In an hour, the weary company emerged from scrub growth and tall reeds. Chesh looked upon the magnificent city of Og for the first time. Strong Myobian wind blew from the northwest. A vast expanse of water dotted with sandy swamp islets stretched out before the youth. White knight chess castles, a hundred feet tall, adorned many of the islets. Streamlined pod-shaped wooden crafts glided across shimmering silver-blue waters, caressing reeds with their bows. Members of the frog-like culture floated across the water-like spirits or ghosts atop wing-shaped hoverboards. Many Ogtavians hummed merrily in cricketish tones. Giant cretaceous dragonflies with burnt-orange bodies and deep-purple velvet heads hovered and darted among the smaller cattails like lions hunting in a veld.

"There we can meet my father, there!" Deedo pointed to one of the small islands. On its shore stood a group of Ogtavians. They hopped up and down in jumping jack fashion. Atop the castle tower, a medieval banner waved in the breeze. It was light green with an orange crescent moon on it. As if she read the princess's thoughts, the myst beetle swam toward this islet. She climbed out and lay down to let her riders dismount. The once-missing Ogtavians and their princess were greeted with warm broad smiles and froggish cheers. They all wore bright-green tunics, with darker-green pants. The monarch was different only in that at times a glowing, translucent blue crown appeared above his head. The Ogtavians exchanged slight bows, which was their way of saying "Happy ways." Ogtavians do not shake hands; they do not care to be touched by others.

Deedo gave a brief explanation of Chesh's presence. Her father, the monarch of Og, bid the youth to join them in a celebratory feast to honor the safe return of his daughter and his fellow Og dwellers. He eyed the unique stego beetle as Chesh slid casually down. The youth paused to pat Peeny and give her a small handful of peanuts. Her mouth opened into a crescent smile. The beetle gestured downward with her head. Chesh set the unshelled nuts on the ground before his friend. *She must want to savor them*, thought Chesh.

When he turned to the Ogtavians, they where googly-eyed with gaping pink cave mouths. Chesh gave a slight bow as he approached the monarch. As they walked to the arched doorway of the white tower, Chesh had to ask out of a naturalist's curiosity, "I see that your homes, or castle towers, well, dwellings, where you live, I mean, well, they are made from what looks like massive blocks of the same white sand that we are walking on. How, I wonder, did you build them, ah, sir, I mean, Monarch Wapiti?" inquired Chesh.

All Ogtavian eyes went to the monarch as he began to explain. "We mix sand with a pulp made from ground-up, dried swamp grasses. We call the variety we use tus-la, meaning dark blue or indigo colored swamp grass. This grass has a sweet, soothing scent. It is also a natural repellent that any venomous red serpent, spider, or sleg—sleg are crawling or flying things that bite—on Myob can smell miles away. And we do have spiders on Myob. The monstrous kag spiders are the color of our dark-purple nights with thin red poison dart hairs. They grow to be half of the size of this six-story tower before us. The kag lives high in giant pines and cattails. They weave Venus flytrap–like trap cage webs that spring closed on victims, or they can simply swoop down on prey using wings ten times the size of condor wings. We mix the tus-la grass with the honey of the harp-wasp. These substances bond the sand together. Each block is three feet thick. The inside of the tower is cool like a cave in summer and as warm and sandy dry as a coy-at's den during our six months of winter." Wapiti looked at the human youth, smiling.

"Six months of winter!" Chesh exclaimed. "How long are your summers?"

Myob was a new planet to the Earthers. It lay in the Alpha Centauri area of space, four light-years from Earth. Chesh and the other space colonists had only been on the new world for eight months. They came to Myob knowing only that it could sustain life and had both plant and animal life on it. Space colonists had to gamble, as did early Earth explorers and settlers. Some land and perish on hostile, treacherous worlds, while others become wealthy beyond their wildest imaginings.

DRAGONFLY DREAMS

"Our warmer time is eight months long, eight Earth months. Fall lasts four months. Springlike weather is brief on our planet. The ten-or-so-foot deep snowdrifts and snow mountains formed by wind seem to all melt in a few weeks," the Monarch finished.

"Thank you, Monarch Wapiti. I am impressed with these castle towers." Chesh smiled, which he did not do often.

The group of revelers proceeded down wide steps to a large open castle hall area. An orange fire blazed from the center of the chamber. The smell of bacon bark, honey wax, and sand floated up high above. Tapestries of woven reed, mainly indigo, green, and tan, adorned the walls here and there. Some depicted Myobian constellations, others creatures, or scenes of native swamplands; these were all throughout the tower. Ponds, streams, minature oaks, ferns, and blue corn plants blended with cattails large and small. Indigo swamp grass grew from the sandy floor. There were many lush plants. Vines clung to the sandstone walls. A small waterfall caressed one wall as it bubbled into a pond. Dragonfiles, red and light blue, alighted on plants or soared high into the recesses of the domed ceiling to become glinting, moving stars. All was bathed in somber, ambient harp-wasp wax candlelight.

As the Ogtavians and Chesh sat cross-legged around a low circular table, small crickets began to chirp Chopanistic melodies around them. Large wooden bowls containing steaming bacon bark, large orange gourds, and the blue corn were brought to the table. Wooden cups were filled with cattail milk. Honey and a bluish bread was also placed before the happy group. Monarch Wapiti spoke first.

"Fate often weights heavily in our lives, rough-hewn as this table though it is," began the Monarch. "The checker work of life can take us to many strange and wondrous places. We are honored to have with us the savior of my one child and daughter. We welcome you to stay as long as you wish and, of course, your marvelous myst stego beetle as well. We are a simple people, Chesh, although we have had our primitive times—nothing akin to your industrial revolution, fortunately. We have, for hundreds of thousands of years, been an agrarian society. Long, long ago, we created and developed technology such as viddy walls and faster-than-light spacecraft. We

105

sit before you evolved, peaceful, kind, and happy. We value and foster our creativity."

"Long ago, our ancestors realized that negative behavior is a product of violent thought. They knew that if there was another war any wars, after that would have to be fought with sticks and stones. They began to study and emulate ants. They saw that metals like iron can simply, through touch, spur one to violence. Power and domain have no place in our lives. We do not kill. We create. We do not trespass. We believe that happiness is whatever you want it to be. We live in happiness. We believe that everything is a miracle. Do many of your people imagine, Chesh?"

Of course Chesh's wrister would blare out now. Like the youth, it seemed to be undergoing some sort of metamorphosis. "I don't know where I'm goin'. On a winter's journey or summer. Through fire or ice. This cosmic river just pushes me on. Guess I'll find out when I get there. I'll be happy either way, 'cause I'll be goin' swamp ridin', giant cattail climbin' all the while."

Chesh looked at the Monarch apologetically. Wapiti laughed, smiling a wide frog smile. "Do not worry, Chesh. We are casual and relaxed here. It is the way of Gi. Please just call me Wapiti. I was going to ask though, Chesh, if you would consider remaining here for a time to be a teacher of your wonderful, colorful language called the King's English. You see, we of Og have long been able to pick up your planet's wave transmissions. We value your English greatly. We feel it would be a good universal language. We have studied it using printed material long ago obtained by our ancestors on visits to your world as well. To have an actual human for a teacher, now that is a miracle!"

"Thank you, sir. I think I'd like to teach your people English," said Chesh.

All were silent. Deedo recited an Ogtavian zave. "Dragonflies, blue and green, armored, ancient. There is something about dragonflies, something quite valiant."

Everyone began to pass the food and converse in cheerful tones.

"I would inquire then, Mon, I mean, Wapiti, how do you educate your young ones?" Chesh spoke out. As he did so, a blue dragonfly landed on his left shoulder.

"Much like your Socrates taught Plato or like Voltaire conveyed knowledge to others. We believe learning is what remains after one has forgotten everything they learned in school, which is how your Albert Einstien defined learning. Our learning is an active process, more akin to a summer camp than a school. Our learning is an active process where yog, the young of Og, interact with many diverse stimuli in infinite ways. They are taught that anything is possible. The goal, I guess, is to empower them to be curious inquirers who enhance their imaginations and creativity and to be happy. We use viddy screens in learning domes to present the universe. Yog take field trips or go to camp on other planets. We do not allow the viddies to suck them in and drain them of their time and creativity. We teach active, dynamic, logical, thinking skills. We are not strict, however."

"The favorite hero of the yog boys is Errol Flynn, while the girls like Bruce Lee and Dr. Jane Goodall. In short, Chesh, our learning system is loose knit, relaxed, and experiencial. It focuses on both mind and body. We have what you call a type of monk system of martial arts. It is ancient. We call it Gi. Arilio can teach you, if you wish." Wapiti looked at Chesh, smiling, sipping white milk.

Chesh was awakened as the first green rays of Mesos gleamed upon the large Belwit mushroom dome structure that Monarch Wapiti and some other Ogtavians had helped Chesh and Peeny build. The mushroom dome was large enough for Peeny to sleep near her friend. The dome was held up by four thick twelve-foot-tall cattail stalks. On one side was a small reedy inlet pond. Monarch Wapiti's castle tower was about three hundred yards away. A fire smoldered as the princess, adorned in pale-green loose-fitting pants and a shirt the color of the underside of a leaf, strolled up.

"Chesh, are you awake?" Deedo almost whispered.

"Ah, well, yes, yes. Good morning, Deedo. I just woke up," he said groggily.

The regal princess came near him. "Let us go zlotting! Come on, sleepyhead, the wind is up. It will be glorious fun. It will take your mind from your worries!" exclaimed Deedo gleefully.

"Sounds good." Chesh slid out of the reed sleeping nest. Deedo smiled broadly, her eyes lighting up.

The pair hurried down to the water's edge. Deedo handed Chesh a zlotos gourd. It reminded him of his old hoverboard from his younger days on Earth. The zlotos gourds were shaped like large arrowheads. These wind-propelled wings of Mercury-like devices were ancient. They have natural diaplanes and spoilers. They have airholes and baffle chambers within them. When altered, the chambers and openings cause the wind to give the gourds a lift and a great deal of forward thrust. The zlotoses are three inches thick. Three angled holes adorn each side like a twentieth-century Buick.

Deedo explained that her ancient ancestors had feet that propelled them across the swampy planet in such a fashion. They also had wings called zols that, when unfurled from below each arm, acted as sail-like wind catchers. These Darwinian-like evolutionary changes made it possible for the early dwellers of Myob to glide across both water and land. They were also efficient underwater swimmers, being able to hold their breath for an hour or more. These adaptations enabled our caveman counterparts to glean what they needed for their survival. Cattails and swamp reeds danced and swayed joyfully in the fresh moving wind.

It took Chesh three falls to regain his hoverboard legs. Then he was off. The feeling of zlotting was wonderful, exhilarating. Lush plants—indigo, green, orange, and yellow—kaleidoscoped past. Chesh felt eight years old again. He was no longer at the age of tempers and weeping. The pair zoomed around dead stumps and reed beds. At times, a scaly creature with a finned head or a silvery flying fish scurried or jump-splashed out of the way. Once, Chesh looked down to see a shadow as large as a great white shark pass beneath his hover board. He shuddered. Then they were off careening, cutting emerald-tinted wakes among giant cattails and cui-vines. *Free at last!* thought Chesh as he smiled elatedly.

The only real scary aspects of zlotting so far were dodging the one-eyed lobster-like pincers of the cui-vines and the larger Devonian behemoth shadows that occasionally lurked beneath. At times, large fins, tentacles, or reptilian tails broke the surface. Otherwise, what a wonderful feeling he had! Looking ahead, he saw Deedo's long black hair glistening in the morning sun. Her dragonfly friend curved back and forth joyfully in her wake. For an instant, he thought he heard, from between the walls of his cranium, a voice—Deedo's voice. It cried out to him, saying, "Come with me, Chesh!"

Water curled from the rear as her gourd skimmed along. Somehow, thoughts of his father drifted into his head. His right eye began to emit tears. Chesh almost never cried. He hadn't cried since he got hit in the head with a rock or the time a neighbor had put gum in his hair or when he got punched in the nose for the first time by a bully. He had wept with great feeling every time one of his dogs died. The stupid bullying had only served to toughen his invisible shell, giving him fighting skills. Martial arts training gave him the humility and foresight to see trouble coming a long way off and step out of its way. Kids picked on him relentlessly from midschool on. He was different.

The chick to be pecked to death in the barnyard, Chesh, you see, had been born with natural shocks of pure white hair growing from the center of his head. He was a genius with an IQ of 380. This made him a target. This and his attractive Nordic looks. Once he toughened up and became well versed in the martial arts of Judo, Tae Kwon Do, Seven-Star Praying Mantis Kung Fu, and Isshin-ryu Karate, the negative Neadertal-Cromagnon types left him alone. Unfortunately, and not wishing to do so, but in order to defend himself, he had hammered a few bullies, not unwarranted. Suddenly, Chesh recalled something from the martial arts: a good black belt never looks down.

When he looked ahead to Deedo once again and saw the sight of her beauty, a feeling of chocolaty warmth filled his central stomach area or emanated from this area of chi, his tanden. Deedo pulled up at the base of a giant cattail. "Let us climb it, Chesh," she said, motioning upward.

The Myobian princess and Chesh sat, looking out from the mouth of a giant owlet hole. From his perch near the top of the giant cattail, amazing new sights greeted the youth. The giant cattails were spread out, separated by at least a league. Cattails do not like to rub shoulders in the wind. Below, giant blue ferns swayed, waving at the two onlookers. A few orange stego turtles munched lazily on swamp grasses, their blue striped dimetrodon dinosaur wind fin sails undulating in the breeze. Dragonflies, both small and the size of pterodactyls, hovered or darted about. Silver ponds and blue vein rivulets glistened.

"Giant owlets only use their lofts once. They are arboreal as well as aquatic, often diving for prey far below the waters of swamp lakes. They live to be six-hundred of your years old. Many creatures on Myob live a long time," Deedo said, removing the climbing spikes strapped around her ankles with burr vines.

"How long do the people of Og live, Deedo?"

"Most live to be three hundred of your years, some say Arilio is over a thousand years old, no one knows for sure," she replied.

"Oh." Chesh looked at her with a zillion questions, but he asked none.

"Chesh, you are at times troubled by your father's fate. When I was a youngster one of our zi, elder herb, or medicine, women told me a story. The story showed me how to make my woes fade away. It was about a valiant dragonfly knight who was on a quest for giant glow worms to light the way to the sacred caverns of Zulliam, far below Myob's surface.

"Here it was said was a land where blue corn grew over vast meadows. Here it was said was also a city like your Eldorado, where a race of wise wraith creatures called zil-o-zists lived. They were the size of gold finches with dragon bodies, moth wings, and dragon-esque smiling faces. If one became friends with a zil-o-zist, it looked after them forever. Whenever you are feeling down or in trouble, just think of their name or you can use will-o'-the-wisp. It will come and circle your head three times, causing negative thoughts or harm to be gone. Ogtavians with third sight are often able to see these creatures. They appear as small moth-dragons floating in green, red, or purple glowing spheres. You might try this, Chesh. It works well for me. Say it with me now to see. Will-o'-the-wisp, will-o'-the-wisp, will-o'-the-wisp," coaxed Deedo.

Chesh repeated the words along with Deedo. Soon, a small green orb rose like steam from a pond far below. As it came closer,

Deedo asked, "Do you see the dragon with the wings of a dragonfly, Chesh?"

"Yes," whispered Chesh. "What a beautiful blue body. It has the same mettalic blue and green colors as a green darner dragonfly. The wings are spring azure moth powder blue. They are shaped like a swallowtail butterfly's wings. The orange glowing teardrops on each wing appear as menacing eyes, maybe to deter predators."

The translucent creature circled Chesh's head three times, hovered inches from his face, looking into his eyes with fathomless indigo orbs. Chesh heard these words in his head, sung in soft gentle tones by a woman's voice, "Chesh, you are a unique individual. You are the master of your own soul and destiny, and you are responsible for the things you do, and the things you don't do." With that the shimmering creature flew up into the green Myobian sky.

Deedo recited an Ogtavian zave, "Oh, brilliant whirlwind of butterflies, maroon, orange, powder yellow, cloak me from the winter winds. Oh, beings of wondrous flight, green and copper blue, when summer comes, I will dance with you among my garden green. All my fruit I give to you and your violet, velvet Queen. Do you have favorite poems, Chesh?" Deedo asked.

"Yes, 'Stopping by Woods on a Snowy Evening' and 'Eldorado' are my two favorite poems."

"Tell me some, please."

"I think I like these lines best: 'The woods are lovely, dark and deep, / But I have promises to keep, / And miles to go before I sleep, / And miles to go before I sleep." Deedo smiled thoughtfully.

They zlotted back to Og slowly. Chesh had taught English to the Ogtavians for three weeks. He taught around tranquil ponds. He taught around green and orange flamed campfires. He taught in the learning dome. The youth employed many diverse methods: reading, writing, rhyme, and song. Hands-on activities, fantastic puppet shows, games, music, and lots of art. Much kiteflying was done; amazing brightly colored kites were designed. Many, many plays were performed in an amphitheater sand crater. The frog-like young people were both eager and quick to learn. Chesh presented them with birch bark diplomas. They beamed with pride in their humble way.

At the graduation ceremony, he spoke, "Thank you for being such scholarly students. A difference is a difference if it makes a difference, and each one of you did! Always remember these words said by Captain Nemo in Jules Verne's famous novel 20,000 Leagues Under the Sea, Mobilis in mobili or Changing with change. Thank you all." Chesh looked to the crowd of Ogtavians. They rose, chirping a soft, mellow sound in unison. Their eyes glowed blue. Ten-thousand multicolored butterflies soared above, some the size of eagles.

In exchange for his teaching, Chesh received martial arts lessons from Arelio, a grand master of Gi, and the great-great-great-grandson of Zoddy Darma, the greatest sinsa in the history of Ogtavian culture. Gi means that a practitioner of the art always wears their martial arts skills as a uniform, always ready. The uniform of Gi is loose-fitting medium dark-green pants, a lighter-green collarless shirt, and a belt of reed cloth. The belt doubles as a sling. A warrior of Gi always has at least one Gi stone on their person. The stones are crescent-moon shaped. The ways of Gi are the following: (1) breath, focus, relax; (2) remain healthy; (3) look, listen; (4) silence is golden; (5) continuous practice; (6) anything is possible; (7) use the circle; (8) be prepared; (9) face your dragons; and (10) do not hate. The gift of Gi given to him by the people of Og added greatly to Chesh's knowledge of the martial arts. It toughened his body beyond belief.

Chesh, Deedo, Monarch Wapiti, Arelio, and some other ogtavians sat at the water's edge in the warm sand as the last rays of Stesos faded. "As to our language, Monar—I mean, Wapiti, allow me to explain it in this way. My dog, Watson, who was probably the most intelligent dog that walked the Earth, bless her, taught me a great deal about the canine species. I, in turn, taught her much. She was highly intelligent. I taught her to sit using a one-finger hand command within a few days of finding her. She eventually progressed so that when she was three, we could communicate telepathically," Chesh began.

"How do dogs learn language? Perhaps you're asking yourself. They, of course, have a form of language all their own. Relative to human language, they originally learned from cave people. In prehistoric times, ancient canines, like dire wolves, began to be around early humans. This survival behavior likely developed as a result of feeding behavior or hunger, a most base need. Dire wolves would scavenge bones and scraps discarded by man. Man developed trust for them. A symbiotic relationship developed. They served each other by hunting for game more efficiently. Dog and man protected each other. Their combined sense of smell and superior hunting skills allowed them to advance far above other species. Therefore, they became a superior survival team." Chesh paused to view the now-rising brilliant orange Ta, Myob's smallest moon.

"As to the exchange and interplay of language, in the prehistoric days, the spoken word was nil. Gestures, movements, laughter, and groans had to do. We still use these forms of communication daily. Man lost his telepathic link with canines. Language developed based largely on geographic regions, race, trade, and survival. Language changes over time. Each person is a product of their time. No matter what language was thrown at the dog, be it French, English, or gutter-slang American, the brilliant creatures adapted. So you see, Monarch Wapiti, this thing we call language has a very complex and intricate evolutionary past. It is no wonder that when you ask a dog to come, it tilts its head to one side," Chesh concluded, smiling at the others gathered around him. "May I ask something?"

"Please do," replied the Monarch.

"Why do you have three moons?"

Wapiti looked at his daughter. She spoke, "Our planet once had six moons that had broken off and formed when a comet struck Myob millions of years ago. Over time, three of the moons collided, forming the rings of Myob. Much as that which transpired around your planet Saturn. We call the moons Ta, meaning 'little,' Kalistritus, for its brilliant white-blue color, and Mezla-zan, for the mysterious power it has over water. Chesh, will you tell us a story, please?"

"Of course, Deedo. Once upon a time, there came to a small town with houses all of wood a wolf in sheep's clothing. He came like a thief in the night . . ." The frog-faced ones looked intently at the youth as he spoke. The green and orange flames of the fire reflected from their faces.

The next day, Chesh and Deedo left early. They extended their zlotting wings to become two green wisps skimming above silver rivulets. Peeny was nearby. She had given Chesh such a forlorn look that he did not believe he could stop her from coming. The pair of extraterrestrial surfers slowed or retraced their routes so the slower-moving stego beetle could keep up. Duter kept pace with the princess, an ever-vigilant knight. After zlotting on a complex network of tiny rivers, the pair reached Deedo's secret place. The exalted pair reached a large raised island. It was inhabited by giant conifers. It resembled a castle with pine-needle-green walls and towers.

They sat on a sandhill in a circular clearing at the island's center, in what Deedo called the Valley of Te. The te are walking flowers. They are also known as teilurium. Te have the petals of dasies, only much larger. At the center of each te is a glowing brilliant-orange orb. Yellow and green moths hovered about, landing at times in these orange centers to dip long straw tongues down for the sweet pollen within. Soft humming, as gentle as a woman's voice, reached Chesh's ears. It was the te humming as they waved in the breeze.

"Behold, my friends, the te flowers, Chesh," Deedo began. "Consider them for they reap yet they do not sow."

"I wish it was that simple for my people," remarked Chesh, looking at the large purple petals of the daisy-like te flowers.

"I have not studied your Earth for a long time, except for its language. I have been occupied helping my father with a solution for the invasion of these lizard things. Do your people still function within the constraints of social systems based on monetary worth?"

"Yes, Deedo. Disks are inserted under our skin at birth. They contain basic information and register all invisible money transactions. I removed the stupid thing when I left Earth."

"That is sad, for in this state, man produces little that is lasting, truly lasting. It is understandable. Fear, conformity, immorality, these are heavy burdens, great drains of creative energy, and when we are drained of creative energy, we do not create. We procreate, but we do not create," spoke the wise princess.

A spiky large red-and-black winged wasp dove for Chesh's head. Duter snagged it out of the air, a sharp crunch, and it dropped to the sand. Chesh and Deedo talked, laughing often, until the glowing rays of Kalastritus bathed the te flowers in soft white-blue light. The Earth-sized moon reminded Chesh of the moon of his home world.

"We should go back now. My father is somewhat relaxed about what I do. However, I do not wish to unsettle him," said Deedo.

The youth felt he wanted to kiss her. He was becoming very attracted to this princess of an alien world. Her sweet patchouli-like scent made him shiver with pleasure. *Well, you've got to grow up sometime*, he thought. Chesh leaned over toward her. The pair looked deeply onto each other's eyes. Chesh kissed Deedo. This came as a surprise to her—not an unwelcome surprise, just a surprise. Her eyes turned from indigo to summer-sky blue.

Duter landed on her shoulder. Peeny awoke from her slumber and displayed a look of beetle confusion, a hurt kind of look. Chesh rose and walked to his faithful friend. He petted her head then rubbed her favorite spot on her neck. He kissed her to show that he felt warmly about her, as well as to make up for the spontaneous kiss he had just given Deedo. Peeny nuzzled him as if to say "I understand."

The four obtuse, enchanted visitors left their pine castle refuge and traveled on shimmering blue river veins back to Og. As dawn broke, a hundred giant dark jagged-shelled snapping turtles appeared on the hills surrounding the city. A great bellowing rang out. A clamoring went up as the Ogtavians ran to and fro.

"We will not fight. Our creator will save us," Monarch Wapiti cried out to his people.

The dark marauders descended on the peaceful hamlet of sand castle towers. They rode upon the red-eyed snappers like Hannibal's soldiers atop elephants. Each snapper carried seven lizard men. Mounted on the turtle's barbed shells were ballistae that fired iron-tipped harpoons. The ballistae also fired metal fishhook nets with red stinging wasps attached. These beings from Ort are a primitive race. They had long ago conducted wars on their planet, destroying all other races. The planet was turned into a blackened cinder devoid of almost all life as a result. The Ort-al are a cruel, doltish, and hun-like lot. Having little, save rancid water and roasted corpses to sustain them, the smarter ones scavenged technology and parts from the space exploration program of their more advanced lizard species kin, now extinct. By combining these with technology cannibalized from crashed or captured alien spacecraft and back-engineered, they built a small fleet of ships that could carry them to other worlds.

The lizard men carried out raids in order to obtain food, slaves, minerals, and materials to rebuild their dark world. The finned black dimetrodon ships were slow and had only large crossbows mounted on the hulls for weaponry. As primitive as these Viking-like spaceships were, they did convey them to other worlds, where the lizard soldiers not only slew and enslaved many life-forms but these conquerors also brought much sickness and disease with them. The giant snappers bellowed thunderously as wide swaths of hooked net shot out over groups of scrambling Ogtavians.

The frog people ran wildly about, as do ants panicked after a foot has stomped their earthen mound. Many screamed, eyes wide with terror. After seeing their monarch remove his Gi belt and use it as a sling, some chose to follow. Lizard soldiers dropped as deadly accurate stones struck them. The soldiers retaliated by firing harpoons at the resisters. Many Ogtavians were felled. The dark armored lizard men dismounted, brandishing short swords. They slew the people of Og at will. green blood poured over the white sands of the islets. After rounding up the surviving Ogtavians and burr whipping them into the nets, the victors set fire to the insides of the castle towers. Using thick vine ropes attached to the snappers, they tried to pull the towers apart. The sturdy structures would not be brought down. The sleek wooden kif ships were burned.

Out of frustration, or just because it was their way, the lizard ilk made fires and began to roast some of the captives. They ate and guzzled grog from metal mugs. The macabre celebration of torture and feasting lasted until the next day. The Ort-al left when the first green rays of Mesos crept over the western horizon. Thick oily smoke rose above the devastated city of Og as bones charred on the abandoned cook fires from the dark feast. Monarch Wapiti and a handful of survivors, including Deedo, crawled toward the cave of the giant glow worms to lick their wounds. She turned, an alligator tear crawling down her cheek. Deedo looked at her badly wounded father. Heartbroken, she wept.

Monarch Wapiti looked to the green sky. "Why have you forsaken me?" he whispered painfully.

The group of refugees remained in the luminous cave for days. Deedo tended a fire by the cave's mouth.

"Why did the guardian frogs not save us, Father?" she said.

"One watcher scout that survived tells of a red fog that the Ort-al cast over them. Everything the red fog touched died, even plants. Somehow this haze must have disabled our copper guardians," answered Wapiti.

Hearing a sound like soft dog pads crossing sand, Deedo looked up. There stood Chesh. He seemed to glow with a greenish aura. Peeny was at his side.

"How is this? Is this a dream? Are you real?" she said with a look of wild astonishment rippling across her face.

"We are here, Deedo. We have risen," Chesh said softly. A single guardian frog chirped in the distance.

"What happened, Chesh?" asked Deedo.

"Well . . ." Chesh tried clearing his throat. "Sorry, I have a—" He stopped his speech abruptly, searched for a better word, and continued, "I have a lump of coal in my throat."

Deedo quickly disappeared. She returned, carrying a wooden cup of water. Chesh drank it all in one gulp. "Well, to tell you the truth, I'm not exactly sure. I don't remember much after the lizard men got a hold of us. I think we fought. Anyway, when I woke up a short time ago, I found myself in an earthen cave deep beneath the ground. I was in a large cavern. Glowing creatures darted about, purple trilobites, orange centipedes, and such. Cattail stalks, blue corn, loatos leaves, and burberries lay scattered about. Peeny was asleep nearby." He paused, looking to his stego friend. "I followed Peeny out of the cave and she brought me here."

"But, Chesh, you were—" Deedo was cut off abruptly by a sharp look from her father, who moved his head from side to side slowly with a grave look on his face. Monarch Wapiti had, like Deedo, seen

Chesh killed by the lizard men. He did not wish to bring up the power of restoring life that myst stego beetles were said too have.

Duter appeared out of the blue-green sky to land on Deedo's shoulder. "Duter!" she cried. "Where have you been? I thought you were killed!" She stroked the dragonfly lightly with a webbed finger.

The day had been spent in restful thought. As night approached, the small group sat around the fire, eating a dinner of cuca pods, cattail mush, and honeyed blue corn bread. *We must equip ourselves with stego horns*, Deedo thought to herself.

Chesh cocked his head to one side. He could hear Deedo's thoughts clearly within his head. *What the heckal, I'll try,*" he thought. *What are stego horns?* Chesh said mentally in an attempt to reach the princess telepathically.

They are that which cause the giant slime snappers and other creatures to go mad when blown, Deedo thought.

Let us talk aloud for the others must know of this.

Yes, I peep, Chesh replied mentally.

"Some of us may be able to retrieve our taken fellow Ogtavians. If we could obtain some stego horns, they would give us the power to render the slime snappers helpless. I believe that the lizard things are most likely driven mad by the high-pitched sounds of the rare horns. It is all we have, our only hope. Speak freely now. How do you want to proceed?" Deedo explained aloud then looked to her right. The Ogtavians and Chesh sat in a circle; it was their custom when discussing things of importance to talk of them, each member of the circle speaking in turn, proceeding from the right of the first speaker and going around clockwise.

Arilio spoke next, "We will get the taken back. Those who go must leave soon for the people of Og may be taken to other worlds. I shall go."

Lavek, who was known for his skill with the curved sword, said simply, "I too will go."

"I will go. We must get our kin back!" said Shaw-nee, his young froggish face beaming.

Bangal, a young girl with black stallion hair to her waist, followed, "I will go to rescue my people."

The others in the circle, who were Rouge, Alistus, Gladstone, and Monarch Wapiti, all said in some way that they would do anything to save their fellow Og dwellers.

Chesh spoke last. "Of course I will go! I hope that my beetle friend sees fit to come along also. Monarch Wapiti, no disrespect meant, I see you are badly wounded. Logically it would be best if you and the few who are to hampered to go stayed to hold the fort, so to speak. We must travel swiftly. You would slow us down or worse. I hope I have not offended your honor, for you are very honorable," spoke the human youth.

The proud Monarch said nothing, only nodded his head in agreement. The group watched in silence as Monarch Wapiti drew a map to the forest of Zud. "I went long ago with a small force to this dark forest. We searched for the castle where from many evil creatures traveled to Og. Dark winged horrors with no faces. They would come in the night and take crops from our fields. Any who tried to stop them were rent apart by their long sloth claws." Wapiti paused, pointing to a spot within a forest he had drawn in the sand. "Here is where we saw the castle. It became visible for only a few minutes. It appeared outlined by a blue morning fog. You must take care for the faceless ones can drop upon you at any time. We lost most of our Ogtavian force members. We returned to Og. Our seers made the guardian frogs, many of which are perched high in trees and giant cattails. The faceless ones have not been near Og since save for some that were slain by the poisoned darts of the copper frogs. I wish you a swift journey!" Wapiti looked around the circle of orange fire faces.

All of them gazed into the night sky. They watched in amazement as the tiny planet Ni whirled so close to Myob that its three moons appeared as mad cosmic bees attacking a green orb nest. As they had ridden out that morning, all the remaining Ogtavians waved to them and said "Have a safe journey," with wide froggish grins upon their faces. Chesh looked back at them with his eyebrows wrinkling downward in the center. They waved with whatever webbed limbs they could move. The excited group then said good-bye to each member of the rescue party, including Peeny and a giant dragonfly named Cal-i-fax, that carried Arilio into the sky.

Chesh reflected on his time at Og and his teaching. He felt a fiery pain when he tried to recall the attack on Og. He did not like the feeling of hatred; it reminded him of how he had felt long ago when he had been brutally bullied. He thought of the will-o'-the-wisp, of how it looked. He pictured it. The image calmed him.

The seven Ogtavians and Chesh rode comfortably aboard the giant stego beetle. Cal-i-fax carried Arilio high above, scouting ahead for any possible dangers. Peeny stopped each evening near dusk. She always found tree-covered swamp islands that were safe and dry. The small company gathered vegetables, fruits, and mushrooms each evening and loaded them into large saddlebags woven from reeds. After four days, the swamp-woods ended. Chesh looked out over the grassy plain-like terrain that had appeared once they cleared the towering stalks and trees. Strange, dry rounded burnt-orange plants, resembling tumble weeds shuffled past in the wind. Large shallow warm Permian lakes surrounded by windswept purple grasses stretched to the horizon. Looking at the obtuse shadow of the Ogtavians and himself aboard Peeny reminded Chesh of a stegosaur with unusually shaped backfins. He began to whistle "Me and My Shadow," and the others joined in merrily.

As the stars began to twinkle in the darkening violet sky, the small band set up camp near one of the lakes. They sat, roasting an odd assortment of fruits and vegetables on sticks. Some green with yellow stripes, some orange, and blue corn, which seemed to grow everywhere.

Chesh turned to Deedo with a troubled look on his face. "Deedo, I've noticed that since that time after the attack on Og, after I was alone with Peeny, that missing time, well, I've noticed that my senses seem to have changed, altered somehow. My hearing is so acute that I can hear sounds that are miles away. And my nose, well, my sense of smell, today when that basilisk came out of the clouds, the stench almost knocked me off of Peeny. I could still detect it even though the beast had became a dot on the horizon." Chesh paused, sensing the princess wished to speak.

"That is not so unusual, Chesh. The basilisk is a creature known well for its odious and repulsive smells. Its odor becomes so strong when close that one's eyes sting and fill with water. The smells help it to survive, I guess," said Deedo.

"Another thing, Deedo, my eyes, well, my sight, I seem to see things that are close with microscopic accuracy. When I ride atop Peeny and peer out over the countryside, things appear as if I were looking through a telescope. Colors are more brilliant. My sense of taste has become incredible. I attributed this to the fact that I've been eating foods that are new to me. My sense of touch is enhanced also. When Shawn-ee put that mud burr in my leaf bag back at the glow worm cave, wow! I almost jumped out of my skin. Holy cow! I really don't understand what's happening to me, Deedo. I thought maybe you could help me on this, as having all of these vastly improved senses flying at me at once is quite confusing, kind of like a blind man who suddenly recovers his sight, I guess." Chesh looked at his friend Peeny. She was laying with her back to the soothing fire as she gazed, with large maroon beetle eyes, out over the vast lake. Stars shifted above, dancing merrily on the water as well.

"Do not worry, I do not think anything bad is happening to you, Chesh. Perhaps, as you suggested, the new foods are changing you. I often recall and follow the words of the sage Epicticus, of your Earth's ancient Roman times 'Train yourself not to worry about things you can do little about," Deedo said in soothing tones.

The next day, the determined company traveled along the lake-shore north. As pastel-purple Stesos rose, they reached the end of the lake. When Peeny stopped to graze for brief periods, the group gathered foods, mainly the blue corn, which grew well along the shore. In late afternoon, they stopped near a wide grassy hill to graze and gather. There came, suddenly, a reverberating thunder-like noise from somewhere far away on the somber plains. It echoed and began to shake the ground. The youth looked at Deedo questioningly.

"It is the sound of millions of prairie choks. We must take cover. It is a stampede, Chesh!" exclaimed Deedo as the deep rumbling came closer, stronger, thundering out the sounds of a million buffalo in a wild charge. The ground rumbled fiercely as the sound was all around them. Peeny remained calm. Gray-purple clouds marched in over the small band of questers. Cal-i-fax swooped from the torrent copper wings glinting purple lightning. He landed near the group, crouched around the base of the stego beetle's shell. Arilio dismounted and led the gigantic dragonfly so that its wings draped over the small group and the stego. Cal-i-fax placed his armored blue body directly over Chesh and the others.

As Arilio moved to duck under the dragonfly wing, he cried out, "Look, ah, look, what can that be? Look, the storm and stampede are not yet upon us."

First Chesh, then Deedo and several others popped out. They looked to Arilio's startled face then looked where he looked. The purple storm had parted like two giant rogue waves. Between the storm waves traveling fast on the violent winds sailed a glinting figure, a small figure. The outline of a being was suspended below a green triangle of spruce spiderweb netting of great size. It undulated in green ripples. Three sides of the netting were suspended in the air by three large crescent-moon-shaped blue pods. Each pod glowed. Light-blue beams of light danced among black-purple clouds. The airship or kite or whatever it was headed for Peeny and the others.

As the group watched from behind the low sandhill, the creature maneuvered the wind kite by pulling on long twine ropes, then landed almost next to the beetle and dragonfly. No movement came from either of the insect giants. Chesh, Deedo, and likely, Arilio took this as a sign that they felt no malice or threatening intent being released into the firmament by this kite flier, a good sign. The creature was reptilian but not any relation to the lizard men invaders. Deedo recognized this kite drifter as a Hon. *Hon* can mean "being, spirit, entity, or one." The Hon live on an island that floats in the sky, a very large island. Auk-en-shield is the island's name; it simply means "oak-in-shade." Myobian oak trees have indigo-colored leaves. To the Hon, these trees are sacred and posess many healing and healthful properties. The island has many oak forests upon it; some call it Auk-en-lund.

The people of this sky-floating land are almost never seen. They prefer to live away from surface dwellers. They are self-sufficient. The sky beings value privacy and honor. Like the bearwalkers of Earth's past Native American legends, the Hon were said to be able to transform into orange, green, blue, or other colored orbs of light, like ball lightning or swamp gas. In this form, they can travel about unknown. The Hon let forth a breath that may have signaled impatience or frustration.

Deedo boldly stepped forward. "What do you wish?" she said, looking at the Hon.

The Hon was a four-foot-tall creature with glowing powder-blue oysters for eyes. The head was dragon-like, always in a half smile. Behind the eyes, sweeping back were three-sectioned ear fins silver blue in color. She, for the creature was a female Hon, moved as if performing one long martial arts form, flowing like a slow stream at times, then moving like a crashing waterfall into a kicking or blocking motion. The Hon girl had powerful legs and arms. Her upper thighs looked like blue iron. Each hand had three clawed long fingers. Three upward-pointing, curved, rhino horn spikes of gold, apparently armor, adorned the center of her back. The skin was medium blue, adorned with crescent, curve markings that gave it a scaly, chain armor appearance. The creature had three curved indigo scimitar shaped lines running across its chest and stomach. Parts of her body were covered as with armor by a thick light-tan leatherlike hide adorned with wing designs similar to the ear armor. These were at the waist, knee, and elbow joints as protection for these vital areas. Each of the Hon's elbows were tipped with three-inch metallic spikes.

She spoke her name. "Jo-hon." She then made one hand into a fist and covered it with the other hand. She pointed to the large green triangle-shaped swath of net-sail that now lay draped over the small sandhill. The dragon's face smiled more broadly as she moved to grasp the green netting to demonstrate what she wanted the others to do.

"Come on, quick! Grab the net and move it over to shelter our insect friends," cried Deedo commandingly.

The Ogtavians scrambled to obey. They ran. They tugged, looking up to the north, to the ocean torrent of purple lightning-breathing monsters. The ground shuddered as the panicked prairie choks popcorned over the wheat-yellow surface just beyond the small sandhill. The net-sail was light. In less than a minute, Cal-i-fax, Peeny, the

Ogtavians, Chesh, and the stranger, Jo-hon, were safe under the netting. As they had scrambled in, grapefruit-sized raindrops began to fall, knocking some of them to the sand. Now they covered their ears to block out the sounds of hundreds of thousands of prairie choks stampeding over them while being pummeled and felled by cannonball rain. Lightning flashed, illuminating the green cave. None spoke aloud.

Time, which was distorted and off-kilter for Chesh due to the vastly different heavenly bodies as well as Myob's slow counterclockwise rotation, seemed to be going by in days to the youth as he crouched next to Peeny's shell. The net held as millions of the chicken-like choks and an equal amount of the bucketful-sized raindrops pummeled and bounded over it. Then finally, silence. First, the rain stopped, and then the thundering of the prarie choks faded. A dim light crept in through the green netting. Jo-hon flipped a portion of the covering back upon itself and emerged with caution. Deedo, Chesh, and the others followed. Mesos was nowhere in sight. The purple rays of Stesos bathed the weary group. It was near the eastern horizon, about to set.

As the youth looked out over the yellow landscape, he saw thousands upon thousands of dead bright-green prairie choks. To him, it appeared they had been trampled or smashed by the voluminous raindrops. He could smell the coppery-rust smell of the indigo blood that puddled around the lifeless choks.

"No point in breaking camp now. It will be too dark to travel soon. Did anyone sleep under the shelter?" joked Arilio.

None spoke up. All looked weary, save the being from the sky island.

"Okay, well, we all need rest so it is just as well. Let us gather some of these convenient and tasty choks to roast then, shall we?" He looked to the Ogtavians. Many smiled, nodding in agreement. Jo-hon, who already held two plump choks, set them down and began gathering dried grass and wood for a fire.

Chesh spoke as he walked between Deedo and Arilio. "Can we trust this Hon girl? I mean, she won't harm any of us, will she?"

Deedo looked at Arilio as if to say "Would you answer?"

"The Hon value honor," began the dragonfly scout. "That she came to our aid says she means well by us. Rarely, at times, a dweller from the island that is shaped like a shield appears to help a creature of Myob. We should feel honored. The Hon do not speak much, if at all. They may be telepathic. However, since they live the secretive lives of the reed catamounts, I doubt they would reveal telepathic abilities if they possessed them. They communicate through hand and body sign language, like the hand covering she did to explain the net shelter. Judging from the ornamented armor she wears, I would say this Hon is of high status, maybe even royalty among Hons."

"I see, well, she is formidable looking with those claws and spikes. I suppose we should all be thankful and helpful to her. Maybe we can do something to get her where she wants to go now as I see her aerial suspension pods have been punctured, I guess by the beaks of the choks," Chesh offered.

"Yes, of course we will help Jo-hon! She saved our lives. We must be careful to do nothing to offend our welcome guest," the princess said in a commanding tone.

Smoke rose from the fire as two of the plump chicken-like wild foul roasted on hand-rotated wooden spits. The smell of country ham permeated the night air. The Ogtavians spoke of the day's events as they feasted on the tender white meat. They gazed skyward to watch the tiny moon Ta as it charged at Kalustritus like an angry fury. Mezla-zan would not be visible tonight. Red, blue, and green stars made up the canopy of deep blackness above as the Ogtavians, Chesh, and Jo-hon drifted off to sleep not far from the dancing orange light.

In three days, they passed out of the littered prarie. Rhino-sized dark-maroon crickets of the tall grasses munched on the ripening chok corpses. A veld-like hilly expanse lay before them. Small groups of forlorn oaks and ash trees appeared here and there. Ponds and thin rivers appeared. From the top of a sand hill, Peeny and Chesh could see something in the far, far distance, beyond the hills. It loomed like an endless wall of thunderclouds. He wondered what it could be.

"We must stop, Chesh," began Arilio, who had landed nearby. "If your stego friend will allow, we need to make camp. We must make water bags for our time under the dark trees. I think it wise if, Chesh," he looked at Deedo, "and I go ahead to the mushroom forest on the outskirts of the dark forest. We must gather mushroom hide from the belwit mushrooms. With this, we can make large water bags that will hopefully last us in our time under the forest canopy. We must avoid the fetid waters of the once-enchanted Zudian Forest for they are poisonous and toxic and will at least kill you." Arilio looked at Chesh, seeking agreement.

"Yes, we should go. Can we still go today?" replied Chesh.

Riding atop Cal-i-fax, Arilio and Chesh soared high over the yellow and green stippled landscape. The mixture of green and purple sunlight dancing across giant dragonfly wings gave them a kaleidoscopic effect of brilliant oranges and blues. They circled wide and came about heading northwest out over the low hills of yellow grass.

To the youth came an intense feeling of the giganticness of this Myobian world. *Why is everything so large here? Well, many things, mainly insects,* Chesh said to himself. *Could it be because the air here is like that of the Permian era, with a 90 percent oxygen rate? I wonder.* He came out of his thoughtful gaze as Arilio spoke to him.

"Your beetle, like my dragonfly friend, does not like you to part," Arilio started.

"No, she always wants to be at my side, to do what I do, so to speak. I thought she did well for her when we left, and I did leave Deedo some peanuts to tide Peeny over till we return," Chesh said.

"It is good for the others to be on their own. I worry about what is ahead for them. Not Lavek so much. He is a warrior and has taught himself to be skilled with the sword, the Chinese broad sword. Lavek, the woodsmith, admires warriors. He likes your medieval period especially. Many of his ancestors fought in the Zudian wars. He will be all right. I worry most about Shawnee and Bangal. Although they are skilled in the ways of Gi, they are young. Gladstone, a carver of wooden bowls, cups, and a woodcrafter, I don't know how well he'll do against dark, faceless, winged things or the giant Zug spider-bats that Monarch Wapiti spoke of. Rouge will be okay. She is of the seas and crafts fine kif windships. She has achieved high levels of Gi."

"Allistus is also well versed in Gi. She seems shy, and like the rest of us, she has not been in combat. Deedo does not worry me. She comes from a long line of warriors from Myob's dim past. She is a highly proficient martial artist and a dead shot with her belt sling. This Jo-hon, if she stays, will prove to be tougher than us all and experienced at real battle, I'll wager. The Hon are known for their secretive martial art. They are agile, being able to leap ten feet or more straight up. If they can change to light balls, well, look out. I wouldn't want to tangle with a Hon. And you, Chesh, are you ready for what will come?" asked Arilio.

"I'm as ready as I'll ever be, I guess. I hate the lizard things. Hate them for what they did to your people. I hate them for making slaves of other creatures. Yeah, I'm ready!" Chesh finished vehemently, looking Arilio in the eyes.

Looking out of his human eyes, the landscape before Chesh took on the appearance of a vast Renoir painting of ladies of all sizes wearing bulbous gaudy-colored hats. Behind the canvas was what Chesh had wondered about before, the dark thunderclouds. They transformed into towering trees and sequoia cattails. Not trees or cattails like on other parts of Myob that Chesh had been to. These were dark, menacing, gnarled, glaring monsters of trees with thick trunks that contained a menagerie of menacing-bark insect faces. The roots of these trees, as well as the giant cattails, which were almost black in color, grew up out of the murk-mud and tarn pools surrounding them. The roots formed tangles of dark spindly spider legs with openings like caves.

The dragonfly began to ease downward in slow circular loops. The smell of sulfur reached Chesh's nostrils. They landed near a tarn pool. "That is a belwit mushroom, Chesh," said Arilio, pointing with webbed fingers. The mushroom he indicated was as big as an elephant. It's color was soft-powder violet. The cap was wide and spread out. The stalk was thick, especially at the bottom. It was darker in color. The spore's top circle color is a pinkish brown. "We will not take too much. We will do no harm. I will cut and drop pieces to you, Chesh."

With that, he walked over to the belwit, threw a twine rope with a bone hook at one end up, and was aboard the wide leathery cap in an instant. Arilio spoke to the youth as he cut sections from the mushroom with his stone knife. "Chesh, there are some things you should know before we enter the Zudian Forest. Some unpleasant things." Arilio looked down then released a patch of the hide to Chesh.

"Unpleasant things?" said Chesh.

"Yes, quite unpleasant, like do you see that island in the middle of that tarn pool, Chesh?" posed the scout.

"Yes, I see it," answered Chesh.

"Well, it's not an island."

"Oh, wha—"

Arilio cut the youth off. "Believe me, Chesh, you don't want to know. Don't worry, it's only active after dark. Some things are better left unknown."

Chesh looked up at the Ogtavian, somewhat befuddled.

"You see, Chesh, this forest is very different, different from any place on Myob. It wasn't always called the Zudian Forest. In the ancient past, it was known as the Indigo Forest. The trees were mostly indigo blue. One day, a creature appeared. No one knows from where for sure. Maybe outer space, maybe inner space, or maybe it just evolved. I doubt that, for even our planet, which has much diverse life, could not spawn such a thing."

"This thing, in the dim past, began to build an army of hideous followers. Strange piping and fires came forth at night from the winding chambers of the forest as it fell deeper into darkness and decay. Headless off-world humans were seen chopping trees down to clear the land beyond the blighted forest. They used giant insect slaves and other unspeakable things to haul the logs to the shore that surrounds this land that is shaped like a mitten. The thing that was called Zud ordered that a wall be built. Trees were cut or burned. The wall was to go around the continent."

"The fierce winds and frequent tidal waves coupled with the Zudian wars caused the building to stop. At times, odd, misshapened things are seen dragging logs to the shore and continuing to work on the wall. This time in our history is known as the clearings. Many meek creatures of all kinds died or suffered horribly. Species all over Myob began to die out as evil black smoke circled the planet as if from many volcanos erupting. Real frogs, which existed only on Mur, became extinct. Many creatures swam or flew to safer lands."

"After thousands of years, odd, misshapened things began to come forth from the dark forest. Things like the crawling chaos we saw back on the plains. Things like spiders the size of Earth horses. Spiders that were not spiders but macabre combinations of things. Coffin winged with bat heads and bodies covered with red tarantula hairs. There are zog, giant clams from three feet across to the size of small islands. They walk on spindly legs, dredging up prey with a vine tentacle. At the end of the tentacle is a razor beak. Leeches abound in the fetid waters and carniverious plants. Leeches that can wrap themselves around your head. Prehistoric centipede fourteen feet long still live here, deep-red venomous ones with lobster claws. Many inhabit the decaying root bases.

"Man-o-war hang down from branches. Precambrian-clawed, scorpion-tailed monstrosities lurk and scuffle in the murky pitch shallows and more. In short, Chesh, my friend, and by the way, one good martial artist, from whom I learned much, the dangers in the dark forest are overwhelming. You must keep the third way of Gi in your mind always, look, listen, and I would add smell. We face our dragons together. In this way, we shall win." He tossed another leathery section down. It thudded in the dust, sending up puffs of spores.

"I see, and thanks, Arilio. I really mean thanks. I will back you up whatever happens with this forest and the lizard things," said Chesh.

Purple sunlight transformed the stalk and gills of the giant belwit into a deep-violet shade. Chesh looked about at the other mushrooms. Some looked like clumsy, damaged giant bells; others, powdery orange pinwheel parasols. There were green anise funnel caps, morels the size of tanks, fairy cups, pine truffles, rusty leaf jelly, blue spine, bitter oyster, and death caps of all kinds. The death caps grew toward the darkening forest. The wind picked up, swaying the

Renior beings into a shiver. A noise like malignant chatter echoed about the tall stalks.

As they ascended, Chesh heard maniacal owllike cries mixed with shriller-than-possible hyena laughs emerging from the spaces between gnarled, knotted dark trees. A cold shiver traveled the length of his spine. It seemed that every once in a while, Chesh saw a fleeting, winged dark figure, a shiny, glistening figure, a figure that made the pit of his stomach hurt, go past or hover above just out of his vision range. He wondered if Arilio was perceptive of these dark shapes. In the night sky above the blue and green stars of Myob appeared. The planet Trigeon, with its single moon, showed brightly in the eastern sky. A flickering orange light from the fire at their camp guided the dragonfly riders back. Cal-i-fax landed softly. Chesh dismounted and walked to the anxious stego beetle. He gave her several peanuts from his pocket. The scent of country ham wafted in the light wind. Arilio had Bangal and Shawnee, unload the mushroom hides. He gave the meal makers a large slice of mushroom meat from the belwit. He gave the dragonfly and the stego beetle each a large portion.

The Ogtavians had been busy making chok jerky using berry juice and bone marrow. They had also gathered much dried grass for fires and torches. Though voice inflections were difficult to read, Chesh thought he detected out-of-the-ordinary tones of nervousness in the voices of some of the Ogtavians. They would enter the Zudian Forest tomorrow, and they all knew it. After a meal of blue corn, belwit mushroom, and roasted chok, they sat by the fire, looking at the parchment map Monarch Wapiti had given them. Arilio and several others worked on stitching together two large water bags using hide strips.

"My father said we enter the forest here. There will be a tunnel opening," Deedo began, pointing at the map. "He said it is large enough for a creature the size of twenty slothos to enter. We remain on this path. The tunnel should be as large or larger then the opening. At times, the tree vine tunnel will open into vast caverns or valleys. He said to always fear the silent death, falling tree limbs. Watch for webs and detritus being used to mask the way. The castle lies here. It only becomes visible at times, mostly during a mist. The mist grows more dense and frequent the deeper one gets into the forest. The castle was built by giant glow worms. It was called the Indigo Castle for it was made using indigo stone. Many tunnels run under the castle and likely run out under the woods, maybe beyond. There might be an opening fifty feet from us, and we would never know. These ancient worms traveled through earth and rock as if it were water. My father also said to watch for the red eyes of spiders."

After the brief discussion, the weary company drifted to their grass sleep nests. Chesh did likewise; he only made shelters when storms or dream spiders were around. None were far from the fire. When they awoke the low clouds were light purple in front of a wall of green sunlight. All was prepared and loaded. There were four large water bags. Peeny would carry two as would Cal-i-fax. Drying jerky was taken from racks by the fire. The large saddlebags packed with blue corn, choco pods, reed jugs of honey, and more were placed gently upon the stego. Peeny did not seem to mind the extra load, although she eyed the loaders a few times. Shawnee and Bangel set about making mushroom-hide helmets spiked with sharpened bone or sticks. These would serve to protect them from creatures that attack from above, they hoped. The two teens bickered back and forth as they worked. They continued their work aboard Peeny. She moved at a brisk pace over the grassy hills.

Around lunchtime, the mushroom forest's colors appeared in the distance. Behind loomed the dreaded forest. After several hours, Peeny and her riders, along with Arilio and Cal-i-fax, reached the dark, foreboding opening and path that led into the Zudian Forest. The small band stayed only long enough to eat a hasty lunch and survey the entrance. They went in silently. Cal-i-fax, generally fearless, needed coaxing and reassurance from Arilio before he stepped timidly into the gaping mouth that would keep him from the skies. To Chesh, it was like the caverns on Jeptus-one. He felt as if he were in an endless sponge of lichen, trees, roots, and vines much in a state of decay. The tarn water smelled like rotten eggs. Tentacles, fins, and giant lobster claws broke the surface of some of the deeper tarn pools at times. The air grew more stagnant the farther the party proceeded into the haze filled tunnel. Chesh's skin felt like it had been wrapped in warm, moist cotton. At times, glowing eyes, mainly red, could be seen back in a dark shadowy cave opening or far above, lurking in the vines and webs.

Finding dry ground would be tough. Peeny did not falter in this, however. She came upon a raised swamp-island-like mass. It was formed from roots and earth. As far as any could tell, night would soon be coming. It was not easy to estimate time under the dark canopy. The wood was dry. The fire was cheery. The mood was dismal. Shawnee tried to liven things up by placing a sage burr where Bengal was sitting.

"Ha-ha, very funny. I wonder who could have done this," she remarked casually, which was unlike her usual tirade. After the meal, the teens set about making torches while Lavek and the others talked about the possibility of making a kif boat to carry them up the Rouge River to the fort of the lizard soldiers after they had gotten the stego horns from the Zudian castle, if all went well. The wood here burned differently than other wood. It gave off blue and green flames with very little orange to illuminate the smothering eternal night of the forest of gloom. The darkness had become so thick with mist it vailed one's vision. Noises echoed forth. Forlorn night wasps, somber minotaurian crickets, and water reapers were among the recognizable ones. From the pitch-black of a wood cave opening came a known cry. An Ogtavian cry. The company sitting around the fire looked frantically about.

"It's Gladstone! Gladstone is gone!" cried Arilio, jumping up.

Chesh sprang to his feet. "We must search. Come on, I think he's this way." He moved in the direction he thought the scream came from.

"Wait, Chesh, please remain with the others. I shall go," Deedo said.

Chesh looked at her with surprise then nodded in compliance. Deedo and Arilio would go. Then Chesh saw Peeny do something she had never done before. First, she eyed Deedo. Then she lifted her right front beetle leg as if to point in a certain direction. Deedo noticed and went in that direction. It was not where Chesh had headed. Arilio followed with a flaming torch. Chesh wondered if some sort of telepathy existed between the Ogtavian princess and his friend. He felt jealous.

They came upon their comrade just inside a large grotto of fetid murk. He splashed and struggled, trying to get something from his head. Quickly, Arilio drew his stone knife and cut at the tentacle wrapped around Gladstone's face. At the tip was a razor squid beak that snapped opened and closed, making clicking sounds. Brown ichor oozed from the knife gashes. The tentacle released their clawed sucker cups. Waves rippled the surface as the tentacle writhed away and down into the foul-smelling black-brown murk. The rescuers raised the stunned Ogtavian to his feet and carried him to the small islet. He was laid by the fire, where he came to himself.

"You were lucky, Gladstone. That was a giant stinger clam. It would have dragged you down under the mud into its lair to feed on you bit by bit," said Arilio, looking sternly.

"It wasn't my fault," Gladstone said as he lightly touched the blue suction cup marks across his cheeks and forehead. "I was sitting by the fire, well, not far from it. I was munching on a bit of roasted chok when something wrapped around my face and dragged me off under the water. I was barely able to work my mouth free to scream. Thank you, Arilio. Thank you, Deedo. I was almost done for. Oh, thank you!"

"From now on, pair up. Pick a partner, or I will choose one for you. Always be able to see your partner. Choose now before we sleep, and sleep with a cord that binds you both together. We must all do this, and likely more, in order to survive," spoke Deedo.

The Ogtavians paired off quickly. Chesh and Deedo agreed to be partners. Jo-hon, who often scouted ahead or took strange excursions alone, displayed a gesture that she would prefer to remain on her own. This done, all turned in except Lavek and Rouge, who were first watch. The vast world of root caves, tunnels, and Permian swamp water closed in around the small company like some prehistoric ocean-dwelling leviathan. They awoke to a scream from Shawnee. Chesh clearly saw something, a barrel-like clear pinkish thing with tentacles in a ring around its middle, draw itself up slowly from where the boy lay. He raced to him.

Shawnee writhed and thrashed, clutching his face. He was car-
ried nearer to the light. "It looked like a man-of-war with a vine
attached," said Chesh.

"I just got up to stretch," said Shawnee, grimacing in agony. His
face looked like it had a metal rake dragged over it from the chin to
the forehead. Something splashed as light broke through between the
trees high above. They watched silently as a translucent paramecium
creature, of great size, cut back and forth in the tepid tarn, probing
for smaller organisms to absorb. On top of the animal, a dome shape
revolved, emitting a sickly-yellow beacon light, possibly to attract
prey.

"Shawnee, you should have let your partner know you were get-
ting up because that thing that attacked you was deadly," said Deedo,
handing the hurt youth a reed bowl containing soothing green moss
to put on his face.

The Ogtavians set about making a morning meal. Chesh began
loading the saddlebags with as much dry wood as they would take.
The distant Jo-hon helped. She had slept under the netting, which
she had persuaded the group to bring.

After awakening during the night to what felt like his face being
stung by a hail of bees and watching a small swarm of what looked to
be red lightning bugs swirl up into the vast ceiling above, he thought
that sleeping under the net was what they all needed to do. He
thought so much of his idea that he added four staff-sized branches
to his wood gathering. Once trimmed, they fit under the net to hold
it up. He also gathered some moss that Peeny and the dragonfly had
been eating. *It seems that not all of this forest consists of malignant poi-
sonous things*, thought Chesh.

The second day in the dark forest, Chesh noticed, as did the
others, that the mostly red eyes that they had been seeing lurking
in cave holes, soaring above on bat wings, and sometimes dropping
from the high branches and vines of the vaulted ceiling of the wide
tunnel belonged to spiders.

"We are entering what Monarch Wapiti called the Forest of
Spiders, a forest within a forest," said Arilio.

Here, there began to be a bluish mist that darkened the ever-present mist that hung in the stale air, giving a thick haze effect to the ether. The winds that at times whistled down the tunnel so fast they buffeted the riders threatening to knock them off ceased, possibly due in part to the large amount of gray spiderwebs spun over openings and above. Chesh and all, except Jo-hon, had begun wearing the mushroom-hide helmets that looked like the helmets of Roman soldiers or Spartans, except these had sharpened bone or wood spikes protruding from them. The group now resembled spiky crusader knights. Some of the company had taken to carrying the net tent poles and using them to fend off any dark fluttering things, like beetle-jawed death's head moths or swimming centipedes. The tunnel path became dryer here. Water no longer ran in rivulets down the intertwined trees and wide rotting sequoia cattail stalks. Instead, it dripped slowly as from cave stalactites. Brown-gray moss enveloped everything. Malformed mushrooms and rotting puffballs grew profusely, shooting out clouds of spores. New breeds of creeping things slithered in and out of the fetid growths, flashing minute red, purple, or sickly-yellow eyes.

Chesh petted Peeny, saying, "It will be okay, Peeny. I know this is tough on both of us. Thanks for coming." He looked behind him to Deedo. "I hope Arilio and Gladstone are careful riding point up there," he said.

Up ahead in the dark, dark tree tunnel, Arilio spoke out to Gladstone, "Are you looking and listening, Gladstone?"

"Yes, I'm doing my best," he replied.

"If that's true, why then did you not see the azure moth that just wrapped itself around my face?" the scout said, looking at the other Ogtavian crossly.

"What!" cried the startled Gladstone as he turned to watch Arilio release the struggling moth.

"You must use your senses, all of them. Also, since you're facing our rear, please do me a favor and rotate your head once in a while to check on me, as I do you," Arilio scolded. "You must face your dragons if you want to survive this forest of darkness and its ilk. Your dragons are focusing and fear."

Cal-i-fax moved forward slowly in the darkness. He stopped and sniffed the moldy air. He sniffed again and then angled his head so that a large purple eye looked at Arilio. He scratched the ground with his right foreleg. Arilio looked at the other Ogtavian, motioning silence. He gestured that he would go ahead alone. He indicated that Gladstone remain with Cal-i-fax.

Gladstone sat for a long while, trembling. *How nice it would be to be back in my sandy tower, cooking bacon bark and yellow cattail root cakes*, he thought. A soft rustling in the darkness sent a chill down his spine. Grabbing the torch, he stood up.

"Be at ease, woodcrafter. It is I returning," Arilio said softly. "You must come. There is something strange ahead. We will observe."

After a time, a long time for Gladstone, the pair reached a small cavern-like area. They crouched behind a sizable rotting log that had dropped from the cathedral ceiling. The chamber formed of the monsterous tree roots and vines in various states of decay was lighted by a drab-blue lichen that grew profusely on the rotting vegetation. In the dim, bluish haze, Gladstone viewed a horrifying sight. Two headless human bodies lay in the center of the chamber. Not far away were several more bodies, both male and female, sitting, leaning against a low rough-hewn stone wall. They wore only a type of harness that fastened around their shoulders, a thick dark leatherlike hide neck collar and some hide cloth. As the two Ogtavians watched from a round hole in a structure that looked like half of an igloo made from rectangular stone blocks came first a spindle spider leg then a hideous pumpkin-sized gray-blue spider body. It crawled on the human forms.

Arilio and Gladstone saw that the spider had the face of a human, an ugly, misshapened face. A second black-gray thing followed. The second spider helped the first to mount one of the bodies at the neck. By sliding six of its eight legs into control slots, the abomination was able to take control of the headless body. The spider thing was locked in place by straps. Its two front legs, which each had lobster claws, were free. After the second spider's head was in place, both creatures walked zombielike over to a large pile of stone blocks. After hooking a harness to one block, they began to drag it toward the low wall.

Gladstone's eyes went wide with terror. Arilio looked at him and shook his head. Arilio took off his sling belt. He removed several Gi stones from a mushroom-hide bag he wore about his waist.

Glaring at Gladstone, he motioned for him to do likewise. The clever scout waited until the spider-headed bodies were close. He elbowed the wood-carver, nodding toward the Gi belt about his waist. Gladstone removed his belt and laid out some Gi stones. They loaded the slings. The scout gave his countryman a quick "One, two, three" finger count. The two rose with slings whirling. The stones struck with deadly accuracy, felling both spider heads and the enslaved bodies. The red eyes of the spider heads ceased glowing and glossed over. Brown ichor dripped from the wounds. Human arms and legs flailed at the air and the dark moss.

Arilio left Gladstone to watch the area. If any more spider monstrosities appeared, he was to sneak away and get back to the others with word. Arilio would ride Cal-i-fax, who had excellent vision in the dark with his hundreds of eyes within eyes. He would meet the others and bring them quickly so they could pass undetected.

Gladstone sat near the rotting log, peering over from time to time. "I still wish I was back in my castle tower in Og, frying up some bacon bark and yellow sweet cakes," he said to himself as he tightened his grip on the Gi belt that he kept at the ready.

Not sure if it was nearing night or not, and not caring much as the events of the last hours had wearied them all, except Jo-hon, the small company of questers after the mystical stego horns sot a place to rest. They had passed through the chamber of the spider heads with no trouble. They came upon a small grotto on one side of the forest tunnel. The blue lichen continued on from the chamber, where it had begun illuminating the tunnel. A blue-white mist washed and drifted over dark detritus. Peeny and Cal-i-fax lay chewing some of the lichen Chesh had packed for them. Bengal, Shawnee, Chesh, and Deedo unpacked food, cooking things, and dry grass, while the others gathered dry deadfall wood. Deedo's face gave off a green glimmer in the firelight.

"My father said that we would pass through three enlarged cavern-like chambers. The last chamber will have open sky, and the castle will be there," she said.

"Bangal and I could scout ahead and find the next chamber," Shawnee chirped.

"Have you asked Bangal about doing this, Shawnee?" said Deedo.

"Well, no, but I'm sure she would," he said.

"Think for yourself and no one else, please, Shawnee," Deedo replied.

Shawnee stared at the fire, an adolescent pout on his face. Within a couple of hours, Chesh was asleep near Peeny under the green netting. Lavek and Rouge took the first watch. The other Ogtavians slept tethered together as partners. Jo-hon, who had not been seen since before they encountered the spider heads, was still missing.

When Chesh awoke, he had the word *slothos* in his mind as if at the tail end of his dream, his mind had been saying "Slowly, slowly, slowly, said the slothos." He had an uneasy feeling that something was wrong. He soon discovered why. Rouge was missing. Lavek and Arilio stood by the campfire, talking in low voices and examining what looked like a piece of parchment. Chesh woke Deedo, who was tethered to one of his ankles. They disconnected the twine that bound them together and walked over to the fire softly, trying not to arouse the others.

"She can't be far ahead. I'm going to find her," said Lavek, broad sword in hand.

"Going alone is to dangerous. We—" Arilio's words were cut off by Deedo.

"What has happened? Where is Rouge?" asked Deedo.

Arilio handed her the piece of parchment he and Lavek had been looking at. She read it aloud. "I am tired of sitting on the beetle all of the time. I can do more. I am going to scout ahead for the next cavern. See you later. Rouge." Deedo looked at Lavek questioningly.

"You see, Princess Deedo, Rouge felt useless. She means no wrong. She only wishes to show others that she is a warrior. She should not have gone on alone. I must go after her." Lavek tightened his grip on the sword's handle.

"No one goes alone," said Deedo firmly. "Remember your Ogtavian history, in the Zudian wars of long ago, our ancestors made the mistake of dividing their forces, and this poor strategy led to their defeat, as well as to the release of the deadly red fog that wiped out all of the frogs on Myob. The Ogtavians were almost exterminated. We go together," finished the proud princess, looking firmly at each member of the small force.

They assembled near the giant insects, all that is except the Hon, Jo-hon, who was nowhere to be found, as often was the case. The staffs were carried, slings were at the ready, and stones were in pouches. Silently, they moved off through the shifting ground mists. As they went farther, the light of the wood cavernous tunnel grew much more faint. All at once, Chesh and his compatriots were in total pitch-blackness. The sounds of insect screams, scurrying clawed feet, and cracking chitin came at them from all sides. Torches were lit, and their light sent many obtuse and horrible things into hiding. Chesh caught a glimpse of a few. One was a barrel-shaped pinkish obscenity about three feet tall with whip tentacles undulating and lashing out from its middle. Another was a black trilobite six feet in length. A horseshoe crab with enlarged lobster claws was devouring the struggling trilobite. Red spider eyes and others peered out from dark recesses. Chesh spotted a dim light ahead. No sign of Rouge except for a few footprints spotted by the skillful tracker Arilio.

As they approached the opening that emitted a sickly-yellow light, Peeny suddenly stopped and laid down. Chesh, who had been walking just ahead of her, turned and tried to coax her on. The myst stego beetle lay firm. "We must go on," said Deedo decidedly. Chesh stayed with his friend after much whispered discussion. The others, including Cal-i-fax, proceeded through the opening. The Earth youth listened as he comforted Peeny and gave her one of the precious peanuts. All was silent. Then *woosh, crash, thud thud* sounds rang out. The Ogtavians cried out to one another. Chesh could make out the sound of the giant dragonfly's wings. He moved to the opening about thirty yards ahead and peered in. A chaotic scene was before him.

Cal-i-fax was flapping his wings in panic against the high-vaulted ceiling of a cavern so vast that Chesh could not see its end.

The reason the giant dragonfly panicked was that a fifty-foot thing that was half-centipede and half–ant lion was after him. It was translucent, and about one quarter of the way down its gullet was their lost companion, Rouge. She was no doubt dead. Her body had been partially eaten away by acid juices. Her handsome face had become melting green wax. The Ogtavians stood ground bravely, hailing stones at the centilion with their slings. Arillio fired at the thing's eyes with a tricross weapon he had made. An arrow protruded from one eye. Lavek slashed viciously at the smoky, clear chitin with his broad sword. Bangel struck it with a staff, as did Allistus and Gladstone. Shawnee slung rocks with deadly accuracy, aiming for the head and eyes. Deedo did the same.

Just as Chesh looked back at Peeny in a rush of thought that told him to go in, sounds of cracking burst forth. Something was emerging from the vine-choked ceiling. Something whirling. Debris dropped. It was a large—well, as large as a person—translucent blue sphere. The sphere had something within, something like a whirl-wind of swirling, flashing, shiny black with glints of silver. A small tornado. The sphere reminded Chesh of the sphere that the small winged dragon-like insect that had calmed him had been in so long ago. The sphere floated. It hovered. It moved from place to place faster than human eyes could see. It moved as does a hummingbird, becoming invisible at times.

Then as she hovered in front of the insect beast, delivering vicious kicks and strikes, Chesh saw that within the sphere was Jo-hon. She became a whirling dervish of spikes and razor claws. The Hon struck and moved. When the thing's mandibles gnashed at her, the sphere appeared to wink out and reappear always at a vulnerable target area. Now Jo-hon struck the throat, which was protected by a chain mail armor exoskeleton of clear chitin. Brown blood burst forth from a deep slash as Jo-hon vanished. The centithing glared at the Ogtavians with large orbs of yellow death. Those using their slings had let up for fear of striking Jo-hon.

The centilion raised one of its saw-toothed lobster claws. As the claw struck in a sweeping motion upon the Ogtavians, the blue orb appeared at the elbow joint of the clawed arm. Chesh watched as Jo-hon severed the elbow joint with one silver-tipped front kick. The claw, stained with the blood of Cal-i-fax, fell to the ground, spurting brown blood upon the stunned warriors as it convulsed and snapped. The highborn Hon struck again at the neck of the hideous leviathan. Brown ichor burst forth from gashes opened by rapier-clawed crescent kicks. Front piercing kicks to the bulbous eyes soon blinded the massive creature. The centilion reeled, gnashing the air with its surviving fore claw. Its mandibles opened and closed, frantically seeking that which harmed it. The massive head dropped first. Followed by the front of its body.

As it lay dying, the pincers that ran the length of its body continued to grasp for a last chance at vengeance. They would go on opening and closing for days after the centilion died. Chesh and the Ogtavians were quick to move in. Lavek cut his partner from beneath the translucent chitin and flesh of the thing. Cal-i-fax began to descend cautiously. The orb of blue fire darted to a wide cone-shaped depression in the center of the chamber. Chesh and Arilio rushed to help. Looking down into the trap, they watched as Jo-hon finished off a half-dozen smaller centilions. Pincers, claws, and chitin flew up from the pit, swirling like autumn leaves, as Jo-hon delivered kicks and strikes so fast that her limbs became whirling blurs. As Jo-hon ascended in her bubble, several giant trilobites scurried down the sides of the cone trap and began to consume the remains. She floated to the Ogtavians as Chesh and Arilio followed. The Ogtavians greeted Jo-hon with their arms extended up and anglewise from their bodies, which means "welcome" and "thank you." The secretive Hon merely nodded her head in reply. Her smile displayed an arsenal of silver teeth.

"I thank you deeply. You saved Cal-i-fax, and I am—we are—grateful," said Arilio as he tended to several wounds and some rips in the sail wings of his loyal companion. He had tears running down his froggy cheeks. Peeny peeked in through the round opening to the cavern of slaughter. She walked over to Chesh timidly and laid down just as mud from a mud storm far, far above began to drip from the vaulted ceiling of rot-black wood. Glowing orange-blue dendrites slithered in and out of the decomposing wood on millions of centilegs seeking nourishment, making the trees trunks into obtuse, whirling barber poles. Furry grey slipper creatures crawled across the dark earth. A black-gray forked tongue slithered out from a hole and circle-grabbed three of them. Arilio rose using only one leg. He raised his tricross bow high into the air. "On to the Indigo Castle!" he shouted.

Gladstone shot up followed by the others. Each warrior raised their favored weapon. Chesh, his vine whip chain with a Gi stone attached to the end. Deedo held up her sling, as did Allistus. Lavek, his broad sword. Shawnee and Bangel held staffs aloft. Cal-i-fax raised a mantis-clawed arm slightly. They set out after burying Rouge in a quiet cave floored with indigo mushrooms and green and red berry hollus vines. The small company munched on trail grok from their pouches as they pushed on in silence.

Chesh thought about his friend. *I will not abandon my loyal, patient friend in any way. The more I understand her, the more I see how like me Peeny is. I must be understanding, not scolding. Still, I wonder why she would not enter the cavern. Was it for fear of the centilion? What else could it have been? Maybe these centilions can harm myst stego beetles. I wonder.*

They moved on in the bluish darkness an indomitable juggernaut. They must obtain the stego horns for that is their quest.

Not far ahead, down in the lower giant worm carven tunnels below the Indigo Castle, some disquieting entities reeled and gyrated disturbingly around a large orange-flamed pit. Among them were pinkish barrel horrors with tentacles extending from their middles. Some of the faceless, bat-winged shiny-black things moved or flew above the others. Many of the slave spider heads milled about. Others resembled ancient Paleozoic life-forms, with pincers and crab claws that had just crawled forth from the lush oily swamps.

One was Zud. The appearance of this ruler from some distant unknown world was much more horrifying than that of any of his followers. He was nine feet tall. His head took on the shape of a half sphere made of sickly green translucent chitin. Two evil looking large dark purple eyes were near the top. Extending from the top of his head, near the eyes, two thin arms with elongated, jagged, crab pincers, reached skyward, as if seeking prey. Below the eyes on each side of his segmented body three smaller arms of chitin with pincers wiggled hideously. Where human arms might have been were long segmented arm like structures that had what loked like elongated giant clams partially opened, at the ends. Protruding from each clam hand were sharp black stingers. Zud's body consisted of semitransparent rounded sections that got smaller as they went down. The thirteenth section, at the bottom gave the appearance of fins, that looked like the tail of a giant walrus. The Zud thing could hover and float above the ground or water like the wretched pink barrel horrors that had tentacles extending from their middles.

This beast from another time and place, another planet or galaxy, or even some other universe, no creature knew for sure; most resembled a Gigantostraca or sea sorpion from the Earth's dim past. These prehistoric sea beasts existed during the Ordovician period, 500 million years before the present. They were primitive chordates that dominated the warm shallow seas and lakes that covered the planet at a time when the Appalachian mountains were beginning to form, land plants began to grow and fish first appeared. Trilobites, brachiopods, and other marine invertebrates, ruled the seas. Zud moved up some stone steps, and from an elevated throne of putridity, the thing that was called Zud looked down. Down upon the moving gyrating mass of Paleozoic Era chordates and other obscure monstrosities that wriggled and crawled around the pit of flame. Faceless black things blew into bone-white pipes, sending haunting, unknown melodies into fetid, smoke-filled air. Unsettling frantic drumming spurred the undulating mass on as it echoed through the dark abysmal openings in the decaying walls. Zud had long ago decreed this night to be sacred. It was a time when the three moons of Myob—Ta, Kalustritus, and Mezla-zan—lined up. This only occurred once every Myobian year. Zud told his followers that if they danced around the sacred orange fire, along with performing other unspeakable rights, they would gain powers. Powers that would aid them on the course

of destruction and domination that this ruler who came from some distant place had chosen for them.

He had had his army destroy a vast amount of the trees on the continental land mass once called Mur. Most of the trees were used to build a wall. Zud postponed the building of the wooden wall that was to go around the continent because his legions were no match for the furious Hon warriors. Their protective spheres made them invincible. Zud was now, and had been for a long time, trying to slay or capture a Hon so that he could discover the secret of the spheres that his enemies could strike out from, yet nothing could penetrate the sphere to harm the warrior within. He knew he would never defeat the Hon without this knowledge. This mysterious ruler had fought other battles on other worlds. Zud was as old as time itself.

The massive chitin-armored ruler motioned with a pincer fore claw. From deep recesses in the sides of the chamber came some of his minions carrying squirming, struggling large insect creatures. These captives were quickly run through with spears of metal and placed to roast above the flaming pit. Oily black smoke billowed forth, swirling up and up the central chimney of the tall castle keep above.

It stretched out before them as wide as the mighty Mississippi river. A ribbon of unmoving silver. The intrepid company had come out of the long tunnel of rotting fungus wood and spider heads. The terrain became one of ancient tree stumps and fetid tarn pools. At times, a grotesque scorpion claw or scaled head broke the surface of one of the dark pools.

"How, oh how can we ever cross this!" Deedo spoke in anguish, looking down at her webbed toes.

"We might fly across a few at a time. However, our beetle friend is far too heavy for Cal-i-fax to carry. If he can't swim it, what will we do?" Arilio looked at the giant beetle.

Deedo looked at the youth with questioning blue eyes. "I will not desert my beetle friend. I wish to help you as well," began Chesh. "She and I can head north then try south to see if there's a place we can cross."

"We must go on, you understand, Chesh. Wait for us. If we do not return, you must go back the same way we came. I wish you and

Peeny could stay. We will see you soon." Deedo looked sad, as did the others.

Jo-hon spoke, "This is the castle mote."

About fifty yards down the river's shore a creature appeared from a clump of black stumps. It was in appearance similar to an armadillo with chitinous moose's antlers. It moved on six beetle legs. Its shell of powder blue was highlighted by bright-yellow spikes running along the edges. The moose beetle sprang into the gleaming river. It began to swim across. The mirror surface around the antlered creature started to ripple and boil. Hundreds of small silver-bodied flying fish with mouths of needles swarmed over the helpless moose beetle. The swarm vanished. The antlers floated on the shiny liquid for a few seconds until an ominous dark tentacle dragged them below.

Peeny glowed almost indigo in the dim blue light. She looked at Chesh affectionately as she rose. Her underside was caked with rich dark-indigo-colored soil. Bangel, Shawnee, and Alistus went with Arilio first. They had the small catapult strapped on also. Cali-fax's translucent wings carried them on a slow assent up over the silver ribbon of death. Tens of thousands of jumbled conglomerations of insect, crustacean, and mollusk life-forms surfaced, striking out with claws and tentacles at the ether just below the dragonfly. They reached the other side safely. The three passengers quickly dismounted and unloaded the catapult. Shortly, carrying Deedo, Lavek, Gladstone, and the ballista, the giant dragonfly headed out over the mote, guided by Arilio. Again, a menagerie of obtuse horrors struck up at them in vein. As they landed safely, the stego beetle looked at them curiously, as if to ask "What about us?" Her legs began heading for the silver water. Seeing this, Chesh ran after his friend, waving his arms and shouting "Stop! Peeny stop!"

Just as she entered the silver liquid, Chesh jumped onto the back of her shell, his eyes wide with terror. Not far from shore, the frenzied things that lived in the mote scrambled, fighting to get near the fresh prey. The smell of scales, fins, and sea slime permeated the air. A strange thing happened at this time, however. A thing that went undetected by Chesh, who had scrambled up to the base of Peeny's neck and clung on for his life. The myst stego beetle's dinner-platter maroon eyes, usually serene, suddenly began to glow a piercing green. Instantly, the predatory things that pursued Chesh and Peeny disappeared. The beetle and her rider were not bothered again as they crossed the ribbon of silver. The Ogtavians jumped up and down, cheering as the Earthling and his beetle companion came ashore. Silver droplets ran off Peeny, splashing into the sand.

The once-immaculate castle of polished indigo stone towered before the warriors. It stood in the center of a large expanse of open country dotted with tree stumps and tarn pools. The castle's keep tower, now encrusted in rotting moss, rose three miles into the green Myobian sky. Predatory vines clung to the walls and towers like parasites. They undulated in the winds, snapping mandibles and whipping tentacles into the fetid air. As the small company moved toward the ancient structure, reeking vapors emanating from the tarn pools stung their eyes. It would take several hours to reach the castle on foot. They were all thankful for the stego's help. When they found the spot where Monarch Wapiti had said the secret cave opening to the castle's underground tunnels and grotto caverns was, the Ogtavians and Chesh were surprised and dismayed to find that it had been sealed off with large boulders. The warriors crouched and spoke softly to one another. They were down in a ravine not much more than a mile from the castle's walls.

"We will have to attack the castle and hope to surprise whatever lies within," said Arilio.

"I agree. We must," Deedo said. "What do you think, Chesh?"

"I think, and have thought long on this, I think we need to attack as quickly as possible. Surprise is a good advantage. We should strike on two fronts, the air and the ground. Arilio, Cal-i-fax, and some others will swoop down raining crossbow bolts, arrows, and stones down on the enemy. Meanwhile, the second force will strike. Lavek has taught Bangel and Shawnee how to use the catapult. We must gather rocks for it. I think it best if Arilio and his airborne force concentrate on the keep, seeking ingress, while the ground force hammers away at the wall with rocks. Some of us can scale the wall using vine ropes. Whoever gets in must seek and carry off as many of the stego horns as they can. If we can kill this Zud beast, we'll all be better off," Chesh said as he breathed more deeply than he thought he ever could.

Chesh and the others looked in the direction of the castle. The single keep tower stood in the center of a circular wall. The wall was about eighty feet high. The castle was elevated on an earthen mound. The wall had parapets and six smaller defense towers. Murder holes and arrow slits gazed out over the decimated land like evil faces. As they watched, the castle seemed to shimmer and shudder as it became surrounded by a bluish haze. The dark structure began to undulate like cattails in the wind. It was seen through a glass darkly. A deep indigo glass. Then the castle was gone.

"Where did it go?" asked Shawnee.

"Castles do not wander as do creatures. It is there, cloaked in invisibility, Shawnee," Arilio replied, smiling broadly. "We must move now. Now is the time." The scout looked at his princess, Deedo.

"Yes, we will gather Gi stones and catapult rocks. Arilio, keep watch with Bangel. Look to the skies for we have seen no sign of the faceless ones my father spoke of. Either they are so cunning and secretive that we cannot detect them, or they are simply not around. In any case, we shall take no chances. All must keep an eye to the skies. When we have enough stones and rocks, we will travel closer to the castle. Peeny can drag the rocks in the green netting. Fill your pouches. Wear your quivers and carry your bows at all times now. Evil creatures can take many forms and may lurk anywhere. Remember the oily, winged, faceless black things and keep an eye above. Once we move out to the castle area, no talking—hand signals only. When next the castle becomes visible, we attack. Cal-i-fax, Arilio, Alistus, and Gladstone from above. The rest from below." Deedo looked at each member of the small force for a nod of confirmation.

As they moved into a tight circle to speak a last time before heading for the castle, the Ogtavians and Chesh, as well as the two giant insects, all looked up. The blue-hazed night sky cleared, revealing a brilliant canopy of stars. Green, red, and blue stars. A deep drumming became audible. It sounded like Myob's swamp mud heart was beating. A faint, mysterious piping drifted on the wind as it brushed cobwebs from them.

"Look, the moons are lining up!" cried Shawnee, waving his web-fingered hands.

"Yeah, neat," chimed Bangel.

"This must be the day of light then," said Gladstone excitedly.

"Yes, somehow it is. We lost track of time and the days in all of that darkness. The day of light, Chesh, is like your Earthen Christmas, only instead of it being the darkest day of the year, it is the lightest. The daylight lasts forty-nine of your hours. The three moons, Ta, Kalastratus, and Mezla-zan, line up. They shine many colors down upon Myob. It is said that creatures, even ones seldom seen, come out on this day and scurry happily about or soar up, up into the lights of the moons. No creature, not even the relentless saber-toothed yog-bog zligguts, will harm another creature on this day. It is also spoken that in the time since Zud appeared, the evil ilk that he has spawned do go about terrorizing and slaying both predators as well as meek creatures to feast on when the moons become alligned. It is on this day that Zud holds a hideous dark celebration, maybe simply to mock the ones he desires to conquer. His minions dance and cavort about an orange flame in maniacal exultation. This is good for us. And better yet, the castle, look there, it appears again," said Deedo.

Slowly, as if being reborn into the world, the castle reappeared. Its keep tower formed first, growing from its base to rise above the vast forest of webbed dark tunnels and trees with desperate, angry bark faces. As the deep drumming and ominous piping drifted up from the catacombs below the castle, the small band of warriors moved out. The assault began with the catapult and ballista firing from the ground while Cal-i-fax, Arilio, Gladstone, and Allistus, holding the orange and green banner of Og, ascended to a point above the keep tower and circled it, unleashing a hail of tricross arrows, Gi stones, and flaming rocks. A rush of rubbery wings told Arilio to look about them for dark shapes. He fired into several of these. From the spaces where the dark shapes had been came shrill cries of pain.

All at once, the three dragonfly riders were enveloped in a whirling torrent of the bat things. Claws ripped into their flesh. Gladstone put a large Gi stone into his sling. He swung it like a mace and chain.

As he swung it in figure eights above his head, many of the faceless ones were struck. They cried out and spiraled toward the ground, spurting rust-colored blood. Allistus stood whirling much as she had watched Jo-hon do, striking out with kicks and knife hand blows at lightning speed. Arilio fired, making his every bolt count. Cal-i-fax hovered so he could focus his mandibles on the attackers. After grabbing them, the dragonfly king simply wrung the black beasts out like dirty dustcloths, which he tossed into the wind.

"Look, Chesh," Lavek said as he pointed frantically to the keep tower's top. "That's too many. They will never defeat them!"

A tornado of the black bat things poured forth from the tower. In an instant, Cal-i-fax and his riders were consumed by a dark thundercloud of oily, fanged beasts.

"We must keep firing!" Chesh shouted.

As they watched, the mass of mayhem swirled like enraged hornets. Inside the dark mass, Arilio struck out with his stone knife in one hand and three tricross arrows in the other. Gladstone continued to weld the Gi stone mace. Alistus landed every kick and punch with lethal force. Cal-i-fax ripped four and five dark ones apart at one time with deadly swipes. Although the valiant warriors slew many of their attackers, the *snicker-snack snicker-snack* sounds of the razor claws of the faceless ones as they ripped through first protective mushroom hide, then flesh echoed within the dark cloud of death. The coffin-winged beasts began to target Cal-i-fax's wings with a sinister purpose. Once enough holes were cut into the translucent wings, the dragonfly would spiral down like a dying moth.

Something caught the corner of Chesh's eye. From the forest's edge, a long distance away, a blue beam issued forth. In the blink of an eye, Jo-han's sphere appeared next to the swirling mass. She became a whirling dervish of strikes and kicks. Silver claws tore and rented dark rubber flesh. Fanged bat-like heads made of chitin rained down from the cloud, along with wings and legs. So many did she fell that as the ground force paused to watch, they could see swaths being cut into the deadly tornado of blackness. Rust blood hit their faces in droplets. Jo-hon's presence rallied the trio inside the dark cloud of attackers to fight harder, seeing victory rather than defeat. Arilio put a new bolt clip atop the tricross. He fired, machine-gunning into the foes. Cal-i-fax, greatly angered by the damage done to his wings, cleared a path using his clawed mandibles like scythes. Seeing all this, the others gave a loud cheer from below. They fired rocks and flaming ballista arrows with renewed energy.

Soon the dark mass became a tattered group of frantic flies. As they made for the tower's chimney, some of the faceless things shuddered and dropped spurting brown blood. The remnant of the black hoard vanished into the oily smoke. Led by Jo-hon, Cal-i-fax soared in pursuit of the faceless ones. They did not slow down upon reaching the top of the keep. The dragonfly king dove for the circular smoke hole opening in the center following Jo-hon.

Arilio turned to the others. "Wrap a strap around your hand and hold on like you've never done. Get as low as you can!" he shouted.

An instant before the dragonfly hit the opening, his silver-blue chitin armor eyelids snapped into place, protecting hundreds of miniscule eyes within eyes. The oily opening was not large enough for Cal-i-fax to enter. He crashed through, splintering the indigo stone floor around it. Darkness encased the three warriors as they descended through the chimney of stone. Now they raced just ahead of the falling indigo blocks. Dismal cries of death echoed around them. The downward shaft turned into a wide stone tunnel made by the ancient giant glow worms. Straight down it went. Choking smoke and unknowable stench permeated the already fetid air. Gladstone's large frog eyes opened wide when the fanged face and a bat wing of one of the fleeing things entangled him for an instant, dancing about his hunched body like spider lightning.

Down and down they flew as if on the crest of a wave, behind which frothed a torrent of rock, bodies, and debris. Seeing orange light far below, Arilio tightened his body down against his valiant friend. A great rush of air surrounded the dragonfly as it flew out of the shaft. Instantly, Cal-i-fax darted to one side to escape the flames of the fire pit. He hovered then began moving over the menagerie of grotesque beasts in hunting lines, reaping them like corn. Striking out with bear claws of steel, Jo-hon tore into any of the armored insect crustaceans that tried to attack the blue-and-green dragonfly, sending a shower of crab claws, pincers, and tentacles into the air. Alistus whipped Gi stones at the enemy with deadly force. Gladstone did the same. Arilio unleashed his tricross bolts as his eyes darted about the large cavern for any sign of the stego horns. The torrent of indigo wood timbers and stone blocks crashed onto the pit of flames.

As the smoke from the bodies of many bat wings and other ilk burned along with the wood, enlarged clouds of blue-gray smoke burst forth from the keep's chimney. Seeing this smoke spurred Chesh and the others to action. They ceased firing projectiles and charged forward en mass toward the dark fungus-encrusted wall. Shawnee carried the orange-and-green banner of Og proudly. Encountering no resistance, they reached the wall and threw hook vines aloft. Up and up they climbed to the top. Amazingly, no arrows, rocks, or fire oil poured down on them from above. They climbed over and crouched on the battlement walk.

The sight was one of chaos and horror. Some fifty or sixty of the spider-headed things moved about, frantically bumping into one another. Some ran amok, hacking and cleaving the air with swords. Others were on fire. Some had nearly severed arms dangling. Many lay on the ground, legs severed, with gashes streaming brown blood. Thirty or so ballista arrows lay burning amongst the carnage. Catapult rocks littered the ground. As the mindless spider heads ran about in terror, they slashed at one another with their hooklike blades. Smoking caterpillars of great size issued forth from the windows and door of the keep tower, adding to the mayhem. Chesh looked at the enemy with fire in his eyes. Led by Chesh and Deedo, the others charged down some steps into the confused defenders. They formed a Spartan V-shaped wedge. Chesh felled several spider heads with his whip chain and then took up one of their swords. Lavek swung wildly with his broad sword, sending oily limbs and hairy heads flying everywhere. Some of the heads, merely wounded, scurried off on spider legs. Shawnee and Bangel dealt out lethal blows with their quarter staffs. Deedo became a tornado of death as she whipped her weighted sling through the smoke, ripping into the frenzied monsters. She kept an eye on her two young comrades and dropped any of the enemy that posed a threat. Below in Zud's cavern chamber, blue-flamed fire spread out over the immense rubble pile. Creatures trapped by the indigo stone blocks and burning timbers shrieked and writhed. The smell of shellfish permeated the air. Most of the grotesque soldiers ran on insect legs for the openings to tunnels that led above. Among them were locust-headed hominids with cloven hooves, long white worms with sand crab heads and huge pincers, giant leech abominations, and many six-foot-long red-eyed spiders dark and hairy. Carboniferous centipedes fourteen feet long tore away at any that got in their way.

"Get the Zud thing, get the Zud thing!" cried Arilio as he fired. *Phit phit phit.*

Immediately, Jo-hon halted her slaughter and looked at the gigantostraca, Zud. It seemed to glare back at the Hon warrior with mesmerizing large ancient purple-black eyes. It snapped its palm-tree-leaf-sized fore claws. Then it, the thing that was Zud, rose, standing upright on fins that resembled feet in the early stages of development. As Jo-hon floated toward the prehistoric monster, it raised one of its shell-armored arms. From the spike at the arm's end, a purple lightning bolt lashed out at Jo-hon's sphere shield. It did not pierce the sphere.

Just as Jo-hon reached Zud, a swamp-earth-colored centipede the size of a triceratops lurched from a dark opening behind the gyrating beast king. Its pincers were each fifteen feet of jagged, razor-edged chitin. They snapped the smoke-hazed air, seeking the Hon. Then with a swish of cyclone wind and a parting of smoke, Cal-i-fax burst forth and smote the centipede with one invisible swipe of a mantis arm. His blow severed the thing's head, sending putrid brown ichor out with such force that the Zud thing fell and writhed in it seeking purchase. It was then that Jo-hon struck. Her sphere shot to the fallen leader. Gladstone, Allistus, and Arilio watched as the chamber held no more foes to be slain. To them, it looked like Jo-hon had turned into a series of small blue pinwheels. These flaming pinwheels moved about the grimy-green crustacean. Zud began to writhe and strike out blindly with claws and lightning bolts. The sounds of horses' hooves stomping on a thousand clamshells rang out and echoed about the cavern walls as the thick armor protecting the evil beast began to crack. Brown-yellow liquid seeped from the cracks as they widened. The purple platter-sized eyes burst. One final shudder accompanied by a death rattle from some Permian world of eons ago and the Zud invader crumpled into a million jigsaw pieces. The sacred stego horns lay on shelves in a small recess carved into the cave wall near Zud's throne. There were a dozen in all. They had the shape of the horns of bulls, the differences being that these horns, which varied in size, were colored glowing indigo, with three tan stripes adorning each. The tips of each horn had been removed to allow air to pass through. Arilio gathered them up and put them in a mushroom-hide sack.

Above the pink-skinned obscenities with tentacles around their middles began streaming out of the openings of the smaller wall towers. Smoke, putrid and oily, poured from the doors and windows of these towers. Other hideous soldiers of Zud streamed out with them. From the chimney holes in the towers flew the faceless winged things. There where, perhaps, a hundred or more of them. Most, sensing their gray-green Permian leader that killed with lightning was dead, flew out into the night.

"Look out above!" shouted Chesh.

Lavek turned his eyes upward just in time to hack one of the bat things in half. The battle raged on fiercely until, from above, illuminated by the fantastic light of the moons, Cal-i-fax appeared. Jo-hon floated nearby in her blue sphere. Cal-i-fax, with his riders aboard, went immediately to where Deedo was. Shawnee and Bangel had each been wounded, and the valiant princess was warding off foes with a sword in each hand. Alistus sprang from the dragonfly's back and tore into the enemy with the hook vine claws she now wore on her hands and feet. *Phit phit phit phit,* the deadly tricross cried out, sending a wave of the dark creatures to the ground. Jo-hon circled above Deedo, the others lashed out and cleared a swath around them. She then whisked over to the large wooden castle doors. The powerful Hon threw off the lock log and pushed the gates wide open. The menagerie of writhing beasts wielding hook swords, bloodied claw arms, and swirling barrel tentacles slowed their pace. For an instant, they seemed to be taking stock of the gore around them. Then the defenders of the castle, which was not truly theirs, bolted for the opened gates. A mass of brown, black, pink, and swamp-slime-green creatures streamed forth.

"Let them go! Let them go!" Deedo cried out over the turmoil.

The brave company stood their ground, lashing out with a sword or claw whenever they or one of their comrades was threatened by a cephlopodian appendage or a clumsy deserter. In minutes, the horde was gone, and Chesh, Cal-i-fax, and the others stood bathed in a brilliant blue light. The light radiated from the castle tower. The fungal growths that had encased the structure for centuries crumbled from the castle as it was reborn. Being very fatigued, they ambled off to where Peeny had been left. Shawnee led the way with the tattered banner held high above his bandaged head. The stego beetle was safe and rose from slumber to meet her loyal friend. Chesh snuggled her neck area tiredly and held out a single peanut to her. The beetle's eyes smiled at him as she took the peanut into her mouth, shell and all. She lay awake while they slept. All that is except Jo-hon, who had vanished.

They were awakened by the green rays of Mesos. As Chesh and the others cleared the sleep from their eyes, they beheld a mysterious transformation. Although the tree stumps around them had not sprung up into trees again, they had turned to a almost-luminescent deep-indigo color. Chesh wondered if the phenomenon of the three moons lining up had somehow burned the dismal fungi and mold from them. He was astounded as he looked at the castle. It stood immaculate, indigo, shimmering forth the light of its bygone regal days. The mote sparkled with clear green water. Purple-winged butterflies sailed the wind in whirling groups. Magnificent red or blue dragonflies darted about, landing on brilliantly colored mushrooms and lily pads that had sprung up overnight. All were amazed and made Ogtavian "Woo" and "Yowee" sounds as they looked about.

"This means we'll not have to go back the way we came or have to cross that river of death. We should seek a path east now," Arilio said proudly. "We go to the wooden fort of the lizard pirates. The fort they call Fort Apache. We must make haste for all we know, our fellow Ogtavians may be taken away today."

"We will eat as we travel. Is Cal-i-fax able to travel?" said Deedo, looking at the scout.

"One way to discover. Come on, Cally. Come on, old friend." Arilio pulled slightly on the dragonfly's harness. At this, the some-what-battered king of the dragonflies shot up like a rearing horse, waving his mantis mandibles into the air. "He's fine," said Arilio, looking to his princess.

They disassembled and packed the catapult and ballista onto Peeny, who looked unpleased about having the contraptions strapped to her shell. As they moved off to the east, casting glances back at the castle, Chesh began to whistle "Yankee Doodle Dandy," and the oth-ers chimed in with obtuse froggish whistling sounds. Brilliant-orange dandelions the size of palm trees shot up from the indigo haze that drifted across the ground.

As the merry company ambled along, Peeny at a brisk stride with Cal-i-fax hovering just above, Arilio recited an old Ogtavian poem about dragonflies. "Dragonflies, blue armored, ancient. There is something about dragonflies. Something quite valiant."

The company munched on choco pods, dried bacon bark, and blue corn as they cruised along, watching the renewing swamp-woods around them burst forth with new life. Bright powder-blue daisies ten feet tall appeared before their eyes. At times they were enveloped in weeds and plants that grew under them. Horsetails grew to be a mile high in a matter of minutes. Green wasps the size of hands darted past the heads of the beetle riders. Armadillo-sized beetles mainly resembling giant stag beetles or June bugs scurried busily about. Some were yellow with blue stripes like Peeny's. Others were purple and orange, the same bright orange as the dandelions. Bumblebees, six feet in length, hovered as they gathered pollen from a panorama of emerging prehistoric flowers. The air hummed with the sounds made by their wings. Swallowtail butterflies cavorted in gentle swirls among the returning plants. Giant sequoia cattails emerged from the rich ground, pushing forth indigo shoots. The metamorphosis of the indigo forest was an amazing sight.

As the purple light of Stesos faded, the stego beetle pulled up at a Permian lake. It stretched farther than the eye could see. The clear green water displayed a sandy shallow bottom. Swallowtailed, winged fish sailed above the surface, making crescent curves as they snatched insects, leaving rainbow wakes. Chesh felt as if he had stepped into the Pennsylvanian period on Earth 325 million years ago, when reptiles evolved and insects grew to giant sizes. When coal swamps formed and the earth was covered with shallow seas. Wasps the size of pterodactyls soared above the surface of the green mirror lake, dipping for the silver-winged flying fish. Pig-sized bumblebees gathered pollen from indigo flowers that resembled upside-down bells. Sand-tan lettuce mushrooms sprang up like small walls.

The weary company set about camp chores as the purple rays of Stesos bathed everything in its somber rays. After a generous meal of mushroom steaks, blue corn, and cattail biscuits, Deedo spread the parchment map out on the ground near the flickering blue flames of the cooking fire.

"This is Wotan Lake. It is green because yellow water from the Erie Sea flows into it and mixes with the blue water from the Indigo River. This then is why the River Green, which we seek, has crystal clear green water. The River Green flows southward. My father said that the river has some rapids and something he called the curllys. He also said that we should build rafts or kif ships to travel down the river. I think we should build a raft for the catapult and ballista as well as for supplies. I do not know if Peeny will carry us on the water." Deedo looked at the gently resting beetle. Peeny munched on a coco pod near the lake's edge.

"I agree. I think we should go ahead with that plan, and if Peeny does not carry us, we can build the raft large enough to carry her," said Chesh.

"We could build a kif ship using mushroom hide and some of the new wood that is growing around us. We can make it large enough to carry our stego friend and tow a raft as well. Cal-i-fax and Arilio can scout above as before," finished Lavek, looking to Arilio.

"Yes, he has healed from his wounds almost overnight as he has done in the past when injured," stated Arilio, looking intently at the map.

"The moonfly feast will soon begin in this area. Many red ants will be about gathering the flies for their young. They will eat also," said Jo-hon, peeking over the edge of an indigo flower nearby.

Everyone in the small group looked at the Hon in astonishment. She had never really said much before. *Could it be that seeing the Ogtavians fighting as spirited warriors prompted her to speak?* thought Chesh.

"The red ants? My father did not speak of them. This area is largely unexplored by my people, so we know little about it," said Deedo, looking directly into the deep, glowing pools of indigo that were Jo-hon's eyes.

"The red ants are the size of the giant slothos. Few opponents can best them as their saw-toothed mouths radiate with fiery phosphorous, causing their bites to be fatal. They can chew through solid rock," Jo-hon explained. A six-inch night wasp hovered near her head. She speared it with one of her silver claws and munched on it as one would munch on a candy bar.

A hushed murmur went around the circle as the Ogtavians contemplated what they had heard. Chesh had been pondering the words "Slowly, slowly, slowly, said the slothos" for some time now. He was very interested in this possible telepathic link between himself and his beetle friend. *Could she be trying to tell me that it is best to move slowly here on Myob to survive? That's my best guess. Seems logical,* he thought. Chesh had thought about the beetles telepathy ever since they had left the castle via the Zudian way, a log-paved road which reminded Chesh of the Apian Way of ancient Rome.

Chesh had, as he rode upon Peeny, thought deeply about her. She was his main interest and driving force in life now. She was his whole life, and she made his life whole. Caring for the stego released a warm chemical, like when he ate chocolate or coco pods. This flowing green warmth warmed his chi and made his whole body and brain feel like a windy summer day. He decided that he would make more of a conscious effort to enter her mind, so to speak, telepathically. He had noticed that ever since the mysterious cave experience, he somehow shared with Peeny the pictures he could see in his mind, which had become much more clear and pronounced, more vivid.

When he heard the words "Slowly, slowly, slowly, said the slothos," he now had visions of a gentle giant sloth, blue like the one he had helped. The slothos munched on coco pods, foraging gently among the tall leafy plants while soft winds swayed the trees, which were bathed in the purple light of Stesos.

"Are you with us, Chesh?" Deedo said, looking at the youth.

"Ah, well, I am now. I was thinking about Peeny. Sorry." Chesh looked at the princess apologetically.

"What plan do you think we should follow? Do you like Lavek's idea of making a raft to carry the ballista and catapult? Some of us could ride on the raft and use the weapons to repel boarders and fend off any hostile creatures. Does that sound good, Chesh?" The princess paused.

"As the current flows south, I see the logic of a raft," Chesh replied.

"Yes, a raft, and Bengal and I can gather rocks for the catapult around here. We could also make arrows for the ballista and our bows while we travel. We will need to cut arrow shafts too. Oh, that is, Bengal can help if she wants to," interjected Shawnee, shivering with froggish excitement.

For a few seconds, all the Ogtavian eyes drifted to the valiant Jo-hon as if seeking approval. The Hon took a large bite from a coco pod, making a loud crunching noise. She spoke not.

"We all agree on this plan then?" asked Deedo. The Ogtavians and Chesh nodded up and down to say yes. "We shall rest now. It may not be safe to forage for supplies and materials in the dark. We begin at first light. Please rest," instructed the princess of Og.

The small company bedded down on dried grasses not far from the blue-green flickering fire. They awoke to some of the most marvelous breakfast food aromas they had ever smelled. Maple syrup, bacon bark, cocoa, oranges, and wheat cakes wafted out over the hazy warriors. Opening his eyes in astonishment, the youth from Earth saw an amazing sight. Stacked neatly near the lakeshore were piles of freshly hewn logs. They were from blue-leafed maples. Nearby was a miniature pyramid of rocks. A large stock of ballista shafts sat on the sand as well as a quantity of kruis vine. Jo-hon, who never seemed to sleep, sat near the fire, moving the bacon bark about with a silver claw. Behind her Mesos shot large green bolts into the fading darkness.

Sleepily the froggish people rose and went for morning swims. Chesh joined them. Peeny and Cal-i-fax watched alertly from shore. Red dragonflies and blue dragonflies darted above the lake's surface, snapping up purple-winged butterfly fish. The small company spoke quietly of their plans as they ate the wonderful food. They all thanked Jo-hon earnestly.

Upon rising, which was done in unison, Arilio sood up,raised his tricross high and shouted, "On to Fort Apache!"

It was not long before the spirited rescuers had constructed a large raft and departed. Chesh, Deedo, and Gladstone rode aboard Peeny, who had shown no reluctance about heading out onto Wotan Lake. On board the raft were Lavek, Shawnee, and Bengal. Arilio scouted above on his dragonfly steed. Alistus joined them at her request. Jo-hon was around someplace not visible as usual. Condor dragonflies hovered curiously nearby. Some darted up to fly around the giant dragonfly and his riders.

Chesh recalled a poem aloud, "I must go down to the seas again, for the call of the running tide / is a clear call and a wild call that may not be denied."

The Ogtavians turned their greenish faces toward the sandy-haired youth, soft indigo eyes aglow.

"Oh, sorry," said Chesh. "I was just thinking out loud. That's a poem from long-ago Earth."

"Will you teach us a new song, Chesh?" Bengal shouted from the raft.

"Sure. Try this one: 'Valiant traveler sailin' on bended knee, looks out over wavy green sea. He sits sharpening his harpoon. He'll have it ready long before noon. Then on and on for the search continues, the endless quest for the mighty white whale.'" Chesh took his wooden flute from his belt and began to play a lively sailor's tune. The Ogtavians carried the song on, guided by the flute's notes. Their song echoed out over the crisp green water as the loyal beetle carried them onward.

"Wotan Lake is seventy miles across one way and one-hundred miles across the other. It is an inland sea," said the mysterious Jo-hon, appearing from nowhere in her blue bubble shield. She hovered like an enlarged faerie just in front and above Peeny, who paid her no mind whatsoever as she paddled.

"In which direction does the mouth of the River Green lie?" Deedo said, looking at the Hon.

"Follow Mezla-zan," Jo-hon answered.

Deedo pointed to a green star shining in the green sky. It was the moon Mezla-zan. It appeared in the northeast. Chesh and Deedo looked at each other with miffed expressions. They had each realized that the stego beetle was headed directly for the green moon.

I wonder, thought Chesh, *I wonder if Peeny somehow knew we needed to head this way, or if she simply chose this course randomly.* Chesh looked ahead to the vast Permian sea. Jo-hon floated upward and vanished. Chesh glanced behind them. Bengal and Shawnee were running about the raft, practice fighting each other with their staffs. Lavek was busy putting points and leaf feathers on some of the bolts for the ballista.

Far in the distance, the Earther saw the shoreline, a melting band of brilliant colors. He turned to look forward across the wind-swept green sea. The sea changed, and as the first purple rays of Stesos began to melt the skies into azure, the wind rose. The water became choppy. Strange sea dwellers began to show themselves. Thousands of semitranslucent corkscrew eels burst forth to feed on schools of small orange winged minnows. Things that looked like gigantic flounders with massive lobster claws and bloated insect legs lurched from the water, devouring anything in their path with three parallel sets of shark teeth. Once in a while, long maroon spikes of great sharpness broke the surface, spearing prey and vanishing. Chesh tried to see what denizen lay below the spikes. However, he was only able to make out large dark shadows, the size, perhaps, of whale sharks. These journeyers on a lake similar to one from the Pennsylvanian Period of Earth 325 million years ago when insects and reptiles evolved, coal swamps formed, and shallow seas began to withdraw. These insect riders had no idea of the dangers they would soon face.

Cal-i-fax swooped down out of the afternoon sky. "Watch out ahead. There are tens of thousands of those spikes. I can't make out what creatures lie beneath them, but their shadows look big," shouted Arilio from atop the hovering armored green-and-blue dragonfly.

"We have seen some. We will just have to avoid them," answered Deedo.

"Maybe we should go around them. Can we circle around them, Arilio?" Chesh asked.

"We could," Arilio answered. "It would be a big circle, though. The spikes cover a good ten of your miles each way," clarified the scout.

"Yes, and the green moon that is our guide lies directly in front of us," Deedo interjected.

Purple curlicue eels popped up around Peeny, and the raft as they inhaled hundreds of the tiny winged orange minnows. Odd sounds came to Chesh. Sounds of the water churning as if from the paddle wheels of many hundreds of Mississippi paddle wheel river-boats. He soon saw the cause. Ahead a mile or so were the spikes. They stretched as far as the eye could see across the wavy green expanse. As they got closer, the youth watched as the maroon spikes spun around or stabbed into the air like a thousand bloodied medie-val swords, impaling whatever was in the sea or air around them. At times, a saw-toothed octopus's beak-mouth at the end of a monstrous tentacle came from the water to rend or rip at the wriggling prey.

Now as they closed in, Chesh became very concerned about his gentle friend Peeny. Although he tried, he could detect no mental message or image of any kind from her. As they reached the brink of this sea of spikes, Chesh and the others could see it more clearly. Thousands and thousands of maroon spikes, some poking up a few feet, others shooting up thirty or forty feet above the green water. At times, the spikes would rotate like the spokes of a wheel displaying a variety of creatures, mainly some sort of aquatic-insect combination organisms. Many writhed and convulsed in pain or vainly tried to free themselves from their impalement.

Arilio, who hovered nearby, accompanied by Alistus, pointed toward one of the whale-sized shadows. In its spindle spikes, Chesh could plainly see one of the grotesque pink barrel things they had tangled with back at the Indigo Castle. It was dead. On another spindle spike was one of the black faceless atrocities. Its rubbery body and wings trembled. The spindle whale rotated, sending both creatures below.

They were a hundred yards from the spindle whales. Chesh began to panic. He tapped on Peeny's shell, saying, "Come on, Peeny, let's turn that way. Come on, Peeny, let's go around. Let's go that way," he pointed eastward. The myst stego continued forward. Chesh began to pound on the beetle's shell. He slid up right behind her head. He bent near it. "Peeny, come on, for me, turn. We can't go through those things! Come on, Peeny, please. Come on, Peeny, please turn!" Chesh took some of the precious peanuts out of his pocket and made shell-crunching noises with them.

The Ogtavians looked on with wide-eyed froggish anticipation. Fifty yards, twenty-five yards, and still the giant beetle did not waver in her course. Chesh looked back at Deedo; fright was in her eyes. In that instant, the youth missed the slight glint of glowing green that appeared in the extreme center of the pupils of the large maroon platters that were Peeny's eyes. When Chesh turned around, an amazing sight took him completely by surprise. Silhouetted against the purple twilight, the spikes moved, parting like the Red Sea. A path of green water opened up before the beetle and her riders. A river of open water that was banked on both sides by towering maroon spikes. In retrospect, Chesh wondered if he should have used one of the stego horns. Then he pictured the spindle whales rotating in crazed frenzies and disregarded the afterthought. Peeny, the beetle, paddled forward at a relaxed pace. The Ogtavians stared out at the spiky expanse, displaying looks of astonishment. Some of them may have been puzzling the why of this event. Chesh surely was. The Earther had been deeply mystified by the parting of the spindle whales. He, at the time of the event, had tried to send a strong telepathic message to Peeny. It was a mental image of the beetle turning eastward and paddling off. If the stego had received the message, it had no effect on her actions.

Chesh recalled receiving no telepathy from his beetle friend at the time of the occurrence. He would continue his quest for a mental link with Peeny. The first time he recalled hearing the "Slowly" message was just before they were attacked by a giant centipede. Then again prior to their capture by the lizard soldiers. He recalled hearing it again when Peeny refused to go close to the opening that led to the centilions' den. He had also heard the message, like a soft rustling wind, just before they reached the Indigo Castle. Each time Chesh had heard the words, it seemed as if a warm, soothing gush of green healing, comforting liquid radiated forth from the area just behind his belly button, the area where Chesh's chi was located. The feeling—which the youth could only describe to himself as one of the most complete humility, safety, and contentment he had ever felt—lasted for a long while after the mental message faded away, flowing through his systems like lazy blue waves smoothing white beach sands.

As Chesh looked out to the purple horizon, he sent a mental message: "Peeny, thank you." He kept it simple. He also envisioned Peeny and him back when they just met at their first campsite. He sat, laying against the stump near the campfire, tasting cattail roots and feeding them to his newfound friend, along with an occasional peanut or two. Millions of crickets chirped songs of ancient Myobian eras. Then, wham! As if struck in the forehead by a six-inch June bug, a vision of Chesh reaching into his mushroom-hide pouch for one of the few remaining peanuts and handing it up to Peeny as she paddled came clearly to his mind's eye. His whole body shook like a wet dog. He looked at the back of Peeny's head. Nothing out of the ordinary. Chesh took a peanut from the pouch and handed it up and around to the stego. She turned her head slowly, and as she cast a glamour at the youth with affectionate maroon saucer eyes, she took the peanut slowly with a smile.

The small company traveled throughout the night. The light of the three moons chasing each other like mad hornets aided their sight as they looked out over the sea of maroon spikes. Occasionally, splashing could be heard as a spindle whale rotated. The cries of unfortunate creatures that had been speared by spikes reverberated off the water, voicing their dismay. It was a long, tiresome night for the Ogtavians and Chesh. Cal-i-fax slept peacefully on the raft built to carry him. When the green rays of Mesos broke over the horizon, they paddled out of the spiked maroon predators. The forlorn cries of lake creatures that chose to tread the same path could be heard behind as the spindle whales closed in on them. The heat could turn a human into a mean meat carrot. Chesh knew this well, having lived on worlds that got very hot. That was why the cooler breezes alerted him to a seasonal change.

"Deedo, how long do you think we were under the canopy of the Indigo Forest? It seems much cooler to me."

"One looses track of time passing when in dim darkness. We, I think, were under the trees for perhaps two or three weeks. Our Myobian autumn approaches. A time of crickets chirping orange-tan songs. Grasshoppers, dragonflies, and bees are very active at this time. The days grow shorter. The winds grow stronger. Gray-green dragon clouds march across the skies."

As Peeny paddled on, the Ogtavians watched as Cal-i-fax, with Arilio on board, lifted gently up from the raft in tow to resume their scouting.

"I wonder why Arilio is so different from the others, why he and Cal-i-fax lived outside of Og," querried Chesh.

"Arilio is different. Hardened like sapphire by past occurrences. His family was killed by a giant horseshoe crab-beetle that had legs fifty quaguets long and was the size of four of your elephants. Cal-i-fax was flying by and seeing the slaughter swooped down and slew the horseshoe monster. The scout and his loyal dragonfly king have lived in a cave ever since. Millions of honeybees live near the cave. Arilio plants lavender plants to provide the bees with pollen. He then harvests honey to give to others. The honey is soothing and splendid. Cal-i-fax relishes the lavender honey as your Peeny loves peanuts," Deedo shared.

"Ahhh-ha," said Chesh. "Thanks."

A purple hue invaded the small windswept waves of Wotan Lake as Stesos rose from the west and Mesos was swallowed by the eastern horizon. They glided slowly along through the green sea.

"I suppose we are safe now. Your myst stego would stop if there were danger ahead," said Deedo, glancing toward the beetle's head.

None were in a position to perceive the brief glimmer of pinpoint glowing green that appeared in each of Peeny's normally placid maroon platter eyes. A flash of green and blue appeared above. It was the dragonfly and his rider returning from scouting ahead.

"The way looks clear ahead. We saw many of the silver flying fish. Several wasps the size of Quetzalcawatis flew past us. This may be a sign that we are nearing the northern shore." The massive dragonfly knight lighted gently down upon the raft and began to chew on some cattail reeds.

Chesh recalled a song from his family's seafaring past aloud, "I must go down to the seas again, for the call of the running tide / is a clear call and a wild call that may not be denied."

The Ogtavians faces glowed green as they all turned in his direction, their inquisitive soft indigo eyes aglow. "Will you teach us a new song, Chesh?" asked Bengal.

"Sure, try this one. 'Weary traveler sailing on bended knee, looks out over the shifting sea. Who knows, who knows where he'll be when the tide turns.'" Their song echoed out over the windswept green sea serpent waves.

"We believe life is about giving more so than taking," Deedo said as Peeny glided gently through the emerald waters. "I believe this way or concept is ancient or more than ancient—elemental. Perhaps your myst stego friend somehow, within her mental makeup, has this way of being. Perhaps it is a survival instinct or something more, perhaps a balance between giving and taking links her with the universe itself or the matter or force that shapes the cosmos. Maybe it simply helps Peeny and others like her, if, in fact, their are others like her, to survive or more. What if in return for maintaining a careful balance, they are somehow endowed with exceptional abilities, or in Earth terms, *magical powers*. I am unsure. I feel as you do, Chesh. Your beetle friend is very special."

"That is an interesting way of exploring what Peeny is, you know, what makes her up. I am starting to agree with you, though. Relative to the spindle whales parting, it may well have been nothing to do with Peeny. As you said, a dragonfly of Cal-i-fax's size is a very rare sight. The whales may have, out of fear of an unknown thing, parted in order to allow the things traveling below him to pass, sensing that the two entities were connected as they traveled the same course. I have not, as yet, scratched the surface of what Peeny is and how she is," Chesh said as he maintained a forward lookout into the darkness of night that had green mist ghosts haunting its winds.

"I agree." Deedo broke off to look in the direction of the raft behind. A loud splash and a yell rang out. Shawnee and Bengal, who had tired of fencing with wooden swords and of honing their skills with the quarter staffs, had fastened hooks and vine line to their staffs and had been fishing. Lavek, who had been working to make a tricross bow similar to Arilio's, dropped it and ran to help the youth. Shawnee who was being dragged rapidly through the water, let go of the fishing staff. As he did so, a denizen surfaced within ten feet of him. It was dark purple and rounded like a turtle shell. Atop in the center, a sickly-yellow light pulsated out into the darkness like some monstrous squid tentacle. It may have been the thing's eye. Regardless, the sea monster opened a large saber-toothed mouth that was half of its body size and lined with circles of teeth like the mouth of a lamprey eel. It made a sound, like a foghorn, like a tyrannosaurus. It steamed toward Shawnee, giving off the stench of a giant squid rotting in the sun.

Before Deedo could react, the dragonfly king streaked down to within a few feet of the purple thing. *Phit phit phit*, Arilio fired, piercing the glowing eye. Lavek jumped feet first into the water, welding his sword to finish the thing.

As they gazed up at the blue-azure and orange rings of Myob with the ever-present emerald Mezla-zan and the planet Regalian, a polished blue stone, Deedo talked of time. "It is an ancient way of my people, a way to peace and tranquility that Gi masters practice at all times. Time shifting is akin to the mental state one may achieve through practice and meditation. It is being in the here and now, existing within present time. It is when one has become so good at the self-control of their own Qui that they reach a pure state. One can make the lake within themselves rough and choppy or calm and smooth. Similar to the *Mizu-Gami* (water goddess) of Isshin-ryu Karate. I guess that is how I would explain time shifting. It is how

I feel when the wind is gliding me along a silvery river on my zlo-tos board. One way to think about it is that animals, creatures, and insects exist in present time using their highly specialized senses for survival. Think of it like putting yourself on cricket time or sloth time then moving as fast as the strike of a mantis, if you wish. Do you grasp the concept, Chesh?" Deedo settled back into a lying-down posture.

"Yes, I think so. I've given this idea of time standing still a lot of thought in the past, especially in connection with honing my martial arts skills. Thank you, Deedo, for explaining it to me." Chesh lay down to sleep as well.

The Myobian darkness was their blanket. Gladstone watched the shallow sea surface for any threatening creatures as Peeny paused to float and sleep. Chesh was awakened by Deedo, who was the third watcher. Peeny was already underway. The raft crew scampered about like startled rabbits. Cal-i-fax had slept floating on the water not far from Peeny and was now carrying his riders aloft to their aerial crow's nest. The green rays of Mesos burst forth, displaying a swirling white-capped sea. Winds whipped at their ears and cheeks. Orange-brown cumulus clouds of Jupiterian proportions moved quickly above. The air smelled of conifers.

"Chesh look, look ahead," Deedo said.

Chesh rubbed the sleep from his eyes and beheld in the distance a grayish wall. The wall was not the land of the northeastern shore; it was dense fog. "Looks like we'll be fogged in for a bit. We'd best signal Arilio. His steed needs to be tethered to us or swim near us. We do not want to lose each other." He looked at the princess, yawning.

The stego beetle gave no indication of veering from her course. By early afternoon, the intrepid company had reached the fog. It towered before them a gray-black wall, extending up and on the sides as far as they could see. The mud-colored sky suddenly became illu-minated by jagged, dancing purple spiderweb lightning. The waves glistened as they became more choppy, resembling a million monks with windswept hoods of foam. The giant beetle did not hesitate; she pulled the raft along with much force.

"Arilio, shouldn't you tie Cal-i-fax to us somehow?" Chesh yelled up to the dragonfly rider, who was hovering fifteen feet above the turbulent surface.

"He could be more hurt by a tether than by being free, I fear, Chesh. If the forces of the storm batter us about when he's fastened, he could be hurt. I'll not have it, lad. I doubt he would either. Thanks, though, for thinking of Cal-i-fax. Perhaps we will swim nearby with tucked wings. Insects can sense much that we cannot and, I think, will remain close even within the fog." Arilio smiled down at his human friend as if to say I appreciate the compassion toward my friend.

Just then, as a purple flash lit the faces of the warriors. Chesh looked back to the raft in time to see Shawnee's head become enveloped by a blob of mud flop. He appeared to be wearing a tan beeny type hat of thick brown goo. The teen's eyes looked like blue ping-pong balls with yellow dots as they bulged from the surprise of the concussion. In an instant, they were ferried into the gray haze. Chesh reeled around to the front as his vision suddenly became so clouded that he could see nothing. He drew a hand to his face. It came into view six inches from his nose. Chesh recalled in a red flash the words of Arilio: "He could be torn apart." He would not let this happen to Peeny. "Lavek!" he yelled at the top of his lungs. "You must come aboard Peeny. Please bring the others. We cannot risk losing you!"

In a moment or so, he heard Lavek's voice at close proximity, along with excited screeches and yells from the two young Ogtavians. "We'll tie ourselves on," cried Lavek. "Quickly now, you two. Become secured. We're here, Chesh. I've lashed the catapult and ballista down well. We'll see how they hold."

The skilled swordsman let out a long sigh of relief. The winds whipped the faces of the members of the small intrepid company as they hunkered down. Peeny paddled onward as purple lightning flashed, causing deep, reverberating thunder. A million mudpies could be heard splashing into the waves. Gladstone made the mistake of looking up and caught one in the forehead. He quickly put his head down and covered it with his arms.

"Still with ya, Chesh," Arilio would call out periodically.

The storm went on the rest of the night and into the next day, although it was hard to tell day from night from beneath this canopy of gray haze. On occasion, Chesh popped his head up, risking a mudpie surprise to look about. Most often he saw just gray. Once, one of those beacon creature's purple pulsing beams reached out like a gigantic ray arm, casting an eerie pale-yellow light upon them. On another peek, he saw an orange orb float above them, hover for an instant, then shoot off. This orange light suddenly made him remember and think, *Where the heck is Jo-hon in all this? What the heck happened to our friend?* Then he thought, She'll come out okay, land on her feet. She always does. Besides this is her land, her territory. *She's probably already reached the northern shore of the lake, has a camp ready, and is frying bacon bark to boot!* Chesh relaxed, pressing his cheek against the warm shell of his beetle companion. He drifted off to the sounds of the wind and the waves. Shouts awakened him.

"It's there, just ahead, seventy strides or so," Arilio cried out. Chesh raised his head. His back felt heavy. He felt it. Oozy mud, as he thought. It felt wet and a bit warm. His back did not ache or hurt. *Amazing that I slept through a mud glob hit! Holy cow, I must really have been tired.* He listened. A whooshing noise came from somewhere in front of his aquatic steed. A sound like an immense waterfall or massive waves breaking on a beach, yet different somehow. Added to the water sounds were strange whistling noises the youth could not identify. The waves had calmed. Ghost flashes of purple illuminated the gray cotton. He heard distant thunder and no mud blobs fell, which was fine with the entire company, all of whom had been pelted in some way by the glop. Alarm juice rushed through his nerves, jolting him more awake.

"Chesh, can you get the beetle to turn?" asked Deedo from the gloom behind him.

He thought for a second then replied, "I don't know, Deedo. She's been right on the mark so far. I say we stick with her. You told me that these myst stego beetles are more ancient than you know. My logic tells me that her long-honed survival instincts may help us most."

"I do not know, Chesh. I do not like those sounds. They strike fear into my bones for some unknown reason," returned the princess.

"Besides, Deedo, I don't think I could get her to change her course. She's either stubborn or she knows something we don't know."

"I agree," said Lavek, "with you both. I fear the sounds, yet I trust the stego."

"We say go with Peeny," Arilio said, floating within ten or so feet of the main group. The others chimed in affirmatives from their various perches. "I think, though, that we should strap ourselves down like there's no tomorrow, because there might not be."

"Yes, and I agree. Lavek, please cut lengths of kia vine," Deedo requested. "If there was danger ahead, your stego would surely not go forth," concluded Deedo with a glance toward Peeny's head. The myst beetle returned her look, a slight green glow flashing from the pinpoint pupils in the center of the normally placid maroon platter eyes.

Lavek, who had lashed himself down at the very backmost portion of Peeny's shell via the web netting that wrapped around the stego and fastened gently in three places under her, suddenly spoke out, "Who's there?"

"It is I, Chesh. Just checking to make sure everyone is secured. You're the last. Have a safe ride wherever we are bound. I'm going to tie in up front," Chesh replied.

The winds rose, becoming screaming sirens in the youth's ears. Closer now, the roaring became deafening. Spray hit Chesh's face and arms. It felt warm. The world went topsy-turvy. Chesh detected Peeny being lifted and spun as if they had entered a giant spinning tunnel of water. At the same instant, the fog vanished, allowing the giant insects and their riders to see what lay before them. Their beetle craft hung suspended on the crest of a long, massive wave tube. It went as far as could be seen, a green tunnel of swirling water. It seemed from the motion and views that they were in a corkscrew or curlicue of water, the waves of which all flowed in the same direction. As Chesh looked into the clear green water, he began to make out obtuse shadowy forms, some quite large, toothy, and frightening. Occasionally, needle teeth protruded from the froth, reminding Chesh of deep-ocean denizens. Some possessed antennas with glowing eyes. Many of the whirling things' jagged giant lobster claws often broke the tube wave's surface, snapping out blindly. The warriors fended any threatening appendages off with quarter staffs. The faithful beetle used her powerful legs to remain steady in the rushing torrent. Looking to his right and back, Chesh was happy to see Cal-i-fax keeping pace with them. The raft, along with the stego horns, however, was gone.

Chesh unstrapped himself and sat upright. One glance behind had told him a grim tale. The Ogtavians aboard were still tethered down. It was their faces that told the tale. The froggish people's eyes bulged with terror. Their expressions were those of frightened animals. Their normally placid faces were pulled back, like stretched rubber or bread dough that is stressed by many gravity forces pulling the skin back toward the rear of the skulls that lay beneath. And rightly so, for as Chesh's eyes went through their dark adaptation to the new surroundings, he plainly saw the horrors that lurked within the water walls.

Hundreds of Myobian creatures flowed by at different speeds, apparently unable to handle the current and waves as well as Peeny. At times, they appeared as dark nebulous forms. When closer to the surface, they became more identifiable. One that came often into Chesh's view, and perhaps the most common, looked like an ankylosaurus with fish fins and the head of an elephant stag beetle. It had long insectoid legs and a single glowing, sickly, miasmic amber eye that was at its front, dangling from a tenticle-like appendage. Its coloration was slime gray. Another thing, more horrifying in its aspect, was a creature the Ogtavians identified as a mist jelly. Ranging in size from one-inch deadly box jellies to large whales, they undulated, waving six deadly squid tentacles. Clear purple eels with rooster heads and long corkscrew bodies, which could pass through a creature-like gamma rays, leaving a hole the size of a cantalope, wriggled dangerously close to the warriors and their insect companions.

Many of the life-forms that flowed within the proximity of the voyagers were dead. The smells within the water tunnel were of putrid shellfish and disregarded kennel offal. Millions of hawk-sized mosquitos, mostly dead, created gray swirls as they were washed along. There were flounder fish with insect legs, mandibles, and the teeth of lamprey eels. The ultraviolet purple eyes of giant leeches peered menacingly at Peeny and the others. Zillions of orange-winged minnows whirled in mini tornadoes throughout the crystline waters. Many of the obtuse creatures in the menagerie snapped at them as they were swirled along.

Somehow, Cal-i-fax had managed to stay in sight of them. Chesh could see when they were close that Arilio sat proudly upon his winged steed, showing no fear.

"Arm yourselves," Deedo shouted from the tumult.

The Ogtavians' heads and bodies shook, awakening them to their situation. Lavek wielded his sword. Gladstone chose his sling with a heavy stone as an elongated mace and chain weapon. Deedo did likewise. Shawnee and Bangal wielded their staffs. Chesh chose a staff as well as it allowed him to push vicious denizens away as well as strike. He could keep creatures away from Peeny's head also, which was foremost to him. As they were moved along with great force, the youth, holding the staff centrally and batting right and left with it like some mad kayaker, was able to take out any creatures that threatened the occupied beetle's head. He soon noticed that only dead or helpless creatures came within close proximity of the stego's head, or body for that matter. The live ones, if forced close to Peeny, struggled to get away. *Curious*, thought Chesh.

Splat! And the youth saw only a wall of darkness. *Had it become night so quickly?* he thought for an instant. A grimy, cold, slimy feeling suddenly alerted Chesh to the fact that something covered his face. In a flash, by hands much quicker than his, the flotsam, flesh-colored horror, which was half-octopus, half-scorpion and had wrapped around his head, was removed. He could see again.

"Bleck," said Deedo as she tossed the thing aloft.

"Thanks, Deedo. I appreciate it," Chesh said as he wiped yellow-brown liquid from his eyes and nose.

On and on the company whirled as if in the curl of a giant wave that carried along, within its walls, zillons of creatures glowing purple, green, or orange. As the light grew dim, the luminescence increased. As night fell, the lights intensified, transforming the immense water tube into a kaleidoscope of swirling colors. Sleep, of course, was out of the question. Without warning, as if bursting forth from a Myobian volcano, the giant insects and their riders came out of the swirling water tube. It was dark. They were surrounded by glowing-eyed things. Deedo explained that these glowing eyes were the eyes of the shadow foxes, the deadliest creatures on Myob. They would feed on the things that flopped or floated in confusion. Peeny swam forth. Arilio's Cal-i-fax swam off to the port side two leagues away. Chesh relaxed his grip on the staff that was once light-wood colored. Looking up, he saw green Mezla-zan. Peeny was headed straight for it.

In a bit, they came ashore on a sandy beach. The beetle took them in over a vast expanse covered with writhing horrors that had been recently expelled from the whirlwind tube. Many scurried off over the reed dunes or returned to the sea. Reaching a sandy hill-top higher than most, the company dismounted and slept near their insect companions. As soon as the first green rays of Mesos raced out over the dunes, the myst beetle was up. She nuzzled Chesh awake. Groggy, he watched her trying to pick up a mental image or some-how draw her words from the firmament. The beetle walked over to a dead sea turtle. She nuzzled it so its face became visible.

"What, Peeny? What can you be saying?" Chesh said, frustrated. *Let's see*, he thought. *The turtle is dead. That's not a good thing. Does she mean we too could be dead?* Peeny snapped at a flipper. "Wow! I've never seen her do that before! Seems obvious to me now. Deduction: Peeny does not eat turtle, to my knowledge, so she must be saying something is going to feed on these bodies, which makes very logical sense. Had we been less weary, perhaps we would have thought of this. In any event, whatever comes to feed on these creatures may, and on Myob, probably will, feed on us. We'll take no chances. Thanks for the message, Peeny!" said Chesh to his companion as he tried to visualize a peanut in his mind. He rose, gave Peeny a peanut, for which she eyed him affectionately, then the youth announced loudly to everyone, "We've got to go. Danger is coming our way!"

As the intrepid crew moved off over low hills on their chitinous steeds, twelve-foot-long semitransparent Gigantostraca, or sea scorpions, emerged from the waves and began to scavenge. Shortly they reached the River Green. Arilio and Alistus took some coco pods and dried bacon bark and soared off into the green sky to scout the river. Realizing Peeny must be at least as hungry as he was, Chesh handed soft, fresh cattail roots up to her as she paddled faithfully on. At first, the terrain was reed-covered sand dunes. Chesh noted that the reeds were green, the first green plants he had seen on Myob.

The Ogtavians chattered merrily about their past adventures. They munched on some old blue corn from the dwindling supplies. As the purple rays of Stesos intermingled with the green, a soothing melancholy came over those upon the stego beetle. The air smelled like autumn leaves and maple syrup. Reeds swayed, moved by light gusty winds. Even the intrepid Peeny slowed her pace. The gentle motion of slow gusty winds swaying the reeds along the sandy riverbanks sent some of the wanderers off to sleep. They rotated watches.

After a day and a half of restful tranquility, the company looked out onto an amazing landscape. Giant cattails loomed in the distance. Gentle mud pod creatures that looked like six legged turtles with powder blue shells, grazed and foraged among weeds. Belwit mushrooms, soft tan hide topped with moss green grew everywhere like transfixed dinosaurs. The giant dandelions were there too, only they had changed. They had become burnt orange and released wispy white seed pods. Pumpkins the size of elephants appeared here and there. Sand-tan lettuce mushrooms held pools of water within their concave tops. Horsetails of about twenty feet in height reached for the green sky. Odd plants of purple hues looking like large garlic bulbs grew on the sandhills that made up the land. The river was fifty to seventy-five yards across. Often, smaller rivers or streams branched off to form ponds or swampy bogs.

Geez! This reminds me of the Dead-Stream Swamp, where Watson and I roamed for so long. Man, I'd sure like to see one of those Jefferson salamanders again, thought Chesh. The hollow tones of mud pods croaking came from the banks. Hearing the sounds of wind and wings, Chesh came out of his daze. It was Cal-i-fax returning with Arilio to report his intelligence.

"Something strange ahead about ten miles. Something I've never seen before. We saw what look like red castle towers. They are almost as tall as the giant cattails. Creatures moved among the structures. Creatures three or four times the size of Peeny. They were red, the same orange-red color as the castle towers. What these things could be, I have no idea. Cal-i-fax seemed puzzled by them also." The dragonfly landed close and kept pace.

The waters of the River Green had, as yet, displayed no threatening beasts. They forged on. Later in the day, the river crested some low hills of sand and reeds, and the mysterious red towers lay ahead of them. The structures varied in height; some were a mile high, while others reached up perhaps two miles. Their circumference was ten times that of a single giant cattail. Gigantic creatures ambled about. To Chesh, they looked like barn-sized red ants.

"We have no plan!" Lavek began. "We must have a plan to deal with these monsters!"

"You know what they say about plans . . ." replied Chesh.

Their plan was suddenly put into view by the gentle beetle as she, from fatigue or hunger, headed for the river's west bank. The terrain was one of low hills with large mushrooms, reed plants, ponds, giant pumpkins, and some towering giant cattails and horsetails. Maple trees with indigo leaves grew in island-like groups. Much of the land was open. The winds chased leaf tornadoes about in wide corridors. The stego ambled ashore and lay down at the edge of a cattail pond near what looked to be a rotting giant pumpkin. She selected some choice cattails, plucked a few out, and munched contently on the tender white roots. As the company unloaded the gear and supplies, purple twilight fell upon their shoulders.

"Hey, look!" Shawnee shouted.

"Quiet, you wamp!" said Arilio somewhat softly. "We don't want those red things to hear us, or any other creatures, for that matter."

"Okay, sorry," whispered Shawnee. "Look here, though," he said as he pointed to an opening that had been hewn or formed at the base of a cottage-sized pumpkin that was faded orange and wrinkly.

"Be careful there," Deedo spoke commandingly. "We do not know what may dwell or lurk within."

As quickly as the princess had spoken, purple-black clouds charged in. Flashes of purple-silver lightning illuminated the countryside. In the distance, the thuds and thumps of mud globs or heavy raindrops could be heard drumming upon the ground.

"Quickly, into the gourd. Shelter our large friends with Jo-hon's kite. Bring our supplies. Hurry now!" Deedo shouted.

Chesh grabbed an armload of blue corn and ran in. He and some of the others shuttled things in as grapefruit-sized drops of rain began to pelt the sand around them. As Chesh reached for a section of mushroom hide, a raindrop hit it about dead center. Before Chesh's eyes, the liquid went straight through the hide and into the ground, leaving a hole as would a powerful acid. He lost his grip and ran to the dark opening, yelling to the others to do the same. In a flash, almost the entire company was in the pumpkin shelter. The flames of the fire that the teens had gotten going flickered and danced on the fibrous white-orange inner walls of the pumpkin. Chesh stood by the fire.

"What the heck was that? What was in that raindrop? It ate right through the mushroom hide and down into the ground, I don't know how far. Hey! Wait, where's Arilio?" He jumped up and ran out. The youth checked on Peeny. She and Cal-i-fax lay side by side near the pond. Arilio was just finishing tucking the green netting over and around them both. Fresh cattails lay in piles near their heads. Chesh looked at Arilio, his eyes said *"Our creature friends are safe."*. They both rushed into the shelter.

After the two had been seated, Deedo spoke. "The drop of liquid you encountered was blick. Rarely a storm will contain some of these droplets. They are composed of strange matter. This strange matter originates and comes from the eighth ring of Myob. A small moon called Blickus orbits within this ring. In autumn, usually some storms include this added effect. The droplets can be distinguished by their faint purple glow, if one has the time to see it. We do not know how far the droplets go into the ground when they strike. Some say the purple droplets go through our planet and exit, only to reenter the purple blue rings of our planet. We should avoid them," Deedo explained as she placed blue corn on the fire, husk and all.

"Will Peeny and Cal-i-fax be safe?" Chesh asked, rising and moving toward the opening.

"Be at ease. Jo-hon's kite is impervious, as are our creature companions. The pumpkin, fortunately for us, is impervious to the droplets. Most plants are," stated Deedo.

The youth wanted to ask Deedo why he had not been told about these deadly drops sooner; however, not wanting to upset the princess or add any negativity to their situation, he decided against it and simply shrugged his shoulders with a miffed expression upon his face and sat back down. Looking around, Chesh saw that the inner walls of the giant pumpkin were paper-bag brown and wrinkly. Something or natural process, perhaps of decay, had hollowed the large vegetable structure out. The air was sweet and smelled like a pumpkin pie baking, which made the Earthling feel both hungry and comfortable.

Gladstone, who seemed to always be hungry, munched a piece of the inner wall as he sat by the fire. Deedo gave a sign, telling the others that their much-needed meal of blue corn, cattail root stew, and bacon bark was ready. After the meal, Chesh and Arilio got up from time to time to check on their friends. Soon all, except for Lavek and Alistus, who were on guard, dozed peacefully off to the pattering of rain.

The green sun of Myob was full up when most awoke. Chesh and the scout had taken the last watch and were about. The rain was gone, leaving only wet ground and puddles. Peeny and Cal-i-fax were both still in deep slumbers.

"I'm going to scale that horsetail and reconnoiter the country-side. Anyone want to come with me?" Arilio asked.

Lavek, a tall Ogtavian, shook his head no. He had already begun to gather wood to use to construct new assault engines. Luckily, his tricross had survived. He had already made several arrows for it.

Shawnee, jumping up and down, shouted, "Yes, yes, I want to go!" Arilio made a thumbs-up sign.

"I am staying to help Lavek," said Deedo.

"I, too, shall remain to help," Alistus answered.

"I'll help," Bengal chimed in.

"I'm too plump. I might be seen. I will help with the weapons also," explained Gladstone.

The two insect giants had awakened and moved to comfortable spots near the clear green pond. Several mud pods, noticing the two large insects, moved off, making annoyed chirping noises and extending their bright-orange sail fins.

The view was a good one from atop the mile-high horsetail. They were at the entrance to a vast valley. It stretched almost as far as their eyes could see. Chesh, who happily came along, saw ponds and streams glistening green. Groups of mushrooms of great size grew in clusters, as if holding whispered conversations. Oaks, maples, and blue birches did likewise. Giant cattails and horsetails towered over all, all that is except for the reddish castle towers. The valley was rimmed by a great forest of maples, pines, and other Myobian trees. The leaves were painted in brilliant burnt oranges, blues, maroon hues, and varied purple shades. The three scouts could plainly see many ants moving about. Some marched in lines, carrying leaves behind them on what looked to be large sleds. Others appeared to be repairing the towers using leaves. One long, curiously weary line of ants carried what looked like baskets filled with coco pods. These were carried in saddlebag fashion. They all marched to a structure that was build over the river. On an axel was an immense water wheel that looked like it had been build by giant Cyclopes. When an ant reached the waterwheel, it dumped its load in a large hopper.

No other creatures seemed to be about, with the exception of an occasional large dragonfly and the mud pods. The mud pods acted much like grazing buffalo or deer. Chesh, Arilio, and Shawnee looked at one another in amazement and then descended.

"That Ka-tuse would make a great house," commented Arilio about the horsetail.

As the purple rays of Stesos appeared, bathing the valley of the giant leaf-cutter ants in paler light, it transformed the massive ants into maroon giants of some prehistoric cosmic past.

"What if some have wings?" Shawnee spouted as the group sat in a circle with no fire. Much hushed discussion went round. The general feeling was that the company should withdraw obliquely and circle this valley to later rejoin with the river and continue their course eastward. The day wore on in silence.

Darkness came. Myob's three moons appeared and cast their orange, green, and blue colors to intermingle among the planets powder blue and light autumn orange rings. Having munched some cold vittles and being very weary, the warriors and their insect steeds drifted off to sleep. They awoke abruptly to Lavek's loud voice. He was the last night watch, along with Allistus. Chesh felt his shoulder shaken and opened his eyes.

"Up, friend Chesh, up now! Hurry for your beetle is going!"

"What!" cried Chesh, snapping to himself. The youth jumped up. He saw his beloved beetle companion heading for the river. Thinking, hoping she was just getting a drink, he ran quickly to her. "Morning, Peeny," he said, walking alongside.

She regarded him with a sudden glance. The beetle lowered herself as if to have Chesh climb aboard or to be loaded. After much scurrying, rushing, and loading of saddlebags, along with themselves, the intrepid rescuers were again off. Arilio and Alistus were upon Cal-i-fax in the water as well. The sun was bright. The wind rushed into their faces, they were testing the new hats that Shawnee and Bangel had made because they awoke around halfway through the night and could not return themselves to dreamland. These hats were made from leaves and looked rather like witch hats without brims. They were floppy. Soft mushroom hide could be unfolded to cover the ears or ear membranes. The Ogtavians' ears were particularly sensitive to the cold, and so the flaps.

Instead of heading away from the ants and their red sand towers, of course, Peeny continued eastward. The members of the small company looked at one another, miffed, their mouth corners curved down. At first, there was much dismay and discord about Peeny's choice of direction. This ceased, however, as they rounded a bend in the river and became clearly visible to the giant ants. The ants either did not perceive them or did not acknowledge their presence. Chesh could see that the ants traveling to the mill were still in a never-ending line that extended out of view. In the far distance, it looked to Chesh like a number of the massive red creatures were climbing their tower castles, possibly effecting repairs. The stego was paddling fast. They would soon reach the mill and its huge wheel. They would have to leave the river and go around.

"What if the ants attack?" asked Deedo.

"I don't really know, Deedo. All I know is that Peeny has not failed us yet. She knows much of lands and creatures that we do not. Surely these ants have seen or sensed or smelled us by now. If they wanted to defend their territory they would have attacked en mass by now. Instead, they pay us no mind." Chesh patted his large friend.

"Be ready, everyone. Be ready with loaded slings and your senses as we cannot be sure what these ants with mouths of fire will do," Arilio cried across to those upon Peeny.

Lavek secured the arrow holder onto the top of his newly made crossbow. The others placed stones in their Gi belt slings and made sure their other weapons were at hand. The waterwheel mill was made entirely of leaves—orange, maroon, and yellow autumn leaves. The wheel served to operate a pistonlike affair that brought a large rock down on coco pods, crushing them into fluffy light-brown powder, much of which was carried off by the wind, putting a wonderful chocolate smell into the air. The powder was used in a glue paste that held the ant's leaf structures together. The treasured coco powder was also the only food eaten by newborn ants. The chocolate powder was quickly swept off a large flat rock and into leaf baskets that were carried by other worker ants off toward the castles, some of which towered so high they touched the moving clouds.

The leaf-cutter ants did not hesitate in their work as Peeny, dripping, exited the green waters to circumvent the mill area. Just as the two giant insects and their riders came abreast of the red ants, the stego did an odd thing. At least to Chesh and the others, her actions seemed out of the ordinary. She paused and shook violently, almost throwing the young Earthling and the others off. They hung on excitedly as if riding a bull or bucking bronco, eyes wide, mouths in grins that were not grins. The shaking stopped. As Peeny moved off, accompanied by the dragonfly, Chesh noticed that several of the coco pods as well as some ears of blue corn had broken loose in the commotion and fallen off to the sandy soil.

It was then that the oddest of odd things took place. A giant leaf-cutter ant, somewhat larger then the others and having larger, more threatening mandibles, looked to the small company and their insect steeds. He moved away from what seemed his position of overseeing the labor. He moved toward the coco pods and spilled corn. The gargantuan ant nudged one of the pods with the tip of a twenty-foot-long curved mandible. He moved it. Rolled it around. He extended his head into the air as if to sniff, then with glowing blue eyes, looked again at the insects and their riders. At the same moment in Chesh's mind, he felt a calm warmth, an awakening. And he heard, really heard the words, "Thank you for the Du-tee-us seeds! Our young, thank you. The builders of our castles thank you. Our winged queen thanks you and looks down upon you from Meg-en-tee-us, the tallest of our castles. Go and come as you wish. Oh, and our queen says she likes your hats!" the mental message ceased.

The Ogtavians and Chesh all nodded as if to say "Thank you." They had all received the mental message somehow. Deedo and the others of Og, as well as their human companion, would have liked to linger in the valley of the ants. However, they were still true to the taken comrades that they sought to rescue. Any debate about their actions was muted by the giant stego beetle, who did not waver in her course.

As soon as the giant red ant had completed its telepathic message, Peeny proceeded eastward on the River Green. The scent of chocolate wafted along with the wind currents. There was a sandy smell also. The river widened. The current slowed. Occasionally, some of the red giants could be seen along the riverbanks, dipping large leaf baskets into the water then heading rapidly for one of the castle towers to aid in repairing the damage caused by the strange matter that fell within the rains. Other ants could be seen dragging litters of fresh fallen leaves from the orange and blue forests that surrounded the valley.

The river became wider. Gentle mud pods ambled from sand caves. Powdery-blue clouds drifted across the green sky. Arilio raised his tricross with his left arm and cried "On to Fort Apache!" once more. The others joined in, somehow their cries sounding somber.

"Why could I hear the red ant's thoughts so clearly?" Chesh asked, turning to look at Deedo.

"As I mentioned before, Chesh, many creatures—I mean lifeforms, for I must include plants—on Myob are telepathic. Some, and I think most, are not. Or if they are, their telepathy is so secretive and encoded that it may never be detected. My hypothesis is that the smaller the creature, the more disguised its method of communication, for survival, you understand. In the case of the giant red ants, well, they probably have few enemies, like your prehistoric brontosaurus. These gentle giants have their very size to protect them. I believe you heard the ant's message, as did we all, because the ant chose to allow you to hear it. One way to think of it is that the giant ant broadcast on a frequency that we all could hear in our minds," concluded Deedo.

"Thank you, Deedo. All that you said makes good logical sense," Chesh replied with a smile.

The waters of the River Green flowed tranquilly along. The light winds caressed the bodies of the small company of intrepid warriors, bathing them in chocolate powder. Dinosaur red ants moved with purpose, toting the precious pods and repairing their towers. Somber mud pods grazed and looked curiously on. Arilio and Alistus, after making sure that the ants would not react negatively by taking a short flight, scouted ahead. Upon the beetle's shell, there was a discussion going on. Lavek felt they should go ashore once they reached the forest and build, at least, a catapult.

"If we were to stop just long enough to gather wood, I could make a catapult or a ballista. As we are, by the rough map, three days from the stronghold of the lizard soldiers, the Ort-al, we must be prepared, I think," said the woodcrafter with a note of anxiety in his voice.

"I choose this as a good plan, Lavek. That is, if Chesh's special friend will accommodate us by going ashore. Chesh?" Deedo said, looking at Chesh questioningly.

"The wooden assault engines served us well against Zud and his ilk. I'm not so sure I can persuade Peeny to stop, though. I'll try," said Chesh.

"We should watch, listen, and smell now for dangers as we move on and the terrain changes," said Bangel.

"Yes, very good, Bangel. Thanks," Deedo commended the youth.

"Yes, yes we should," chirped Shawnee.

"I agree," said Gladstone, nodding, the orange fluff ball at the tip of his horn of plenty hat bobbing up and down with his head movements.

Peeny, the beetle, paddled along with the soothing current and seemed to Chesh to be following the giant dragonfly with her gaze. Violet Stesos had arced half of her journey across the dinosaur cloud sky. The winds began to pick up. Leaf tornadoes extending a hundred feet high or more began to invade the gentle valley. The red giants displayed no apparent alarm as they ambled about diligently, attending to their various chores. Chesh, who had drifted into a gaze that was trancelike had had his mind on his recent telepathic experience relative to Peeny and himself. His conclusion was that with the ant's telepathic message, he had received no mental images of any kind. Therefore, Peeny's telepathy was clearly of a different nature, being as best as he could tell a combination of words conveyed to his mind, and perhaps the minds of others, coupled with visual images that seemed to accent the words sent. He could not help but think that the state of peaceful inner chi, or being in the here and now, related to the mental conveyance of messages somehow. A long, somber, wolflike howl jolted Chesh to full awareness.

"What the heck was that?" Chesh blurted out.

"I'm pretty sure that was the cry of a Kellow. Kellow are wheat straw yellow with swamp mosses growing upon their shells. They have the faces of gentle deer and six paddle-like legs. The Kellow graze upon seaweed and near-shore swamp grasses. We have them around Og. We call them water deer, swamp deer, or moss deer, in Ogtavian, of course. Many predators feed upon them," said Deedo.

"Thanks, Deedo. It's good to know they are harmless. Their cry sounds a bit fierce, though," Chesh remarked.

"It is suppose to," Deedo explained, "to deter predators."

"I see, yes, I should have known that, yet one always wants to make sure on an alien world," said Chesh, resuming his attentive watch mode. They were, perhaps, three miles from the blue, orange, yellow, and maroon wall of leaves that rimmed the valley.

Oddly, the River Green was flowing uphill, defying Myob's gravity, which was not always the same all over the planet. Cal-i-fax soared out over the crest of giant pines, maples, and oaks. Curving in a wide arc, he came about around them and landed next to the paddling myst stego.

"Our path looks clear for the next ten miles or so. We saw only the gentle moss deer grazing or swimming. If there are any flying creatures, the leaf winds have grounded them. A storm is headed our way from the east. Just rain, I figure." Arilio was wearing his mush-room-hide poncho, which dripped a bit of rainwater from it as did his Zeewichit or leaf hat. His had a orange daisy-like flower, quite a large one, at the pointed tip. It whirled in the wind a Myobian pinwheel.

The gleaming emerald rays of Ni, their guiding star, in this case a planet, was shown dimly through the veil of haze. The amber planet Trigeon could be seen as well. Chesh, the Ogtavians, and the giant insects reached the summit of the river hill. The River Green became level once again. It flowed at a slow pace. Trees of brilliant blues and oranges lit their way. The somewhat-weary company all dawned their mushroom-hide ponchos as rain began to pat lightly down upon them. Several Kello paused from their grazing on weeds to look up at the passing strangers, their yellow eyes aglow across the water. Trees whispered secret ancient Myobian messages wrapped in rustling leaves. The sound soothed the youth and made him drowsy as the rains turned to a mist that encased them in a cottony cloud.

Peeny, accompanied by Cal-i-fax, who had stayed in the water, headed for a swampy inlet, seeking the finest in cattail roots. A bevy of wet wind-driven leaves sloshed across Chesh's face as the drizzle turned back into a dripping rain. The winds chattered through the trees, whisking leaves off on their cartwheel journeys. Chesh noted mentally, *Hmm, no telepathy that I can detect. Logically, Peeny was hungry, maybe tired as well, so stopping for a respite makes sense. Heck, I wonder if Dad's okay. I wonder if he's alive. I think he probably is. I would have felt something if he had died, like I did when Mom was crushed in the ice cave. Since we seem to have gone through a Myobian season change while under the dark forest canopy, I fear that the lizard things may have taken the captives off to another world to be slaves.*

"Oh, I do not know," Deedo said, having sensed Chesh's thoughts. "The Ort-al are cannibalistic and worse. We must hurry! I have a feeling, an inclination, an intuition, or something that we really should make great haste. No time for fear now, just caution."

Ka-smuf-wamp, a huge gob of oily, wet large blue leaves almost engulfed the youth's head, bringing him out of his mental wanderings. He cleared the wet leaves from his eyes and face and said "A good martial artist always keeps his head up" calmly to himself.

As the members of the company drifted off to sleep under green netting shelter in the mist rain, chirp-barks echoed about the rustling wind in the leaf forest. The barks of shadow foxes.

"What were those creatures chirping last night? Tree frogs? Oh, I forgot, you have no frogs on Myob. Well, does anyone know what they were?" asked Chesh, rising.

"They were the barks of the shadow foxes. I can sense them. We have them around Og sometimes. They have never harmed anyone. They seem to watch. They are curious," Deedo said.

"Yet they are the most dangerous creatures on Myob. You said so yourself!" returned Chesh, a bit upset.

"They are, Chesh. The shadow foxes cannot be killed, that, I know. We were all, all of us Ogtavians, aware of their presence, yet we sensed no badness from them. They came not near us as they did not at the small lake at the end of the curlicue nightmare. Our mind color would have turned bleak as seeing through a glass darkly, alerting us of their bad intentions. These creatures are very like the gray foxes of your Earth. They are so secretive that they are almost never seen. I was surprised they allowed us to see them at the lake. I do not understand why they leave us alone. However, they do," finished Deedo.

"Couldn't you have maybe told me this a while ago?" Chesh mildly scolded the princess.

Gradually, the small company drifted into their respective dream universes, except for Arilio, who stood first watch along with Cal-i-fax and his hundreds of eyes within eyes of deep blue. "Sorry, Chesh. We should have told you," Arilio chimed in.

Peeny paddled loyally all through the greenness of morning. The youth and his companions noticed less and less of the mud pods along the river's banks. The forest of brilliant autumn tree giants shifted to less hilly land populated by the strangest plants Chesh had ever seen. There was only one kind of plant. Deedo and the others were not familiar with these plants that stood from nine feet tall to about fourteen feet tall. The lower parts of the plants were a kind of rotting pumpkin-pale orange. Near the top were dark green speckles. The plant's centers were pale purple, which darkened as it descended into dark murkiness. The large trumpet cone plants undulated in the winds and soft rain. They appeared rubbery and fungi-like.

As the banks of the river became darkened by walls of these odd plants, if they were plants, Chesh noticed that near the base of each plant, a dark root arm or leg extended. Upon slow and measured observation of the conical plants, Chesh saw that this appendage, through the use of a sharp-hooked end, allowed the plants mobility. Chesh watched as one of the plant things suddenly, with only a slight sound, shot its hooked leg into another plant and dragged it so that it fell, the top end splashing into the water. A hollow sound like a dinosaur crying out from a tar pit reverberated among the dim hollow tunnel, mud bog world that the cone plants inhabited. It was a forlorn death cry given as the putrid burnt-orange plants closed in upon the one that had been dragged down.

As the purple hue of Stesos faded from the gray-green rain sky, the wise stego beetle pulled up on a small sandy islet in the river. Arilio and Alistus had returned before sundown. Arilio reported that he did not like the cone plants. He said that several times when Cal-i-fax flew close to the ground, hooked legs shot up, almost hooking his winged steed. He had seen also that the things could shoot some kind of seeds or projectiles from their cones. The plants would at times expel these spores along with a dismal brown mist. Any winged insects in the vicinity would then drop as if suddenly turned to lead, disappearing into the sea of carnivorous plants.

The company, growing more weary and fearful of the cone hor-rors, watched as one of the retched plants shot its hook into the green waters and pulled forth a gelatinous purple-orange striped creature, its tentacles wriggling wildly in the air. Opting to put up the emerald netting and sleep near the giant insects, the group ate a quiet meal of honey cattail bread, bacon bark, and popped blue corn and quickly drifted off to sleep. Lavek and Gladstone took first watch.

Chesh had a vivid dream that night. So vivid that he was awak-ened by it. He shivered, yet he did not feel cold or wet under his mushroom-hide covering. Recounting his dream, Chesh visualized and recalled the dreamscapes. They were traveling through a tun-nellike path among the funnel-hook plants. It was dim and gray and hazy. He was aboard Peeny, with the Ogtavians. Cal-i-fax followed with his two riders. Water dripped upon them. The path was enclosed by dismal cone plants that were much bigger, being thirty to forty feet in height. The River Green was nowhere to be seen.

Then Chesh's dreamscape changed. He drifted up an incline. Then from a hilltop, he saw a valley below cleared of the wretched plants. Within the valley of dark mud and rotting stumps was the fort of the lizard soldiers. Some of the soldiers walked around the log walls. *It looks like something out of the old West*, Chesh thought. Oily black smoke poured forth. Looking inside the opened gates, the youth saw many soldiers, and in his dream, he heard their gluttonous laughter as they joyfully slaughtered and roasted a variety of helpless struggling creatures at one of three big fires that burned within the fortress walls. Lastly, Chesh viewed several log poles behind the central fire. He could not make out exactly who or what was tied to them through the oily smoke rising from the fire. Chesh knew, as if by instinct, as he peered through the gate, that Peeny was not with him. That he was alone! And that truly scared him. It scared him to his very bones. That is the fear that had awakened him so abruptly from his troubled sleep.

What can this mean? Is this a premonition of what is to be? Chesh thought. He was nudged from behind by one of Peeny's legs. The massive beetle leg was moving back and forth as does a dog's during the deep sleep of dreams and nightmares. Chesh turned over to face Peeny. He watched as her eyes moved back and forth under the thin tan membranes that covered them. Slowly, the beetle's platter eyes opened, looking directly into Chesh's. For an instant, a millisecond, a greenish light illuminated the mirror in the youth's mind. He seemed to see a distorted vision of the last thing he had seen in his own nightmare. A vision of the fort seething with mayhem and carnage within. This vision differed as it was from a vantage point high on a hill overlooking the valley of Fort Apache. Chesh came back to his present surroundings. The orange puffball at the tip of his tall elf-like hat undulated as the winds of Myob blew more briskly from the northwest. Green sunrays had broken through the gray marching armies of clouds.

The giant beetle rose and ambled over to a cattail patch. She began to munch lazily among the browning plants. The islet contained none of the orange carnivorous plants. It was also far enough from each of the river's banks so that the moving plants could not reach it. Chesh joined the Ogtavians, who were waking groggily and forming a sitting circle. Wooden bowls of sweet honeyed mushroom meal were being passed around.

"We must be near," Arilio said, sniffing the windswept air. Cal-i-fax, who lay nearby, raised his head and sniffed the air as well. They both looked to the east then at each other. Chesh wondered if they were exchanging telepathic information somehow. He thought they might be.

"Yes, there is the source of the stench on the wind," the scout said, pointing toward a pillar of billowing black smoke. "There lies Fort Apache," said Arilio with a look of hatred and disgust. All eyes turned to look at the dark smoke.

"How far do you think it is, Arilio?" Deedo asked.

"I'd say seven or eight zeoquets, which is equal to around nine miles, no more," he answered.

"We attack in a short time. I do not know if the stego beetle will take us. I do not think she will. We will swim. The catapult and ballista will be carried in pieces strapped to us. We must stay clear of the riverbanks and those hook-shooting plants. Once we get as close to the stockade as we can by water, we will go ashore and hack our way to an area where we will assemble our assault engines and gather projectiles for them. We will attack after observing our enemy and choosing a time when we can surprise the Ort-al. We must use surprise! Agreed?" The princess looked around to the others, who all nodded in agreement.

Indeed, Peeny did not go. Chesh had reconciled himself to this fact. He would go. To himself, he thought, *I will go. I shall face my dragon with indomitable spirit and cunning. I shall survive. My beetle friend shall survive.* He repeated these words until they stuck to the sides of his mind or reverberated around inside his head.

As they entered the waters of the River Green, Chesh hoped that he could keep up with the Ogtavians, who could swim for days and sleep floating on their backs. Cal-i-fax swam along with the intrepid warriors. Some of the larger parts for the catapult and ballista were tied aboard him. Arilio rode upon the armored giant dragonfly as well to scout as best as he could from his elevated position. The morning air felt cold and crisp as it blew in gusts around the intrepid company. On they swam with the gentle current, never going near the river's banks, which were lined with undulating, putrid-smelling, stinger funnel plants.

As Deedo and the others got closer to the wooden fortress, an acrid odor permeated the air. After a time, perhaps two hours, the river opened up into a large swampy pond. They could see the fort. It was made of logs sharpened at the top. The shape was a large rectangle. Crudely hewn guard towers stood atop each corner. The massive wooden gates were, fortunately, open. Chesh and the others slipped in among the reeds, choosing a spot that would, partially, anyway, conceal the dragonfly. If they had been spotted, they did not know. Common sense told Chesh that if these lizard soldiers spotted them, they would rush out of the fort attacking.

As the warriors moved about preparing their weapons, Chesh was able to glimpse inside the gates. He could see that a very large fire burned in the center of the fort. Halfway between the central fire and each of the sidewalls, fires burned belching out oily black smoke. On a large spit over the fire in the center, two unfortunate Myobian creatures twisted and writhed, sending forth shrill alien sounds of agony. Chesh gripped the wooden handle of the short sword he had carved tightly. He felt the moisture from his sweating hand. There was no waiting, no hesitating. The catapult and ballista sat positioned and ready with rocks and long-shafted arrows nearby. Deedo moved to each one of them, whispering last-minute battle instructions into their ears. She came to Chesh.

"Shawnee, Bangal, and Allistus will operate the catapult and ballista. We will charge on the ground, you, Lavek, Gladstone, and I. Arilio and Cal-i-fax will attack from above. We will finish these Ort-al and be back in Og soon!"

Chesh looked deeply into the eyes of the princess and said "I hate to hate" as his tears dropped to the ground.

They were up and sprinting as fast as they could, the four of them. Arilio flew just ahead to create a distraction and begin his assault. *Phit phit phit*, his tricross spit out arrows. Cries of pain and confusion began to ring out from the wooden structure. They were about fifty yards from the gates when the first leather-armored lizard soldiers charged. The Ort-al were a couple of feet taller than the Ogtavians. Each soldier had two short swords, one in each clawed hand. The swords, which resembled scythes, whipped about, haphazardly cutting the air. Chesh and Deedo began felling the scaled beasts using their Gi slings while Gladstone and Lavek met the attackers with swords. As he hacked several of the lizard things' arms from their bodies, Gladstone was thankful for the days of training he had put in with Lavek. The four warriors fought like Viking berserkers.

Soon they were within the gates. Chesh put up his Gi sling and short sword and began firing the two hand tricrossbows that hung from rope that ran behind his neck. *Phit phit phit*, dark soldiers fell in waves. Cal-i-fax swooped repeatedly as Arilio fired into the panicking soldiers. The scout also rained fire pods down upon the enemy, turning many into writhing torches. Massive ballista arrows aflame and large rocks fired by Shawnee and Bangal mowed down lines of the lizard ilk. Then Chesh saw his father. The air reeked with the smell of burnt creature flesh and burning chitin. Oily black smoke clouded the youth's vision, yet through it he saw his father tied to a stake behind the central fire. Blood ran from many wounds on his face and body. Chesh swung his sword violently, lopping off a lizard arm and slicing a neck, then he plunged the short sword, blade flat, into the chest of a taller lizard soldier. He watched as a ballista arrow struck a soldier to his left and mowed down ten more. The catapult's flaming shots sent lizard soldiers reeling as they burst into flames. *Swit-swit-swit*, the dragonfly swooped, slicing many of the enemy into pieces of flesh and armor that dropped to the ground, forming brown pools of ichor. Arilio's arrows felled the Ort-al like a scythe felling wheat.

As Chesh hacked away at the defenders, he caught glimpses and flashes of action within the battle. Alistus was off to his right, nearer the central fire. She appeared as a whirling dervish, arms and legs with razor-sharp blades attached to them sliced all around her, sending gore and detached limbs into the fray. He saw Gladstone swinging his Gi belt as a mace and chain. His arms were a blur as many dark armored ones were hit with crushing blows. Deedo spun about like lightning, welding her Gi belt as a mace in one hand and slicing foes with death swipes of her stone knife with the other. Chesh figured there were eighty to a hundred lizard soldiers in the fort. Then his eyes fell upon a sight that, if any sight were to, should have demoralized him to his soul. As he slashed a soldier across the face, to his right he saw behind the fire a sort of sus-pended metallic cage. Within the cage was Jo-hon. Her eyes glowed with rage. Chesh immediately began to work his way toward his comrade. He yelled at the top of his lungs "Jo-hon! Jo-hon!" and pointed with his sword, hoping that Deedo and Gladstone or Arilio might see Jo-hon.

Hack, slice, stab. Hack, slice, stab. Chesh began to cut a path. The lizard soldiers were slow. Their gangly, flexible arms had difficulty maneuvering at such close quarters. They fought with swiping windmill motions that could be evaded easily. The Ort-al did not use their projectile cone flingers or hook nets. They would have injured many of their own. That they had been drinking bradrook wine and eating mass quantities of flesh prior to the battle added to the slow, clumsy state of the fort's defenders. "For Og!" the cry came from Chesh's rear. He glanced back toward the gates. It was Lavek. He welded a broad sword in each hand. Chunks of armor and flesh, arms, and heads flew about his flashing blades. Shawnee and Bengal were off to the sides of Lavek. Before he turned his head, Chesh glimpsed Bengal kicking one opponent and dropping him then felling several more with her quarter staff.

From nowhere, Alistus dropped into the mayhem a swirling whirlwind of death. Screams of pain came from bloodied mouths of the leather-clad ones. Chesh tried to work over toward her. He saw severed limbs flying out of the torrent where the Ogtavian woman spun as a whirlwind, welding razor-sharp crescent-shaped blades in each hand. She had spikes of indigo wood vined to each knee as well as trispikes on her ankles. *Phit phit phit*, Arilio's bow spat arrows as Cal-i-fax killed with his mantis claws, shearing heads off or removing an arm and hand that held a sword. Chesh and the others began to cut their swaths toward the cage that held Jo-hon.

In the heat of battle, Chesh heard cries from behind from the main gate area. He recognized the voices. They were the voices of the two teens and Lavek, who yelled in unison "For Og!" The youth battled on, slicing and hacking as would a Roman centurion of old or a Spartan. In an instant, it seemed, Chesh was joined by his comrades. They formed up into a triangle and wedged in the direction of the cage. The lizard soldiers converged on them like deadly vipers. Their slinky arms windmill-swiped wildly. Some whipped rocks and

debris at the Ogtavians with young cone-hook plants. Having no
shields, these soon began to bloody Chesh and the others, especially
around the face, and where they had no protective mushroom-hide
armor. The blue-and-green armored dragonfly landed on the cage
and began to tear at the bars with one mandible while using the other
to slay the enemy. The scout sat atop his insect steed, methodically
mowing down lizard men with his tricross bow.

Noticing that some soldiers were squat and stout, while only
a few were taller, perhaps eight or nine feet tall, and further that it
was the tall Ort-al who shouted commands while pointing to areas
where soldiers would then move, the scout began to target these lead-
ers. *Ka-thwank*, an arrow struck one in the center of the forehead,
sending a gush of brown blood forth. "Aaahugg," the thing cried as
it dropped. The acrid black smoke clouded the youth's vision as he
swung his short sword deliberately. Confused alien cries of pain filled
the air. Chesh felt that he was running on automatic. A sword-weld-
ing robot. He felt no exhaustion, no pain, although his face bled, as
did several slashes and wounds he had received. He could hear Arilio
cutting loose with his tricross. The shots felled lizard soldiers that
surrounded the wedge of warriors.

Chesh glanced left to fend off a swirling blade. He took the sol-
dier out with one lightning stab that pierced the dark armor. Before
he looked again to his front, he caught a glimpse of Gladstone being
slashed across the side of the face. The brave Ogtavian did not cry
out as he fell. Chesh saw this clearly. Slice, he slew two soldiers in
front of him. His head moved at the neck, looking to his comrades.
Shawnee wielded his staff like a windmill propeller in a gale. He
popped three Ort-al in their noses with a staff end; they fell dead as
stones. Bengal clomped her weapon down on the heads of several
Ort-al, dropping them as well. Lavek swung his two broad swords,
swirling into the mass of enemies, cutting swaths littered by arms and
legs, then he reformed into the wedge. Deedo used a short sword in
her left hand to slay and fend off attackers while whipping Gi stones
at taller commanders, sending them shrieking and whirling or drop-
ping them outright.

The lizard soldiers stopped using their blunderbuss like projectile flingers. As Cal-i-fax tried in vein to loosen the cage and lift it aloft, the lizard things suddenly pulled back. Through the smoke haze, Chesh could see the dark armored soldiers forming into a Roman phalanx about fifty yards from them. Many looked up as a dark shadow moved over them from above. Looking up, Chesh froze as he saw what came. It was the faceless bat horrors. The shade creatures grasped within their claws one of the gigantic black nets. He put his sword in his belt and grabbed the two-hand crossbows that hung suspended around his neck by vine. The youth began firing at the faceless ones. Chesh's bolts struck with deadly accuracy, causing two of the dark ones to cry out, lose the net, and spiral to the ground. Arilio fired. Deedo targeted the things as well. Then darkness and pain over took the youth as the hook-filled net enveloped the valiant warriors and Cal-i-fax. The giant dragonfly struggled to get free, tearing his wings in anguish. Blood ran into Chesh's eyes as he lost consciousness below the dark veil.

Sometime later, he had no idea how much later, Chesh came back to himself, sort of. *I'm upside down,* he thought. Blinking and dislodging dried blood from his eyes, he saw the central fire of the fort before him. Roasting on a spit was a blackened creature. He could smell the cooking flesh. He vomited. Shaking himself back to reality, the youth began to perceive the dire straights he was in. He was lashed to a wooden-log stake. To his sides in a curve of stakes, his fellow warriors were tied as well. The valiant dragonfly was held almost flat to the ground by staked-down spiker vines. Chesh felt pain in his gut as he saw Arilio, suspended nearby, tears running from his eyes. Looking to his right, Chesh saw his bloodied father. He, likewise, was bound with vine to a stake, as he had been during the battle. Chesh struggled violently.

Ka-wap-wap-wap, he was lashed in the face with what felt like dried rose bush branches. Although he received a harsh drubbing with the thorn branches, it did bring him more to the reality of his surroundings. Through blood-encrusted eyes, Chesh saw all his fellow warriors except for Alistus and Gladstone. To his right were first his father, then Deedo, Bengal, and Shawnee. On the left were Arilio

196

and Lavek. Turning his head farther, Chesh saw the valiant Cal-i-fax with spiker vines woven over his armored body and wings like spiderwebbing. The Hon warrior lay unconscious in the metallic cage. Chesh thought, *They didn't get Peeny! Good!* as a number of the lizard soldiers nearby eyed him with scaled eyes. Chesh pretended to pass out from the pain of the whipping. Acrid smoke pierced his nostrils. *I saw some of those giant snappers that the Ort-al use for hunting slaves,* thought Chesh. *They were staked just beyond the gate. I also glimpsed some of the bat-winged things among the rejoicing lizard men and circling about over head. What must have happened, I think, is that the sinister black flyers must have formed some dark alliance with these lizard things. A patrol or some patrols that were out searching for victims and possibly for us returned. We were too occupied with our battle, so the onslaught of creatures above with nets was too swift for us to perceive and prevent, thus we were captured. It's academic, I guess, yet I feel we are not finished. What, okay, what can I do?*

Although the youth's predicament was seemingly hopeless, he did not give up. His mind raced with ideas of what he might do to put his friends and father in good stead again. After an eternity, Chesh heard a change in the tumult of the Ort-al celebrating their victory around him. As Chesh opened his eyes, he saw the daylight had a purple hue; it was evening. No lizard things were very near nor were any watching him. They were focused on the three fires, and for the reason that having drunken their intoxicating brackish mead all day, they now grew hungry. A struggling mass of Ort-al to the left were engaged in moving the cage containing Jo-hon using a vine rope and wood scaffolding so that it could be swung over the fire on that side. She lay unknowing, eyes closed. Chesh moved his head and saw Lavek struggling until he was knocked unconscious. He was then tied to a pole and suspended over the fire on Chesh's right. Bangel, tightly bound with spike vine, was being taken to the central fire. Ghastly cheers and cruel mocking words issued forth from the lizard ilk and the noxious smelling faceless things.

In his mind, like a gentle wave, came the melodic words "Slowly, slowly, slowly, says the Slothos." Through the open gates of the wooden fort Chesh could see Peeny standing, pristine, immaculate, atop a hill overlooking the fort. She wore a cruel grin on her beetle face. Her eyes flashed green fire light from their very centers. The light illuminated the myst stego beetle's face in the dimming purple twilight. A flash of green lightning shot forth from each eye. The silent bolts struck the hewn logs of Fort Apache. The entire fort glowed green as if engulfed by Saint Elmo's fire. The wooden structure fell like burnt cloth. Gray ash was left to drift away in the wind. Looking side to side, he saw that Deedo and Arilio also looked in the direction of the giant tan beetle with blue stripes. The armored lizard soldiers ran madly about, crashing into one another from terror, confusion, and strong drink. Their eyes bulged. They swung wildly with the blunderbuss cones in vain attempts to strike the beetle with projectiles. Some tried frantically to load hook-net arrows into the large ballista that had been mounted on the giant snappers. Green beams hooked on to many of the lizard soldiers and their weapons. Shrieks of death spewed into the smoky wind as they were transformed into wisps of gray ash. The snappers, unharmed, ran off as their chains had vaporized as well. Thirty or so of the bat-winged ones flew aloft with a dark hook net to enshroud the attacker. They were turned to gray cloud haze and carried off in the building winds along with the vaporized net.

The remaining confused groups of Ort-al soldiers and winged horrors were then systematically turned to piles of gray dust. Winged things that sought to flee via air gave out shrill cries and became puffs of smoke. The green beams of death swept across the ground, taking groups of the enemy out as one would remove chess pieces from the board upon their defeat. Shrieks and wails of death filled the bleak firmament. The Ort-al were gone. Not one of the faceless bat things escaped. The beams of the myst beetle then went from stake to stake, freeing the captives by dissolving the vine ropes. Chesh, startled by his abrupt fall off the stake, immediately rose. He ran awkwardly and stiffly to the fire where Bangal was and swung the large spit out from above the fire. He slit the vine binding the young Ogtavian with an Ort-al sword. Arilio freed Lavek in a similar fashion. Deedo and Shawnee had succeeded in getting the cage and Jo-hon from over the fire on the left. Just as they did, a green beam struck the iron cage, vaporizing it to gray ash. Deedo and Shawnee flashed in like lightning to catch their unconscious comrade. Seeing this, Chesh ran to his father, who was conscious and looking about with a confused-anthropoid gape upon his face.

Around the perimeter, creatures of all sorts, big and tall, blue slothos, stego beetles, and giant snappers, that were staked to the ground with metal chains and heavy leg irons moved freely as the metal that bound them dissolved when the green beams touched it. The gleeful creatures burst forth with Myobian cries of joy. Many simply roared, snorted, or buzzed as they slithered, scurried, or flew off. Chesh watched as a swallowtail butterfly the size of a barn roof with wings of purple velvet drifted off over the hills. Looking around in a sort of aftermath daze, Chesh saw 150 or more piles of gray ash that had been the lizard soldiers and some of the winged black things. The gentle morning winds blew their small mountain peaks off, sending them away in wisps.

The air smelled of the greasy, acrid smoke from the three cook fires of the vanquished enemy. Arilio, a scout of action, a stitch-in-time Ogtavian, already had the wounded Shawnee and Bengal hauling water in wooden buckets. The water was poured on the rancid fire pits. Arilio, badly wounded himself and using a quarter staff as a crutch, made his way to the cattail pond on the east side of the fort where Cal-i-fax lay, tending to the wounds in his gossamer wings. The loyal scout began to gather cattail roots for his friend. Deedo was rendering first aid to Chesh's father and Lavek. Jo-hon lay in the same fetal posture she had been in when still caged.

Chesh got up unsteadily and walked over to kneel at the side of his father. Blood ran from many slices and cuts on his father's face. His eyes were almost swollen closed. "Dad, it's Chesh," the youth said in hushed tones.

Slowly, with blood issuing from the corner of his mouth, Chesh's father whispered, "I came to find you Chesh, and you found me."

"Yes, Dad, I found you, and we are safe now. I'm with good friends. Just lay back and rest, please. Let Deedo take care of you. We will soon leave this place. Rest and relax. We'll have you back at Noeggsplantation in no time," Chesh reassured his father as he placed a hand lightly on his father's shoulder, which he had never done before. Chesh looked at Deedo, looking directly and deeply into the glowing indigo pools. A greenish tear ran down one of her cheeks. They did not need to speak.

I'll try one more time to reach Peeny telepathically, let's see, okay, I've got it, "Peeny, who are you?" After a pause these words came into the mind of Chesh like a soft summer wind.

"I am a defender of the meek. Happiness is whatever you want it to be, friend Chesh. I like the name you gave me!" The youth's eyes went wide with amazement.

The line of twelve gigantic lily pads floated lazily along. Cattail people shook off the morning frost. As Peeny rounded a bend in the River Green, several of the freed captives jumped into the cool water and took hold of the soft green cushions of vegetation. Using gentle kicking motions they moved the giant lily pad rafts away from the sandy banks of the slow moving river. The cooler water did not bother them as their skin allowed Ogtavians to swim even in icy waters. Eighty-three captives had been rescued from the cave dungeons below Fort Apache. Fortunately, Alistus and Gladstone were among them, both badly wounded. Among the liberated were Zuma, an elder; Mizus, Monarch Wapiti's best friend; and Oblyo, a young Ogtavian, and his sister, Oberon. They rode on the lily pad just behind Peeny. In the center was a cheery orange fire burning upon dried mud. The smell of bacon bark wafted upward into the green sky along with the smoke. Zuma and the others moved about, tending to the badly wounded Lavek, Gladstone, and Alistus. These valiant warriors would be scarred or perhaps a bit lame. For now, they lay quiet, soothed by the sounds of the swirling waters.

Shawnee and Bangel tended to the wounded or ill Ogtavians on the last green sponge pad. They also acted as rear guards. Shawnee paused to watch the silvery-green surface as orange flying fish with pastel-blue stripes arced above the water on their quests for nourishment. As the green rays of Mesos bathed them in radiated splendor, the weary warriors drifted lazily down the River Green. No denizens were observed lurking in the calm-flowing waters. The air smelled of dry cattails and autumn swamp. Cattail people in tan coats waved to them merrily. Mud pods lay along the river's banks or swam slowly about. The wounded rested on the soft giant green lily pads. The badly wounded dragonfly king lay on a large pad as well, being comforted by his loyal friend.

Chesh knew that things were returning to a more pleasant state when he heard Shawnee screech, "Who the heck put the stupid burr in my pants! Come on, which one of you clowns did it! Ooh, ouch, ohh!" he groaned with joyful chagrin. Chesh breathed a long sigh of relief as he looked southward, where he could see endless cattails the color of dried corn husks. Chesh had read no telepathic thoughts or images from Peeny when he led her down from the hilltop. He recalled with a mental visual movie the pin beams of green light dancing about the chains and stakes of the helpless Myobian beasts and insects and the joyful looks on the faces of the creatures as they ran free once again. He recalled her timid look when he first reached the summit of the sandhill. He saw the swath of melted, deformed stinger cone plants that the myst beetle had left in her wake. The closer he had gotten to Peeny, the more the feeling of warmth and contentment grew within the area of his chi. Lastly, Chesh saw a single tear slowly crawl down her face.

He was awakened from his daze into the purple twilight by the feeling of land under the beetle. The company, as usual had little choice in the matter of the campsite. The cone horrors had vanished from the landscape soon after Chesh and the others were some distance from the remains of the fort. They were replaced by swampwoods. Giant cattails reached for the green clouds and three-hundred-foot horsetails swayed high above at times. Rivulets of glistening green branched off from the main river. Swamp ponds and cattails abounded. Permian dragonflies eight feet long, turned powder blue by the purple light, darted or hovered over immense ferns. Many of these landed on Cal-i-fax for a time as if to speak to him. The youth, with his enhanced senses, fancied that he could hear, from a distance, or simply in his mind's ear, the sweet, soft melodic tones of their conversations. And coco pods grew here! The pod trees had appeared just as Stesos came out bathing everything in purple twighlight.

Now the group sat or lay around an orange-blue flickering campfire. Those who could eat munched on rich, thick slices of bacon bark, honeyed cattail bread, and even prairie chok, which tasted delicious. As the Ogtavians and Chesh enjoyed their dinners, many walked or hobbled about, feeding their comrades. Deedo had made a broth of cattail roots and was spooning some into Gladstone's mouth. Jo-hon still lay in a coma-like state. As night fell and darkness grew, an aura of purple light formed around her. In several hours, all, except the watch, slept under a canopy of green and blue stars.

"Come on, come on, all of you! Come quickly!" Arilio called. The green sun had just come up.

Chesh sat up. He looked at Peeny, who slept three feet from him. She was just opening her eyes. He rose, rubbing sleep from his eyes. Looking about in the dim green light, he saw Deedo and the others moving toward an opening in the reeds and bushes about them. Like lightning, Chesh raced to join them. The beetle's eyes followed him, but she did not. They all cleared the brush. Their eyes went wide as the amazed warriors and most of the freed Ogtavians looked out over a field of battle that was comparable to Gettysburg. Thousands upon thousands of lizard soldier bodies lay strewn about, entangled, missing limbs, open-eyed, staring up into the sky, death grimaces on their faces. A strange, miasmic brown-yellow haze drifted about over the carnage. Hundreds of the giant snappers, confused but alive, were scattered among them. Swords, flingers, and hook netting lay mute on the gray sand. Upon closer observation, Chesh saw that many of the bodies had the same familiar slashes delivered by Jo-hon at the Zudian battle. The youth from Earth, Deedo, and Arilio all looked to one another at the same time and said "Jo-hon?" in unison.

Looking up, because a light above attracted their eyes, the warriors beheld a glorious sight. For far above the battlefield appeared a purple orb. As they watched, the orb floated to a position directly over them. It was not fear that Chesh felt, however. Instead, he felt a warmth grow within the area of his chi and radiate through his body and to his hands and feet. The others stared at the youth in amazement for his whole body had begun to glow green. He, not knowing what to do, walked slowly back to the campsite and to Peeny. His friends and the Ogtavians followed. The purple orb, which had gotten larger as it approached them, followed above. All was normal. Chesh's father had awoken. Lavek was asleep. Jo-hon still lay in a fetal position near the glowing indigo flames.

Just then, the purple orb divided, undergoing a metamorphosis into a lighter purple orb in the center with a brilliant yellow orb on the right and a shimmering green orb on the left. The orbs began to become wavy and undulate. Dim forms appeared. The yellow orb became a large Hon warrior clad in yellow armor. The green orb changed. It became a small dragon-like creature. The same small dragon-like creature that had appeared to Chesh so long ago when he and Deedo sat high atop Myob, perched in the owlets' nest in the giant cattail. The purple orb became a Hon warrior also. This warrior was clad in magnificently crafted purple armor, and a glowing indigo crown floated above his head. No member of the company moved as the purple knight in the center spoke.

"I am Zo-hon, the king of Oak-en-shield, the land that floats in the sky. This is my son, Lo-hon," he indicated the Hon to his right. "And this Gal-a-hought, my first knight." The glistening silver-purple claws of his left hand motioned to the form of the small green dragon. "We mean no harm. We have come for my daughter."

"I am Deedo, princess of Og. My father is Monarch Wapiti. Your daughter has saved our lives many times. Our quest would have failed if not for her bravery and skill. We are all greatly thankful." With that the entire group, freed captives and wounded warriors alike, nodded their heads in agreement. "If we can be of help in any manner, please tell us how. And know that from hereafter, all Hon are more than welcome in our kingdom of Og." Deedo's face became very grave, the corners of her mouth quivering as she asked, "Oh, and oh, please tell me, your majesty, will Jo-hon live?"

"I thank you. Please worry not, for we cannot die," answered the regal Zo-hon.

With that, the small dragon flitted over to Chesh, landing upon his shoulder. "It is good to see you again, my friend. You have changed," Chesh heard in his mind. The dragon called Gal-a-hought hovered over to a spot in front of Chesh's eyes as he had when their eyes first met high in a giant cattail at summer's beginning. The others watched in amazement as green beams issued forth from the indigo eyes of the miniature dragon. The beams went directly into the youth's eyes. Chesh lit up like a glowing green Christmas tree. He felt as if he were being changed with wonderful, chocolate-sweet electricity. He felt renewed, formed again.

Had this journey truly been about his reclamation? he wondered. Had it been about inner strengh? His fight-or-flight reaction? Had it been about survival, survival on the alien world of Myob? How he had to change, had to undergo metamorphosis, for if he had remained unchanged, he would not have grown and survived? Chesh thought of Captain Nemo's words: "Mobilis in mobili" changing with change. He pondered these thoughts deeply, for if he knew nothing else, he knew that he was different.

The green dragon rejoined the other glowing entities. The three transformed again into three orbs. They moved in unison over to Jo-hon and hovered above her. A purple sphere formed around the sleeping warrior. She rose. The Hon princess opened her eyes and looked toward Deedo and the others. She nodded as if to say "All is well." Chesh and the Ogtavians returned Jo-hon's nod of respect and farewell. Even the giant insects nodded. As the company watched, the mysterious orbs encompassed Jo-hon and became one large purple orb, which drifted off to the west.

A new day surrounded them; it was crisp and windy. The River Green meandered toward the south, toward home, Og. The Ogtavians were sullen as they stared at the passing banks with blue oysters for eyes. Shawnee and Bangel cooked coco cakes and blue popcorn over orange flames in the center of the last lily pad on the fire base made from rocks that Arilio had shown them how to make. Cal-i-fax, healed, soared ahead with the ever-vigilant Arilio aboard. Mud pods looked out upon the unusual sight with puzzled deerlike faces. Cattails waved and chattered in the fresh green mist.

Sensing the anguish and anxiety of all at the loss of their comrades, which was only now affecting their emotions, Chesh had scavenged a couple of nice driftwood pieces, and he sat in front, atop Peeny, trying very hard to carve the wood into zlatos boards. Lavek, who was now somewhat mobile, strained to watch Chesh from the first lily pad. The teens gazed at mute fishing lines, their minds adrift. Gladstone stirred a large pot full of big red beans. Arilio had flown off ahead. Chesh's father sat just behind Deedo. Being of hearty Viking stock and not being able to just lie around, he had insisted on riding on the stego.

It was he who spoke first, breaking the silence. "I am deeply in your debt. I thank all of you from the bottom of my heart. I don't understand a lot about your planet or your ways. I know we must seem like invaders. I apologize for this."

"We of Og welcome you as long as you do not harm Myob or its creatures," Deedo explained. "I am the princess of Og. My father is King Wapiti," she said, turning to look at the Earther.

"Hey, Dad, I know something you can do for the Ogtavians!" Chesh exclaimed.

"Yes, Chesh, yes, what's that? What can I do?" said Chesh's father, his face lighting up.

"You can get them some frogs!" Chesh said. "The frogs on Myob have all been wiped out. Dad, could you please order a gizzilion peanuts also, some for planting and some for Peeny."

"Yes, Chesh, I will get Peeny peanuts. And as to the frogs, yes of course. Of course! Let's see. Let me think. We still have many different types, although they must be housed in the sun domes on Earth. We also have the DNA of many frogs that used to dwell on Earth in our Noah's Ark bank. I will contact Professor Abbirage at the University of Nature and see what he can do. I mean, I know it's possible. I will viddy him as soon as I get back to the plantation. Thanks, Chesh, what a great idea!" said the wounded man.

Chesh looked up from his knife and the gray-blue flecks of wood. "Dad, I'm going to stay with the Ogtavians and teach them English, if that is okay?"

"I think that would be fantastic, Chesh! And I will not be far."

"Great, Dad, that's fantastic! We'll have you back in no time!" Chesh said, looking again out over the horizon to see giant cattails nodding in agreement.

"Now, Chesh, about this beetle . . ." his father began.

Thunder lizard clouds drifted by. Stegosaurs' of light purple were chased by tyrannosaurs', in the green skies. The friendly winds were with them. Shawnee was the first to hear the warning chirps of the copper frogs, Arilio and his winged steed had returned a short time ago with news that they had sighted the white sand castle towers peering above the swamp woods. They would float in with their companions. The scout had seen no apparent dangers, yet who knows what lurks. Then suddenly the river rounded a bend and there on the bank, by the secret cave stood King Wapiti surrounded by cheering, jumping kindred. The smell of country ham, mixed with chocolate and popcorn drifted through the air reaching the noses of the intrepid warriors and the others. The faces of all aboard the lily pads radiated with broad froggish grins. As they dismounted from Peeny, Chesh and Deedo looked warmly at each other. The youth could almost hear her say "How in the hecka did Peeny know to come here?" Instead of speaking she handed him the new reed sombraro she had been weaving on the last leg of their journey. He smiled and handed her one of the zlotos boards he had carved.

After coming ashore and refreshing themselves with cattail root juice, blue popcorn, coco muffins, and prairie choc, Chesh, his father, Monarch Wapiti, Deedo, and Arilio, sat on the white sand in a circle, speaking in soft tones.

"Mon…, I mean Wapiti, I have some suggestions for the ways of Gi," said Chesh.

"Yes my dear friend Chesh, and what, I wonder, could they be?" the regal monarch quarried.

"I would, I mean we, Peeny and I, would add these words to the ways of Gi, along with, breath, focus, and relax, we would put, look up, and clear your mind. Peeny recommends putting, slowly, slowly,

slowly, says the slothos, after remain healthy. And she would also add, always do things in threes."

"These suggestions are fantastic Chesh, oh, and Peeny, thank you! We shall add them right away. Chesh would you consider teaching our young ones martial arts skills as well as English?"

"Of course," answered the young man from Earth.

Peeny lay by the River Green munching peacefully on tender cattail roots, Cal-i-fax was nearby. A small pile of peanuts was near the gentle beetle's head. Falling leaves of indigo and orange swirled about in mini tornadoes. Purple twighlight bathed the ferns and pines. The tapestry of stars above were blue and green lightening bugs.

The Unknown Valley

The house did have a somewhat forbidding look, as if it where the face of a monstrous raccoon frozen into astonishment and terror by some unknown predator. It seemed to hold a secret, a message from another time and space. The seclusion of the land and pond on which it was located may have had something to do with the oppressive mood in the yellowed firmament surrounding the very old structure. It was as if one stepped back into the Permian Era. The expanse was encircled by a forest of tall ancient pines, maples, and oaks. Poplar trees were plentiful at the forest's edge. The land was sandy and overgrown with wild grasses, weeds, and cattails. There were small patches of tarn black swamp scattered about. A large circular pond skirted by reeds lay in the center of the clearing. Its sides quickly dropped off into dark weedy depths.

Along the east side, spruce pines grew in rows. The pond lay in a low area in a valley of sand washes. Thousands of dragonflies, red-, blue-, and green-headed giants with shimmering blue bodies, streaked the air back and forth on their hunting lines and landed resting on singular plant stalks. Frogs and other reptilian wildlife were plentiful.

I was happy for the seclusion. My favorite pastime was the study of swamp life, particularly insects. I took notes, researched and read about, and at times, wrote scientific articles about these interesting life-forms. My area of interest being one that focuses on highly specialized behaviors. For example, the case of the tarantula spiders and their arch enemy, the digger wasps of the genus *Pepsis*. It is a classic example of what looks like intelligence pitted against instinct—a strange situation in which the tarantula, though fully able to defend itself, submits unwittingly to its own destruction. To me, unusual behaviors are intriguing conundrums. Thus, I am similar to the previous owner. A man of some mystery who had degrees in both botany and entomology. I say *mystery* because, according to the agent who handled the transaction of the property, the man, J. Handicot Jebson, apparently walked off into the deep woods' swamp on one of his many specimen-gathering expeditions one bright summer day, never to be seen again.

Although in need of some repairs and alterations, the secluded house and its surrounding lands meet my needs nicely. It is a sturdily built structure of a basic design used by the Vikings. The house is a simple rectangle with a sharply sloping roof. This slope enables snow to slide off with ease. The house is tall, having three stories and an attic. There is a large root cellar, which I have not yet explored. The walls on the interior are of the most tranquil knotty pinewood. Antiquated ghost furniture sits silently, covered in moss thick dust. The exterior is of overlapped, weathered boards the color of gray driftwood. There is a barnlike shed that will serve to keep the snow from my car in winter. Although remote and secluded, my new home is located only a thirty-minute drive from the local school where I have recently been hired to teach. The drive is a pleasant maze of country roads lined with woods and farmlands.

I had all summer to clean, straighten, and organize the abode to my liking. It was in the course of doing this that I chanced upon the discovery of that sinister journal. I was cleaning out the kitchen drawers. I bought the house furnished, and much of the previous owners belongings had been left undisturbed. I was removing old newspaper from one of the drawers when, discovering a raised area at the back and tearing the paper out, I found a leather-bound journal. It was old and smelled of mildew. What I share with you now is, word for word, exactly as they were written in this ominous account.

Dr. J. Handicot Jebson's Journal

July 24, 1927

Yes, I'll admit I'm a bit odd, different, eccentric even. I cloud watch, listen to the winds murmur, whisper, and chuckle through the trees. And I like cricket listening and ant watching, among other perhaps out-of-the-ordinary things. To most, these pastimes or hobbies would seem obtuse and out of the ordinary. I have changed much since the war. In losing my left arm, I have had to make many psychological and physiological adjustments. My past left-handedness made these adjustments difficult. I know that the stressfulness of these and other adjustments have caused a weakened condition within me. I, however, feel that my state of mind and my somewhat-weakened physical condition have improved greatly in the years following the Great War, the world war in which I lost my arm. I remain somewhat of a misanthrope, and so the remoteness, solitude, and privacy will be comforts rather than handicaps.

My immediate plans are to give the place a one- or two-day clean and arrange things to my liking. Then I will begin to camp first not far from the farmhouse then to venture into the depths of the vast lands called the Dead-Stream Swamp.

July 26

I had begun my day preparing for a long trek into the depths of the Dead-Stream Swamp. I packed a small knapsack with sandwiches, nuts, and carrots. Filled my trusty canteen. Packed such things as my compass, a pocketknife, a magnifying glass, and sample containers. I strapped a machete to my side. I would be gathering mosses, molds, and perhaps some mushrooms. This is in connection with my chosen field of botany. I am a specialist in lichens, ferns, mosses, and other plant life native to the swamplands of the northeastern area of America. I was fortunate in receiving a generous grant from Michigan University in order to pursue studies and obtain samples of many rare types of swampland plants.

The university was particularly interested in a rare fungus mycelium growth called sargasso. It was said, although I do not know if the source is an old wives' tale or a scientist, that this extremely short-lived fungus possesses qualities or obscure chemical combinations that in fact can cure consumption, plague, and numerous other maladies of the human body. This obscure fungus has only been found on two recorded occasions that I know of. Once in the ancient Nordic swamps of Holland, where the finders were the Norsemen. And once by some early Spanish explorers who were in the process of exploring the Great Lakes area of the new world. There is no documented or artifactual proof of the claims of the amazing healing properties of the sargasso mycelium.

Nonetheless, the university has been kind enough to advance me a generous amount of funds. I, in turn, used a portion to purchase the old Haggamar place, as the locals call it. The parched gray farmhouse is perfect for my studies. Its location, in close proximity to the vast swamplands of this area, and its seclusion will allow me to focus, undisturbed, on my retrieval and examination of specialized swamp-growing life-forms. The swamplands lie just north of the largest inland lake in this state. The lake is shallow, having a maximum depth of twenty-eight feet. The water becomes very warm in the summer months. On viewing the lake, one feels as if traveling millions of years back in time to the shallow Permian Era waters that covered much of this land. Waters from which emerged the first mammal-like reptiles. Could this lake possibly have survived from those times? I wonder for I have seen several highly interesting and differentiated creatures in and around its waters.

The Haggamar house is located on a large pond that teems with reptiles, amphibians, insects, and the flora and fauna of the area. The house itself is well built and sound, in spite of its run-down appearance. It has ample room for my laboratory equipment and gear. The oak furniture, although in need of some cleaning, is sturdy and comfortable. The homestead has sat vacant for some many decades. The house and lands had been a farm. According to local gossip and idle chat, the homestead and its grounds were haunted. A witch's curse is said to hang over the place. The witch, who was stoned to death in the late sixteen hundreds, said to her executioners, "All who come to this sacred ground without the protection shall be turned to putrid piles of rotting flesh and bone."

According to local folklore, some twenty or thirty people, and many animals had met their ends in this way as a result of straying onto these shunned grounds. The home itself is said to rest upon a foundation built by a tribe of Cro-Magnon people. Local Indian lore describes these people as animal worshipers of great powers. They were said to transform themselves into bears, coyotes, or man-sized owls. It is also said that the Cro-Magnon could become blue fire-balls and would often slay their enemies in this form. This sinister mythology does keep me observantly alert, yet not so much out of fear, for fear is not much within me any longer, but out of curiosity about the unknown. It would thrill me to come across something undiscovered, whether it be of a supernatural nature or some other as yet unfound nature. Further, this curtain of fear surrounding the place shall serve to keep it all the more private for my work.

August 2

It was 5:00 a.m. when I headed out. with Ajax, my dog. Ajax the strange Mastiff like dog that wandered up out of the swamp woods the second week I was here. I fed him and it was like we had been together for years. He has a broad chest and is very muscular with short coyote tan fur. Odd black tiger like stripes extend vertically down from a ridge that runs along his back. Ajax's eyes are like no other dog's eyes I have ever seen. They are shiny and amber-brown when viewed in the light of day. In darkness they glow with an other-worldly green color that is unlike any green seen on Earth.

The day was the color of shark hide. The swamp was wrapped in cotton fog, cloaking and dampening all its sounds as if absorbed into the dark spots between its pines and reeds. The day shall be hot with much humidity.

We have explored and made camp in the vast green world. The deer flies have gotten so bad in the deep swamp-woods that, had I not applied my fern juice mixture to myself and Ajax, we would have been forced to turn back or make shelter against their viciousness. The tenacious pests swarm like bees around the head and neck and lay in bites so potent that they swell immediately to marble size. The pain and itch lasts for at least weeks. A man alone, unprotected, could be significantly drained of blood by these vampiric things.

August 5

The most exciting thing from our journey is that I have discovered a most unusual, remote spot. It shows promise in being a prime location for the sargasso fungus to grow. In brief, after passing through a long, dry gorge valley lined with pines, dry lichens, and sandy soil, we came upon a secluded valley that was hidden on all sides by steep hills and dense woods. It was a prehistoric land left unto itself. We will make camp in this primeval place.

August 6

I have decided to call this area we have discovered the Unknown Valley. My reasons for this are that the valley may well have never before been traversed by man. This is because of its remote location. We walked over many treacherous windfalls, climbed steep, loose rock gorge walls, and cut through thick brier brush, as well as waded or swam through snake- and snapper-infested bogs and tarn pools to reach the spot. We entered by way of a steep gorge that was choked with dead fall trees.

Ajax and I moved or cut logs and branches. We struggled through tree log tunnels, finally coming into the unknown place. The mysterious valley is vast and surrounded by very steep walls, most of which have pines and some other trees growing almost vertically. I have observed some possibly undiscovered cycad-like plants. These primitive gymnosperms are descended from very ancient plants. The valley is circular in shape and may well have been formed by some cosmic impact, such as a meteor or comet. The place reminds me of an ant lion's concave, cone trap pit. This land that smells of sixty million years of stegosaurs, dimetrodons, and plesiosaurs living and dying seems itself to be a trap.

August 7

In our explorations today, we noted many odd and malformed plants, mushrooms, and lichens. I dog-paddled to the center of the dark cattail pond that we are camped near. The fishing line I use for depthing is three hundred feet in length and weighted. It reached its end never having given a sign of striking bottom. How can this be? While swimming to the bank, I saw an ominous dark shape. It surfaced as I climbed out. A moss-growth-covered snapping turtle, easily six feet in length, glared at my eyes then submerged. I have seen several insects that I cannot explain. A dark-red centipede, two feet in length, with massive mandibles crawled out of a rotting log and moved aggressively toward us. Ajax's barking and clawing of the earth sent it scurrying. An indigo metallic dragonfly three times the size of the largest-known dragonflies hovered over a black tarn pool. I saw a Jefferson salamander just short of three feet long surfacing and submerging in the reed pond near our camp.

"Oh my Dog there's a Griffin dragonfly! How magnificent. It lived 300 million years ago during the Carboniferous period. It's the size of an eagle. The prehistoric insect is flying in hunting lines grabbing and consuming what look like ten inch long cicadas. I've always wondered about the colors of its body. One cannot discern them from fossil evidence. The head and thorax are a brilliant, deep metallic purple. The abdomen shines like brightly polished golden armor. The Griffin dragonfly has appeared in my dreams many times, in many colors. Now it will appear in its true colors," Ajax looked to his human companion, astonished.

We have come upon an astounding place!

August 8

Seeing vultures circling, I took us in their direction. We hiked for some time. The terrain hid many muddy dark tarn pools. The thorny brush became impassable, and I hacked on with my machete. As we reached a small clearing, I saw a deer. We crouched to observe. To my amazement, a wave mist descended and enveloped the deer. The deer vanished from sight. A slightly-purple-colored ripple cloud then moved upward like a swarm of bees, Ajax and I walked to the spot. We came upon a patch of decomposing animal matter. I took a sample. The bones had been reduced to liquid. The brownish ichor was devoid of all traces of blood. Brown and white fur indicated these to be the remains of the adult deer. The animal matter seemed to have been digested. Hearing a rustling in the air above, I looked up, expecting to see the vultures. They were gone. I saw instead a strange purplish rippling effect, like heat waves on sand. The ripples moved in waves undulating in unison. They dove and swooped as flocks of birds do. I do not know what to make of this phenomenon. I am curious about these remains.

August 9

The cries of birds were ominous. A fog hung in the trees, transforming sunrays into long vertical pillars of shimmering haze. Deer flies and mosquitoes brushed by in hordes. Branches, roots, and vine-armed plants grabbed and tripped me as I advanced further into the swamp crater. And the smells. There was one overshadowing stench that permeated the valley's ether. It was a miasmic, fetid odor. It can only be described as a combination of the mold that overtakes rotting oranges, kennel offal, and swamp murk baking in the August sun. At times, the smell intermingled with the odor of a rotting corpse. At other times, a mushroom fungus scent wafted on the slow-moving damp winds.

I have made the most amazing and disturbing discoveries! After careful study of the tail part of the creature that Ajax detached in the horrific struggle, I have come to the conclusion that whatever the stingray-centipede thing is, it is at least an undiscovered species and, at most, not of this world. Within the sinewy structures of the spiked tail end are the elements ozmeium and uridium, which are found only in meteorites. Other unidentifiable elements were also present. How is this possible?

This came about as I was looking for the sargasso fungus. In a still, mossy spot surrounded by a black tarn creek and overhanging spruce pines, I came upon several ancient rocks. I lifted a moss-encrusted stone that was surrounded by gray mycelium growths of grotesque forms. The growths were from six inches to one foot in height. They possessed the singular qualities of sharks' heads with sharp pincers at either side of the mouth. The bodies of these ashy, spiderweb growths were long and tapered, descending in a cone to the hazy soil near the rock. Lifting the rock, I saw a dark shape scurry. It was this oily black thing that sent out an electric eel lightning-blue pulse when I flinched away. I lay unconscious for sometime.

During this time, Ajax had battled the fierce creature. He bit four inches of the thing's tail off in the battle. I could see where the beast had escaped, wounded, down a webbed dark tunnel. Ajax, miraculously, was unharmed, except for cuts and scratches on his muzzle and forepaws. I do not know how he escaped unaffected by the powerful shock of the centiray. Perhaps it had drained its power on me and was weakened. I'm just joyful that no severe harm came to my faithful companion.

Something about the deer that I saw vanish and the mysterious waves in the air struck me with curious wonder. I do not think it wise for us to remain in this valley much longer. And yet I am so intrigued by the wave mist and the ray creature that we must remain here a bit longer. I feel I must attempt to investigate these mysteries. How did the deer come to vanish? How was it consumed? What manner of bizarre and sinister animal is this stingray centipede horror? What is its purpose?

I have cleaned and disinfected Ajax's wounds. He seems okay. I will build up the fire so it will burn brightly all night. When at the pond getting water, I saw lurking beneath the surface, on the small sand shelf that rims the edge, a group of about thirty medium-sized shadowy horseshoe crabs. Since there are no freshwater horseshoe crabs, these must be some species unknown. I go to a troubled sleep. I have my machete and a lighted torch within grasping distance.

August 10

Slept. Woke three times. No signs of danger. Ajax is breathing normally. I walked the perimeter of the camp each time, hearing and seeing nothing threatening. I sit by the fire as the sun shines rays across this somber place. I have been contemplating my next actions and decided the following: (1) I must try to capture the centiray creature; (2) I must gather as much of the sargasso mycelium as soon as possible, as we will stay no more than two days longer in this valley; and (3) I will be on constant lookout for the wave-flock phenomenon, with much caution.

August 10, 12:00 p.m.

I was able to gather six sample bottles of the sargasso mycelium. This was taken from the area under the rock that the ray thing attacked from. I checked for signs of it and could find only some possible claw tracks in the mud. I kept my machete in hand and had a large torch burning nearby. Before I left, I replaced the rock. I also set up a box-and-stick rabbit trap, which I made this morning. I have weighted the box with several heavy rocks. This should hold the thing. I have a bottom for the box trap. Once the creature is inside, I will slide the bottom in place and secure it. Thus, I intend to transport the retched thing back to Haggamar house.

I came across the liquefied remains of what I believe to have been three large raccoons. These were on the far side of the pond from camp. Oddly, I saw no vultures. I dug a pit in the rear of my stick-and-reed hut. It will serve to keep the mycelium damp. I covered the pit with a large rock. I shall wrap the bottles in wet swamp grass and place them in the bottom of my backpack for transport. I have high hopes for the survival of this rare substance. We will eat and rest now as we will leave at first light, whether we trap the centiray or not.

August 11, 3:00 a.m.

Awakened by a horrific commotion. Went to the pond shore with torch and machete. Petrified, I immediately dropped to the ground and put the torch out in the wet mud. As my eyes became able to see in the dark, after their dark adaptation, I saw it all. A bear, but not a bear. A fierce creature much larger than a grizzly, with saber-toothed canines protruding from its mouth and a bone ridge running the length of its back clawed the air wildly. It looked to be a short nosed prehistoric cave bear from the Paleocene period. It clawed the air and made fierce sounds.

Then the real horror came out of the charcoal sky. It drifted down in a slow, arching swoop. The air smelled strong with its fetid scent—its scent of rotting oranges mixed with rotting flesh. The airborne predator's outline glowed an eerie purplish color. It had the translucency of a jellyfish. Its size was that of a whale shark. It has a beetle-like head with massive spiked mandibles on each side of its mouth. The large mouth is lined with rows of long needle razor teeth. It has no fins. The curved, sharp barbs of its deadly tail lash the air. It dives now hawklike. The upper half of the eighteen-foot-tall prehistoric bear vanish. The torso is left spurting blood; it drops. As the cloud beast ascends in a wide arch, I can see red blood and black fur passing along its digestive track. I hear a rustling, the sound of air meeting air, as it moves off to vanish into the ink of night.

From nowhere, from everywhere, a swarm of blue orbs appeared. They descended as an insect swarm. They varied in size, from six inches to two feet. Their appearance is that of a whirling pinwheel of blue flame. People call these light balls will-o'-the-wisps. They move over and dive down onto the remains. I hear whooshing, chattering. The horde of pinwheel lightning drifts as a fog out over the primeval pond. I stand and watch as their shimmer fades into the bottomless depths.

We waited for twenty or so minutes. All was quiet, and suddenly, millions of crickets began to sing. The moon came out from the night clouds. I took the extinguished torch in hand and headed back to camp. Ajax looked at me with a be-careful look as we walked. I feel dazed, bewildered, and fearful. We will gather our things and depart at first light.

As we neared the hut, I was overcome by a familiar odor. The air smelled of orange mold and miasmic tarn. I lit a dry torch using the fire. The fire that burned dangerously low. Cautiously, I entered the wood-reed structure. I saw immediately that the hut had been entered. It looked like an animal had ransacked the place in search of food. Broken glass lay strewn across the floor. Blankets lay about, torn and shredded. Food stuffs lay scattered. In an instant, I spotted the cruel blue shimmer of the centithing's eyes. It slithered from a hole on one side of the rock that secured the sargasso mycelium. The thing shot forth. I saw a black blur. It was upon me, tearing away at my right leg. Its ray-spiked tail lashed at my face. I was hit with a numbing, dizzying energy shock. My body quivered as all went dark.

August 15

We have reached home. I carried the valiant Ajax across my shoulders. He is greatly injured and may not live. I stopped to rest and care for him along the way. Ajax is covered with deep cuts about the muzzle, head, and his front legs and paws. He has several deep lacerations on his sides and hindquarters as well. He rests now. I have cleaned and bandaged his wounds. Minutes ago, Ajax opened his eyes. Although his look was forlorn, I saw a brief twinkle of victorious contentment in his brown-amber eyes. With nutrition and time, I feel and hope that he will recover. Were it not for my faithful, tenacious friend, I would not be here. Ajax fought off the primeval centiray.

When I awoke from the thing's shock on the hut's floor, I found two dozen or more of the beasts horseshoe crab leg pinchers laying in the much-disturbed dirt. Indigo blood was splattered on everything. Bits of oily black flesh and shell littered the floor. There was also much red blood. I quickly bound a six-inch gash in my upper right thigh. It cut perilously close to a main artery. I tended to Ajax's wounds. I managed to retrieve several things, including two unbroken sample bottles of the sargasso mycelium, and departed with my companion over my shoulders. My right hand was at the ready with the machete. The trek back was almost the end of us both. Without a compass, it may have been as it was raining for the four days of walking. I could not have navigated via the stars.

As I write this log in a very exhausted state, I have come to these conclusions regarding the centiray creature. I believe it to be, or to have been, the guardian of the spiderweb larva growths. Possibly the mother. I believe that these growths undergo metamorphosis to become the whirling blue orbs. The luminous, beetle-headed, air-shark organism that dived on the bear, no doubt, is the adult form of this mysterious, unknown predator. This is my current hypothesis regarding these highly specialized, vicious entities. I know not what species the thing falls into. I will keep one quarter of the sargasso mycelium. My purpose is to grow the mycelium. I shall use its spores to do this. The remaining one and one-half bottles will be sent to the university. As to returning to the Unknown Valley, I may not be able to find it again. I took no time to mark my trail. I think it may be best to keep my discovery of it and the horrific monstrosities that dwell within the primeval place to myself. My inner instinct is that some things and some places are not to be disturbed. That by intruding, an event or series of events could be caused to happen resulting in the disruption of the harmonic balance of nature forever. For now, I shall confine my studies of the swamp and its life to this general area. I will watch. Especially, I will watch the skies.

*   *   *

If this journal is a true account, then Dr. J. Handicot Jebson made some astounding discoveries. Prehistoric creatures, a Paleocene mammal, unknown insects and plants, and the centiray along with its hideous spawn, and airborne predators. Could this all be true? Could I explore and find this Unknown Valley? I wonder. I wonder, since these predators that drift and soar through the skies, and may also inhabit lakes and seas, I wonder, could they be from somewhere in the outland of the universe? Could the hundred-billion stars of a hundred-billion galaxies hold the seeds of these life-forms? Perhaps they came upon a comet. Perhaps they have fed off the 850 thousand people who vanish each year. I wonder how many animals disappear. Perhaps these creatures will outlast or outdo mankind.

Green Fire

The winter sky was the dark, dark blue of the distant universe. Stars illuminated it, as if trapped in a web. The crisp air and silence were what the new day would be made of. A large silver-winged beetle streaks across the backdrop of stars. It is seen in the southern sky. It travels from southwest to northeast. At its closest, it can be seen. The shape is as the front of a rocket. It looks like dark comet rock. Trailing from it is a tail of green flames. Sparks shoot from the shimmering stream. A gentle hissing can be heard. After it passes, the air and earth trembles in its wake.

"Come on, Robby, the bus will be here any second!" scolded Robby's mother, Mary.

"Okay, Mom," the fox-like youth answered as he sat down in the chair that once was his father's. The tattered wooden table creaked with age.

"Just peanut butter toast and cereal today, and watch for the bus. Did you hear that noise earlier?" asked Robby's mother.

"Yeah, Mom, it shook the whole house just when we were comin' in from running. I think it was from the thing we saw out over the lake. It looked like a comet or something," answered the brown-haired youth. Then yellow lights flashing, the school bus appeared, and Robby was out the door with a slice of peanut butter toast in his hand.

Everyone at Bobcat Middle School was excited about the thing that had streaked across the sky that morning. It was the talk of the hallways as students and teachers rushed about like three-hundred crickets with books. In Robby's first class, English with Mrs. Martin, the students spoke nervously of the unusual event.

"It rattled the windows in our house. My dad's mad because it cracked our front window," said Amanda Fugle.

"My dad says it was a meteor, and he works for the fire department," remarked a raccoon-faced boy.

"Yeah, they think it was a meteor or comet or asteroid, and it was very close. Wouldn't it have been cool if it crashed here? We wouldn't have school probably," said Billy Warner.

"Well, yes, class, something unusual and exciting happened this morning. I can see we are all very interested in the comet," announced the enthusiastic teacher, her bright-orange flowered dress rustling as she walked up and down the rows of desks. "My lesson plan for us today is to watch a film about ancient times because we are going to start reading a story called *Beowulf* this week. However, I see we have a good prompt for a free write." Most of the students groan. "So instead of beginning the film right away, please take out a pencil and paper, and I will write several thought questions on the board." Mrs. Martin began writing on the board, "1. This morning at my house, when I heard the loud rumbling noise, I . . ."

The hallways were a maze of ants jostling and scurrying to get to their next classes. Then the school day ended. Sunlight came slanting through the windows of the bus. The smell of fumes filled the air. Kids were yelling.

Oh no, she's going to sit here. She has to sit here. There's no seats left. Oh no! thought Robby.

"Hi, my name is Patty Gwenore," the frail elf-like girl said, sitting next to Robby.

"Oh, yeah, hi, I'm Robby Percivel. Your parents bought the big old house on the lake kind of across from us. You're in my first-hour English class and my sixth-hour art class." Robby looked into Patty's green eyes, a feeling like the one he got in his stomach after eating several chocolate bars welling up within him.

A wad of gum flew from the back of the bus and landed in Patty's hair. Robby turned and gave an angry look to the kids who were laughing. "Don't worry, Robby, I've been through this before. I will be okay. I have a blue belt in Tae Kwon Do. I only use it if I'm attacked," explained Patty. The bus stopped. "See ya," said Patty.

"Okay, bye, Patty," said Robby.

Soon thereafter, Robby got another new neighbor. *I like him because he's always with his dog, like Jib and I*, Robby had thought at first. Mr. Grey came to the town suddenly, having just taken a job at the middle school, teaching special education English classes. To his peer educators, Mr. Grey was a quiet man of uncommon thoughts and a wizard among teachers. He bought the small gray cottage next door to Robby's trailer house. Robby often saw the strange-acting man and his dog staring up at the stars in the wee hours. The teen thought it odd that this teacher knew little to nothing about lawn mowers, baseball, or cooking.

He owned a most curious and unusual dog. She was the size of a coyote. The creature had a broad chest, was well muscled, and was the straw-tan color of a coyote, with black stripes much like those of a tiger or a brindle retriever. The unearthly dog's glowing eyes seemed to see to one's very soul. Many shivered when they saw the striped canine and her companion approaching. People often crossed the street to avoid Mr. Grey's dog. After much observation from autumn through most of the snow months, Robby had many questions about the strange pair that lived next door.

While winter still held on in the time of the great March meltdown in Northern Michigan, Robby and Patty discovered something different about their neighbor Mr. Grey. They had hiked way back into the snow-covered swamp-woods of the Dead-Stream Swamp. For them, the swamp-woods was a refuge of enchanted primeval, where mist spirits lurked and owls told long-forgotten tales. The two, who thought very alike, had been hiking into the deep woods often. They walked with Robby's dingo-like dog, Jib, talking about unusual things. They discussed life on other worlds. They laughed and wondered if the universe went on forever or if animals could think as the snowdrift winds buffeted them and sun-glinting pines smiled at them.

"Hey, look, isn't that Mr. Grey and his dog?" exclaimed Robby as he looked ahead down the white road.

"Yeah, it sure is. His dog is the only one like that!" said an astonished Patty.

"Boy, I knew he walked, but he sure goes a long way," said Robby.

A shot cracked into the air like thunder. The shot knocked Mr. Grey back and down into the snow. The pair paused then ran, with Jib leading them toward the fallen man. As they got close, Mr. Grey's dog sat, watching them cautiously. Mr. Grey, who at first seemed dead, opened his eyes and sat up. Robby saw a hole in his orange coat. From the hole, a liquid like blood but not like blood trickled.

"Are you okay? What happened? Are you shot, Mr. Grey? What is that purple glowing stuff?" asked Robby, his voice filled with panic.

"I will be all right. It must have been a careless hunter. Maybe they shot at Watson because she resembles a coyote," reasoned Mr. Grey.

The sun faded as large snow flakes began to fall. The wind swirled them into cotton tornadoes. Patty, Robby, and Jib were just beginning to walk home when the hawk-faced Mr. Grey called to them. "Say, Patty, Robby, may I please speak with you both a moment?"

As they turned, he began. "The liquid that you saw, Robby, was like blood. It allows us to live a very long time, about two thousand of your years. Our purpose is too grave and the consequences too great, not to tell you of them," spoke Mr. Grey solemnly. Watson's gold-coin eyes stared at Robby, Patty, and Jib. "You see, we are not from your world. We have come from far out there." He pointed skyward. "We are here to offer the people of the Earth a place with those who dwell among the stars. Your planet is on the brink of great disaster. The current gaseous interference with your sun's rays will soon make life unbearable for mankind. My world is called Ellium, which means both 'wisdom' and 'happiness.' It is over two million of your light-years away."

The three walked several miles along the snow-covered sand road. Then they veered off along a remote path that got thinner and thinner, eventually turning into a deer trail. The snow covered their tracks. Watson paused and sniffed the air carefully. She then pointed to a spot where dense pines opened, revealing a ravine. The large ravine was filled by a vast expanse of windfall trees. The place gave off rays of desolate remoteness. They circled around along the edge of the mountain of fallen trees. The zebra-striped tan dog led the group into the mass of blackened trees. They passed through a long tunnel of roots and entangled deadfall. The tunnel turned into earth and grew too dark to see. The man from another world lit the way with a bluish disk.

After walking for a short time, they came to a dimly lit cavern-like area. The spacecraft was there. Immaculate and sinister. It was shaped like a giant cymbal. The color at the top resembled indigo blue armor. The metallic craft gradually turned to lighter blue shades lower down. The bottom edge looked like shiny teal blue armor. Mr. Grey had been telling the truth. The young pair gazed, amazement in their eyes. A seamless V-shaped portal slid silently open. They entered. The craft had walls that glowed with ambient emerald radiance. They walked through chambers of different colors—a somber-blue chamber, a violet room, and a soft-maroon area. The group seemed to be going in a spiral direction, swirling toward the center of the spacecraft. A large round chamber opened to them. Cheery green light radiated from the walls. Robby touched the glowing wall, "It feels rubbery," he said. Several curved seats flowed into the smooth control area, rising from the floor on a circular pedestal. There was a large screen that fit concavely into the wall. In the middle of the control area raised on another pedestal hovered a translucent ball the color of green flames. Silence filled the chamber.

The man from Ellium sat, looking at the youths, who were relaxing from their walk. "You have a trillion questions, I know. Please let me speak. I will not take long. I know you will need to be heading home soon. When I have finished, you may ask some questions. Thanks for being there to help me. We arrived not long ago. You know of the comet. Regardless of what was said by the news people, which was, I believe, that a meteor had passed about one hundred miles from here and headed up into Canada. It was said to have then crashed. No evidence of a meteor crashing has been discovered. You are sitting in the meteor now."

The questions went on for sometime until Robby finally said, "Hey, it's got to be getting late. Patty, we better get going. Our folks like us home before dark."

"Is that your real name? I mean, is Mr. Grey what you're called on your planet?" asked Patty as she stood up.

"No on Ellium I am called Galahote. Galahote means messenger, or go batween, like Mercury who delivered messages to and from the gods. Galahote is also the middle English name for Sir Galahad, the famous knight of the round table in King Arthur's castle," explained Galahote with a smile of pride. The two young listeners rose from the luminous blue floor, and after saying good-bye to their friend, began their long journey home. Then on a day when schools in the area were closed because of icy roads and deep snow that blew into three-foot drifts, Robby looked out of his bedroom window and saw strange men and official-looking cars. Plain white vans with small dish devices and antennas were also parked along the street. There were men dressed in military camouflage. *We've got to help Mr. Grey!* Robby thought as he called Patty.

"You should not have come," said Mr. Grey.

"There's guys. They're telling everyone to leave. They look like government men. We think they are after you. We came to warn you," exclaimed Robby.

"Yeah, did they come here, Mr. Grey?" said Patty.

"No, not yet, but I'm sure they will. I thank you both. You truly care about the future of your planet. I respect what you have tried to do. I must tell you that you have placed yourselves in great danger. These men may see you as a threat. These men may feel that you know things that they must keep from the public. They may not let you live freely any longer or worse." Mr. Grey paused, looking out of his big living room window.

"You mean, these men will hurt us? Maybe we should leave. Maybe they will leave us alone," said Patty.

"It is too late. Look outside," said Mr. Grey.

Robby, Jib, and Patty moved to the window and peered out. The plain-looking cars and white vans were parked in a semicircle surrounding the front of the small gray cottage. The vehicles were parked up and down the street as far as they could see. They looked out of the backdoor's window. Armed men in uniform crouched or stood in the swamp-woods.

"I'm sure we are completely closed in. I must go out and talk to them. You will please remain here in safety with Watson. Please do not touch the device on the table," the visitor from outer space said gravely, pointing to an opaque blue oval on the kitchen table. The device had three luminous buttons on it, one orange, one green, and the third purple. It did not look like it had been made on Earth. "If anything happens to me, you must say these words to Watson, 'Watson, Galahote Ullen Vesslo.' You must do this. Your world may be at stake. Remain inside this house, and you will be safe. Please repeat the words," explained Mr. Grey.

Patty and Robby repeated the words spoken by Mr. Grey. The man who was Mr. Grey but not Mr. Grey stepped out into the whispering snow and closed the door. A short burst of shots cut through the air. The messenger from space fell. Watson watched, her paws on a small oak table, to hold herself up. A group of men wearing SWAT-type body armor picked Mr. Grey's limp body up. They carried him to one of the white vans and placed him inside. The van and several cars drove away.

Galahote was taken to Maple Land Army Base in Central Michigan. He was placed on a stretcher and wheeled into a maximum security cell in the base's stockade. The stockade was constructed of cinder block walls three feet thick. The walls were reinforced with steel rod and two-inch-thick steel sheeting. Heavily armed guards were stationed inside and patrolled the stockade's perimeter.

The gray cottage gave off an unearthly glimmer. It had a blue aura. The military had tried everything they knew to gain entry to the structure. Diamond drills, cutting torches, lasers, and finally, the latest high-powered explosives had been employed. Nothing would dent or scratch the glowing blue force field around the little gray cottage.

Patty looked at Watson with hurt in her eyes. She said, "Watson, Galahote Ullen Vesslo." The two youths watched as the black-striped tan creature that was much more than just a dog went out the front door. The men surrounding the cottage were caught off guard. They froze then moved for the cover of their vehicles. They raised their weapons. Watson sat on the snow, glowing amber eyes focused on the aggressive ones. After a minute, she began to move off. The men unleashed a heavy hail of weapon fire. The shots made pinging noises as they ricocheted from a glowing blue force field surrounding the cosmic creature. Hand grenades and rocket launchers were used. These weapons had no effect either.

Watson paused and sat down again. Beams the color of blue ice shot from her eyes. A deep-blue light was cast upon the soldiers and their cars and vans. A shrill ear-piercing sound cut through the air. In an instant, the men and vehicles were reduced to smoldering whitish piles of ash. Watson drifted up into the cloudy sky. She vanished in a burst of speed, heading northwest toward the army base. In an instant, the dog from somewhere out there in the great cosmos sat majestically, looking at the back wall of the stockade building.

"Hey! What's that? A dog?" shouted one of the guards.

"It looks more like a coyote. Let me shoot it. I need the practice," answered another guard as he aimed his weapon at the tan creature.

Suddenly, Watson's eyes became a glowing deep-green color. Ice-blue beams lashed out. A gaping hole appeared in the thick wall. As the soldiers opened up on the heroic dog with bursts of machine gun fire, her head turned toward them with a slow, methodic robot motion. Cold blue rays surprised the soldiers. The men were reduced to small mounds of white ash. Watson entered the building. She cast a violet beam onto the metal case holding Galahote. It vanished. Galahote was encased in a translucent blue balloon-like force field, along with his rescuer. Together, they floated out of the stockade and off into the sky, heading southeast. Like vultures descending from the gray clouds, a group of gunship helicopters converged on the messengers from outer space. They began firing rocket missiles and machine guns at the bluish sphere. Watson's head moved mechanically in the direction of the helicopters. The blue rays touched one and then another, transforming each airship into rusty-brown haze.

At the same instant, six jet fighters, looking like silver-winged death moths, appeared.

There powerful missiles exploded harmlessly as they hit the shimmering orb. The guardian dog did not bother to release its rays of destruction upon them. Instead, the sphere and its occupants accelerated so fast that to the pilots, they seemed to have vanished. The front doors of the gray cottage opened as if by some ghostly force. Galahote floated in followed by his faithful companion. The doors closed. Galahote descended gently onto the soft living room couch. Patty and Robby watched in amazement as a beam of violet with small bright-orange lightning bolts within it came forth from Watson's eyes and encased the space traveler.

After six minutes, Galahote awoke. "Have you been harmed?" he asked.

"We are all right. Are you okay? We thought they had killed you!" said Patty.

"I'm fine. In a way, they did kill me for a short time. But none of that matters now. I regret any harm that has been done to save me. However, in the long term, the few harmed now could save many later," said Galahote. He got up and went into his bedroom. In a moment, he emerged, wearing what looked like a skin diving suit that was the same silver-blue colors as his spaceship. He went to the kitchen sink and drank three glasses of icy water. Encased within a clear blue field of protection, Galahote walked outside, Watson at his side, to address the large military force that had gathered at his doorstep.

"Men of Earth, we mean you no harm. We have traveled a great distance through outer space to bring you a message. We have learned much of your world by studying your radio and television transmissions. We have observed many of your peoples and customs by living among you for a time. It is not our purpose to judge you or your ways of life. We are here to offer you a place in the universal community. We live in harmony. In recent times, your science has progressed, and you have entered outer space. Eventually, you shall travel farther and farther out, reaching planets and galaxies very distant from your own. Your spaceships could be armed with laser or atomic weapons.

This we cannot allow. We ask that you join with us and live in harmony. The primitive warfare that you wage and the destruction you bestow upon your own planet are not our affair."

"Tomorrow this message will be carried telepathically to all of the people of the Earth. All mechanical devices will cease to function beginning at six in the morning, and they will resume functioning beginning at six the following morning. The purpose of this is to give people time to contemplate their future. No device shall be stopped that would cause serious harm to any living thing. If you choose not to join us, your planet will be encased within a force field. If you display aggression toward the inhabitants of the cosmos, all human life-forms upon the Earth will be reduced to piles of ashes," Galahote finished and walked back into the cottage, followed by Watson. "I know you have a trillion questions. I hope to answer many and tell you of such things as air-cars that need no roads and are powered by engines the size of oranges. And worlds such as Diveneaous, where the inhabitants can both fly and live underwater. Rest and eat whatever you wish. For your helpfulness toward Watson and myself, I offer you a ride in my spacecraft. Tomorrow we must leave," said Galahote. The three dined on bacon, eggs, and pancakes and drifted off to sleep. The ever-vigilant striped dog lay in her orange chair with a view out the front window.

Light snow swept the air as Watson led the group out into the morning rays. A blue force field surrounded them. Following at a distance were the officials and military men. They were on foot. It was after six, and the whole world had stopped. No modern weapons would work. Cosmic ray dispersion had neutralized their energy sources. The vanguards of colored metal beetles of all sizes and shapes that went scurrying about, puffing prehistoric gases into the air, stopped. The massive winged pterodactyls of man slowed to a standstill. Centipede trains stopped on their tracks. All the electric veins and paved arteries of the Earth ceased flowing. Watches stopped. Time became a snail.

People enjoyed the tranquil quietness. They talked and ate together on sunlit porches. They ran to lush parks with sleds or picnic baskets, laughing. Birds sang. Trees swayed in gentle breezes. In the evening, people prepared memorable meals in soft candlelight. Many shared food with those who had little or none.

As they walked along the familiar snow-covered road, they chanced to stop as a lone coyote looked out from some thick brush. He showed no fear. He looked into Galahote's eyes, then he looked at Watson and cocked his head. The group moved on silently.

"When will you return?" asked Patty.

"That, I must leave up to Watson," replied Galahote.

As they entered the blue metallic craft, green light enveloped them. Patty and Robby sat in soft control chairs as the ship ascended. In an instant, billions of stars became a kaleidoscope of colors before their eyes. They soared close enough to planets to see the surfaces. The two youths from Earth felt as if they had become celestial spirits. Strange worlds covered with purple forests appeared. They saw planets with endless orange seas and swamp worlds having primeval dragonflies eight feet long. Moons of blue, maroon, and silver gray revolved around Jupiter-like guardians. Nebulas, stars, comets, and much more were all a part of the space feast. The two youths sat happily, watching the sights of the cosmos.

Just as evening approached, the immaculate craft hovered down and settled on the frozen surface of the largest inland lake in the state of Michigan. It was a shimmering powder blue color. Patty and Robby departed. They watched as the silent blue dish rose straight up into clear skies. It hovered for an instant, casting light-blue rays forth, then sped off toward the great tapestry of stars, trailing behind it a comet tail of green fire.

The October Dream Machine

The bleakness of gray rain lay overhead when Timmy Lilly went walking in the six o'clock morning twilight. His faithful cattle dog walked at his side. The changing trees whispered lightly to him, like dark shadow ghosts. He had a small pocket flashlight in case he saw any glowing creature eyes or heard any ominous sounds. Raccoons in musty coats, whip-tailed possums, invisible skunks, and other nocturnal animals moved about in drying grasses and weeds, seeking day refuges. A lone owl's hoots echoed through the branches of ancient dark pinewoods. It is a time of things moving.

He had awoken early. Strange, vivid dreams of glowing green pumpkins, luminescent purple-orange bats, and obtuse, friendly ghosts had danced in his head all through the night. They had showed him things. Things from the firmament. Things that crept unknown under mildewed carpets of autumn leaves. Things from beyond the universe. Now, back in his wood-paneled mushroom bedroom, he took a piece of notebook paper from his school binder and drew pictures, alchemical diagrams that had come or been given to him in his dreams on that late September night.

The voice of a large-headed, fanged blue ghost, who called himself Marley, had said, "Build it, son. Build the fantastic, oblique, amazing thing. Take your time. Do it right. This is the way. Then it will show and carry and whirlwind you far beyond the edge of the swamp where the universe reaches out to red, violet, and green stars. Ride on purple comets with orange tails. Rockets are too slow, too primitive. Build the box, Timmy." The blue Marley ghost grinned and gloomy green light came forth in widening beams from his mouth. "Build the October Dream Machine tonight!"

The school day slithered along like a coppery skink lizard. When things got boring, Tim read tales of Edgar Allan Poe from a paperback he hid behind whatever textbook was in use. Rooster and hen kids bantered and pecked about him in dim, crowded hallways. Then suddenly, the dinosaur fumes of the roaring yellow bus machine left him near home in a small tornado of red maple and brown oak leaves. Tim inhaled a brown-sugary smell that floated on the wind. He flew straight to the spare room. The green room. Which was also his dog's room, although his dog seldom left his side.

Rummaging, dust, cardboard crunching, laughter, and "Here it is! Here is just the box! Perfect size!" His striped red-tan companion nodded in agreement. The twelve-year-old gathered and gleaned. Small Christmas tree lights, blue and maroon yarn, string, lots of batteries, a small electric motor cannibalized from a fan, magnets, a compass, cotton, red felt, peppermint tea, and a clear blue marble. Then they went out to the fall swamp woods behind the gray pre-civil war wood frame saltbox house where dry beetle wing leaves floated like butterflies landing on rustling, browning cattails. They gathered sticks of various odd shapes and sizes. Some cattail tops, dried by the autumn sun and covered with white puffy cotton like seeds. Tim and Qui-quag collected spiderwebs, mosses, leaves, cicada shells, and muddy pebbles that when washed would glow indigo or emerald. Into a paper bag the bizarre assortment went.

Then wind flying, Tim and his companion, raced to his room, their shadows close behind, to build the undiscovered incredible machine. Into his room, his island, his universe. A creature from the Black Lagoon model clawed the air. Pterodactyls, authentically painted, hung from thread, soared among gray plastic UFO models. The sun's ray's streamed in the windows and glittered as they danced over the room's ceiling Tim had painted with stars and constellations that glowed in the dark. A map of Middle Earth on one wall, the only picture. T im and Quequag settled in to begin building their amazing machine on the blue ocean wave carpet.

"What cha doin'? Are you working on some dumb school project or somethin'? What are you doin', you idiot?" asked Tim's sister.

"Nothing, April. Now get out, please. What I'm doing is none of your business. Like your perfumes, yeccck, and your hair spray and scented soaps and cute boys' names and all that girl junk is none of my business! You don't really care anyway. Now please leave. And close my door, please. Thank you, April," Tim finished, calming himself.

Slam! "Okay, okay, I get the message. I was just trying to be friendly like were supposed to be. But okay, be a brat! I hope your project or whatever it is turns out to be a hunk of junk and you get an E or 0 or something. You immature, moron, geekasaurous!" April left and walked back into her Miss Teen world.

He worked in a fever fury, using epoxy glue, the big scissors, blue tape, masking tape, watercolor paints, a yard stick, felt of midnight black and universe blue, green thread, a litter of sticks and twigs trimmed to precise measurements. "Ah, yes, the blue lights must go in these exact positions. The green ones here, here, and here. And the mystical stick and sinew dream catcher on top to pull in cosmic waves from the deepest abysses of the universe," Tim said to his friend. Reed stems and straw; choice red, purple, brown, and yellow leaves; and sapphire or emerald stones lay strewn in a puzzling array upon the carpet of blue.

"Timmy, dinner is ready! Time to eat!" a voice yelled from below.

"No, Mom, that's okay. I'll just have popcorn tonight. I have to finish something, a project. I'll eat in a while. Besides, my stomach is a little upset, and you know popcorn and milk always makes my stomach feel better. Is that okay, please?"

"Yes, but you really should eat. We are having hamburger and mashed potatoes, one of your favorites. I'll save a plate in case you'll want it later."

"Okay, thanks, Mom."

Some felt glued here. Cotton to deaden or block out all sounds. Lights here and there, always in threes, two green and one blue. Small Christmas tree lights, two blue on this side with one green in the middle. What was it the blue mist specter had said? "Always in threes, always do things in threes. Three is a supernatural, mystical, gateway number and more. Three is a number very highly regarded in ancient Chinese societies, particularly by monks. Three can lead one into and out of the corridors of time and space," the Marley spirit had said. Tim painted the sides of the box the dark blue color of outer space. He added special ingredients mixed in for strange purposes. "Will the magnets all move and rotate and line up?" the boy asked himself. A bend of some wire. Some solder connections complete. "There, I think that's got it. They will work now!"

A gentle wasp-wing hum filled the air. Tim's eyes lit up as the magnets circled exactly opposite each other. Other magnets rotated on axis or moved up and down. And well, by Dracula, by Frankenstein, by Wolfman, by Marley, it was done. Nearly done, anyhow. It still needed the finishing touches of sitting all night in an old wooden house—the older, the more haunted, the better. You know, blank dark eyes for windows, a gapping mouth door, creaking wooden attic, mice, bats, cobwebs, and ancient dust. Bats in soot-tunnel chimneys and doors that move. Cold spots. Still needed a solitary night in a haunted house fireplace. Not a stone or steel building. "No, that won't do," the blue specter had shrieked. Or a shack or a shed. Not a church abandoned for decades. Not even in the bell tower belfry. No barn, too many animal ghosts, headless chickens running about featherless and such. But a house!

Timmy would take his machine to the leaning relic called the Hermit House by some kids. A driftwood gray two-story house that seemed to vanish and reappear out of the swamp's dense fog. A vacant place said to have had no occupants since the civil war. That is, except for ghosts. Civil war soldiers; a forlorn widow; strange, mutant children; and dogs of ages past drift through its darkness, dogs still loyal to ghostly apparitions that had tread with them through life. It was way back deep in the Dead-Stream Swamp, with a bog pond for a foundation and owls and salamanders for guests. There, he would leave this enchanted contraption of autumn divine.

The Marley creature had instructed him, "Then on the appointed day, the day you'll know by the leviathan clouds, the yellow-green air and winds so strange they wisp the crumpling husks, the bits of the souls of trees into monster shapes that chase humankind into their caves to hide, on that day, eat the sacred food. The crumb of moldy cheese. The slice of underdone potato. And roasted pumpkin seeds. A bit of corn cob. A moonlight indigo flower. The soul of a deceased toad. But mind, have no hand in its demise. A turning rose. Some cattail roots. Sulfurous, tepid swamp water. Lastly, allow a woolly bear caterpillar to crawl freely upon your skin. Gaze at the green star of the west until it moves on. It's then that all shall be ready. Your situation is good. That day must be spent raking leaves with a rake of wood and bamboo. Inhale deeply of the reviving, rejuvenating, rekindling mossy leaf dust. Drink it with nose. Rub it with hands. A million passing souls wheeling by on cartwheel wind journeys to somewhere, not to oblivion, to somewhere in the far, wide, vast midnight-blue tapestry of space. To the ether. The fermentation vat of life and death. Take in the precious dust and save it for your dreams. And dreams you shall have, my lad. And dreams you have earned, my fine lad."

Tim was raking in the orange-amber light. Twilight leaves drifted down as circular swirling animals. The Marley ghost appeared from a leaf lion. "And, Tim, did you make the pouch? The leather bag filled with dragonfly husks and stag beetles deceased, with September-gone crickets, a pinch of basil, sage, and ginger. With peppermint leaves and tobacco and the most beautiful, to your eyes, of maroon, violet, amber leaves, the magic ingredients of fall drifting past. Did you make the medicine bag and fasten it mobile-like in the very center of the inside of the top of the device? I hope so, Tim. And using exactly the numbers of which I spoke? For this is the heart of the machine. The central pump of the dream machine. Double-check and double-think, my young mortal, for unless this sack of insect spirits and flavor is exact, the whole thing will be askew. Askew and off-kilter, and you would be harmed or disappear into the dimness of time and space. Your soul wisped off to an ancient planet of thunder lizards. Be exact in the construction and mounting of this skin leather pouch, or all is lost, my earthbound young friend," the blue fog apparition had insisted.

And the silken, sad, uncertain rustling of each purple curtain thrilled him, lulled him, unfurled him as he anticipated the trying, wearing, flying. *Had there been a full moon the night he dreamt of the making of this wonderful machine?* Tim thought to himself. *The night when in a misty dream swamp, the blue haze ghost, of Dickensonian dress, had risen in wavelets from a pool of tarn and marl. From black brackish waters. Then after his words and drawings in the air appeared orb lights,* Sleepy Hollow *will-o'-the-wisps. Other apparitions and creatures unknown. A giant sloth glowed reddish, a toad the size of a large stump sand tan with iridescent indigo spots. Thousands of shiny green beetles scurrying among the stars.*

Yes, there was a moon! I woke up and couldn't sleep. Qui-quag and I went out. A mysterious long-ago ether hung heavy in windy trees. Yes, a blue-white moon, it was a ghostly frigate, and at times it appeared to become a ghastly ghoul, a wolf, and witch. Yes, I went out under the rays of that Neptunian orb. Shortly after prehistoric ice age dreams. And dreams of sitting in a distant planet's cave, gazing at a fire. And gliding through pterodactyl eyes. It was after all this that the Marley spirit came.

Somewhere in my twilight world, the Marley thing entered fettered with chains, moaning with misery. "Look at the leaves," I said. At the mention of leaves, he gleamed, he cheered. He danced and glided along with the swirling, falling husks of summer past.

The ghost said "Now that the October Dream Machine is almost complete please, Tim and your wonderful companion, whisk it off way back into the deep swamp woods. Take it to the old secret haunted ramshackle cottage. Place it in the ghost chimney for the night and done it will be." With that the timeless spirit turned into orange and blue haze, then a flurry of deaths head moths, a black shadow short nosed bear, a purple and bright yellow striped velociraptor, and a ball of powder blue light, then back to the fettered haunt made of green haze. As the Marley spirit slowly dissipated Tim heard the words "Go now, go now," echo on the night winds. Tim and Qui-quag crept out of the house and journeyed way back into the Dead Stream swamp to place the Dream Machine in an ash filled ghost chimney where it needed to be. Qui-quag and Tim walked in four-o'clock morning darkness. A million mealy bug stars circled consuming cosmic dust, twinkling. Gray spirit mists crept among cattails and weeds. Mysterious clouds formed into leviathans drifting on the soft winds. The pair walked for miles back into the swamp-woods, down dirt road and trail. Then along an overgrown logging road cut back in 1809. At last, in dawn's first light, they came upon the hermit house. Thousands of frogs began chirping as Tim and his dog stepped into the bog water surrounding the driftwood gray place. Then up rickety, moss-covered stairs. To the fireplace, in the center of the main room. The boy ignored the dripping dark apparitions that looked on, some adorned in civil war garb. Tim reached in and picked up his machine. A dozen pairs of gold-coin ghost dog eyes followed them as they crossed the creaking porch. The driftwood boards of the house cried out to them as they waded away. Tim turned and said "Thank you."

As Tim raked the wondrous patchwork of leaves, he looked to the sky. He looked at the sky to be sure the clouds were right. There, pterodactyls, a plesiosaur bigger then six football fields, a stego, a towering winged lion, a goblin face, gargoyle images throughout. It was the day! It could only be the day. Day of the night that he would wear the machine of October for the first time. He raked and raked and raked filled tall brown paper bags with bright orange, yellow, and marron October leaves.

By late afternoon, Tim had built a wall of bags. "Well, it's not really a science class project," began Tim. He had decided to have dinner with his mom and sister so as not to raise any suspicions on this night of all nights. "It's more of just a fun project I'm working on. I might enter it in the science fair or something," he fibbed.

"What does it do?" asked his mother.

"It's sort of a rest machine. You know, like if you put on head-phones and listen to soft music or stuff your ears with cotton. Then wear a light shield mask and think calm thoughts, like floating on a calm sea or floating through clouds. You know, like a beta wave machine. It blocks out all negative stimuli, and you listen to your body's rhythm and relax. It sorta does that," Tim explained.

"I would like to see it sometime please, Tim. April said that you used some of my things without asking. Please try not to take things without asking. Then things like running out of salt, like we did last month, won't happen. My point is, Tim, don't take things I don't know about, please," scolded Tim's Mom.

"Don't worry, I won't. And I won't even put wet toilet paper in April's bed or salt her milk for telling on me. I really want to try to be a good brother," said Tim.

"Yeah, sure, you dork. We believe you, we believe you," April returned.

"Oh, come on, April. You're always so negative. Leave Timmy alone. If you have nothing good to say, then don't say anything please, April," cautioned Tim's mother.

As they ate, April and her mother talked about an upcoming high school play. Tim ate his beef, potatoes, and pinto beans thinking silently. He was thinking, *This obtuse ghost machine could do who knows what. Has one ever been tried? What if it could astro-transport my spirit to China, the Moon, Jupiter? Wouldn't it be worth it then? Wouldn't that be as good or better then traveling there by rocket? For one thing, rockets take too long. For another, they are too dangerous. Look what happened to Dad. He made the first flight to Jupiter. Jupiter, the destroyer. His rocket, the* Argo, *made it there in three years. He gathered images and samples. He saw amazing sights. His journey was cut short when the deep cold of eons of outer space caused a minuscule weakness in one of the vein-like rubber tubes of the rocket. Then a bubble. Then pop,* yellow ichor liquid burst forth. The spacecraft's blood congealed into rivulets and floated off into infinite indigo darkness. No more spaceship. No more Dad.*

Tim turned his thoughts back to the dream machine. He knew it would not be good to think about the past. *We'll see. We'll see what this amazing, secret, and wondrous machine can do! We'll try it, and then we'll see what we see,"* thought Tim. *And we'll see tonight!* Tim asked to be excused then took his plate and silverware to the kitchen and washed them. He went back out under the autumn creature sky and raked and raked. Twilight closed in around the boy and his companion, Qui-quag.

Night cometh. Tim remembered something the Marley ghost had said: "The thing is with the leaves you can hear things movin'. Movin' in the night. Movin' in the dark. Movin' through the fabric of time. Movin' in the universe." Tim climbed into bed. He kept his clothes on; he didn't know why. Qui-quag jumped up and lay against his leg. He placed the dream machine box where his pillow usually was. He put his head comfortably into the cushioned box. He pushed a yellow button on the left side of the box. The magnets began to circle and move. The green and blue lights blinked in mysterious patterns. "Everything will be okay, Qui-quag," Tim said, petting his friend.

Crickets chirped melodically as the youth drifted off into the land of the night. Tim slept. First, a soaring feeling. Then lights. Flashes. Orange, purple blue, then silver white. Then in some form, in some sea, he awoke. The dreamscape landscape was a Pennsylvanian period beach of 325 million years ago. Primeval volcanoes erupted in the distance. Giant dragonflies streaked through the air. Sunlight danced on the waves. But what was he? Had he changed? He could not see. Looking down, he saw no hands. He was bright-green algae on the water's brewing surface. Then some tailed, swimming microscopic thing of single cell. Now a long eel. Some fins developed, and he became a coelacanth. Then up through the evolutionary ladder he climbed. An alligator. Hungry, he ate fish and crabs. Then the alligator that was Tim drifted into sleep again, a smaller alligator resting at his side.

Next, whirling in a dream that was not a dream. In the vortex of a gigantic leaf tornado, then whirled out with terrific force, he came to rest on a leafy lawn. The place seemed familiar somehow. Tim looked at the turtle-green house. It was the house he had lived in for most of his grade school years. His loyal dog was at his side. Changed to a leaf dog all adorned in a chain mail of colorful leaves. Qui-quag looked up at Tim. "Where now? I wonder, where now?" she said with her eyes. Pumpkins sat on porches, triangle eyes irradiating orange light. Kids as ghosts, pirates, witches, and dinosaurs ran in whirling leaves. He picked up his bag. Glow worms wiggled in the grass. Silent fireworks filled the Halloween sky. Tim felt something behind him. He looked out from costumed eyes. It was his alligator tail. Tim looked down at himself. He was wearing the alligator costume his Mom had made for him when he was a third grader.

"Come with us, Mr. Alligator, trick-or-treat with us!" a skeleton boy called to him. And he did. The group of goblins, a witch, a pumpkin, and a skeleton ran and laughed. They raced from house to house, collecting their treats. The boy in the pumpkin costume scrubbed soap onto some of grouchy old man Cudgle's windows. The porch light came on. They ran. They lit a paper bag with squishy stuff inside, rang the doorbell, and disappeared as Ms. Miginty opened the door of her dark-eyed house. Pausing, the group refreshed themselves with chocolates and popcorn and candied apples. They ran, danced, and sang Holloween songs that they made up. Trees swayed, reaching out with ghost arms. Sweet, pungent piles of ash-orange leaves smoked in gutters on Olivia Street. All the while, the wind whispered above through dry husks of leaves. "It's autumn, Halloween, All Hallows Eve. The time crisp ghost spirits move. Summer's gone, and winter is near. Enjoy the night. Know one thing clear: Mr. October is about. Mr. October is here" was its message.

Then off to skeleton boy's house to enjoy their sweet booty. They played pin the tail on the scarecrow. Umbly peg with dried Indian corn, Star Toss with stars that lit up, unbury the dead, and finally, Timmy was blindfolded and given a broomstick to break a suspended giant pumpkin. When he hit it, luminous spiders, centipedes, shiny blue bats, and yellow pincer beetles showered down. There were chocolates adorned in costumes of gloom. Candy corn, peanuts, and licorice lay piled deep on the floor. A ghastly green pumpkin candy looked up at Tim and winked. He reached down, scooped it up, and put it into his pocket with no thought. Then the kids all went out for a midnight game of ghoul-and-seek. Tim and Qui-quag hid in some pine bushes and soon fell asleep.

The boy awoke. Looking about, he saw that they were no longer in the pine bushes. What had been was gone. He looked about, feeling dazed. "Ah, there you are, Qui-quag," he said to his friend. Her leaf costume was gone, as was his alligator costume. He looked up. The stars had changed. The Big Dipper was there, but in a much more northwesterly location than it should have been. He recognized other constellations and stars like Betelgeuse, but they were all rearranged, askew. Numerous shooting stars painted the indigo sky with their tails. The stars twinkled and shined as Tim had never seen them before. The air smelled of fresh earth, flowers, plants, and something wonderful, a sweetness that was new to the boy. Each breath refreshed him as no air had ever done before. A brilliant grinning pumpkin moon illuminated the strange forest about him. All was bathed in a tranquil blue-white light.

A blue haze enveloped the pair. The landscape undulated as if it were a giant turtle's back. Volcanoes sprang up in the distance, orange-red fountains of molten fire. Shadow ferns and horsetails grew before Tim's eyes, reaching hundreds of feet into the dimness. Winged gargantuan dragonflies darted and hovered in the air. Looking down at his hands, *What am I now? What have I become? My hands are now giant sloth or bear paws. Where are we now?* Tim wondered. He walked over to a lagoon nearby. He looked down at his reflection. "I'm a giant bear, a bear that walked the Earth a long, long time ago. A short-nosed bear, I think. At least I know I can keep us safe because I'm one of the most ferocious of the large mammals that ever walked the earth. But I sure am hungry again and thirsty, I don't know why."

With that, Tim crouched down and tongue-sipped the cool, refreshing prehistoric water. Qui-quag drank also. Standing and turning, he saw a glow off in the forest of ferns. He walked two-legged toward the orange light. Through massive pine trunks and towering cattails. Around lagoons that all seemed to connect in one long centipede lake. Large alligator-like lizards peered from the water or from beneath foliage as they passed. Night moths the size of platters hovered about. Cat-sized beetles shimmered green and purple as they moved slowly along. Thousands of primeval crickets sang to the blue moon. The bear that was Tim crouched and peered through some reeds that obscured the orange glow. He watched as bears, giant sloths, deer, rabbit, grayling fish, great proud beetles, and dragonflies with six-foot wingspans danced and flew around a primordial fire from the bowels of the earth. His bear self, sensing no danger, parted the reeds and stepped out. Qui-quag followed. No angry eyes looked at the pair. Tim, being adventurous joined in.

There was singing in strange animal, reptile, insect, and aquatic languages. The youth understood them through his bear ears. Large dire wolves bayed howls of joy. Mammoth blue crabs and sea scorpions swirled and sang of the seas. Centipedes the size of men undulated in the volcanic firelight. Rhinoceros beetles, stag beetles, and June bugs as big as dogs moved slowly and rhythmically to cicada songs that drifted down from the surrounding towering pines. The creatures feasted on sweet purple grapes, roasted potatoes, carrots, and many odd-shaped and colored vegetables and fruits unknown to the bear youth. Qui-quag ran in circles around her companion as she and Tim stopped to eat. Owls' yellow eyes aglow perched in tree bows. All others sat quietly. They all watched the moon. The majestic, fantastic, spectacular blue moon.

The fire cast the shadows of the menagerie of creatures onto the reeds and tree trunks encircling them. Stars gazed down and winked. A shimmering brook whispered and chattered. This lasted forever. At last into the circle strolled, slowly, regally a massive-shouldered, striped saber-toothed tiger. Tooth tusks gleaming, it lay down by the fire. Then into the inner circle hopped a rabbit minute and small, but bigger then big, not timid at all. It lay beside the tiger.

Out of the darkness of the prehistoric fern forest drifted the soothing chirping of millions of frogs. Closing his eyes, Tim floated off to sleep, as did the other creatures gathered around the ancient fire. Waking slowly into a new landscape, the boy gradually saw, as his eyes went through their dark adaptation, that he now lay in a cave mouth, on a bed of soft October foliage. A fire burned low to ashy wood ambers. Caterpillars having black fuzz on each end came forth from his bed place. Qui-quag eyed them curiously. In their centers were stripes of red rust. He recalled hearing, "These are the caterpillars that appear in late September. You are suppose to be able to tell if the coming winter will be long or short, warmish or icy frigid. The length of the reddish stripe is the indicator of measure."

Tim looked at his companion. She looked back at him. "What now?" was her look. Tim walked over to a small pond nearby. Now he saw himself as a cave-dwelling being. With long hair and a set of big sharp teeth. He had on a fur of some mammalian creature.

I'm a caveman, he thought. And he did many things as a caveman for he knew not how long. Made a spear, hunted prey, carved out a log boat. Ate roasted meats and looked up at the stars with his cave dog. The pair of night journeyers were whirled down the corridors of time. As they became bathed in torrents of lavender moon beams and whisked off by small tornadoes of swirling orange and brown leaves, the boy and his dog lived lifetimes in instants. From Pithecanthropus, to Australopithecus, Neanderthal, Piltdown man, and Cro-Magnon. A Viking berserker armed with a two-sided broad axe and wearing a helmet with horns. A knight all adorned in shiny green armor, wielding a magnificent sword with a blue sapphire in its pummel. Then aboard a tall ship of three masts, cutlass in hand. A Spanish explorer sipping clear water from a fountain of youth, matchlock firing piece nearby. A soldier in the king's red and blue, flash powder exploding smoke before his careful aiming eyes. A Confederate lieutenant, revolver in hand, riding a pale-gray horse. A farmer harvesting corn under an August moon. A World War One pilot in a double-winged plane. And on up the latter. Until they reached a place of great blue-white flashes, not lightning, but lenticular clouds causing bursts and flashes. Great atom splitting bursts bigger then Tunguska.

The sky darkened with dust. A megawinter began. Tim and Qui-quag crawled out from the ice cave. Tim could see his reflection in the ice wall. He had changed. Now his metamorphosis had transformed him into a being with a high forehead, large butterfly-wing ears, and big, deep thinking eyes. *A future man?* thought Tim. The landscape shifted before his eyes. Snow and ice melted into running rivers, streams, and ponds. Giant pines, maples, and horsetails reached for the orange sun. Fern trees grew everywhere. Flowers and marsh plants appeared. Small reptiles scurried and swam about. Carboniferous period insects crawled among twenty foot tall ferns. Eagle-sized dragonflies streaked through the air.

Night fell. Millions of color radiating stars twinkled, green, red, and yellow. Crickets sang. The maple-syrup-scented wind began to blow harder, sending dry fall leaves into the night. A moon like none Tim had ever seen appeared. As he looked at the deep blue moon, it began to descend. The Moon Man stood before the evolved youth and his dog. His face in ways resembled that of a saber-toothed tiger. His large body was like a giant willow tree. Blue light bathed him. He began to speak. His voice was wind whispering up a gray-bone hollow tree trunk. "I came down. I'm Mr. Moon descending from on high. I look about at what they've done, and I begin to cry." Night mist drifted across him.

Tim asked, "Oh, Mr. Moon, who controls the seas and surf and firmament. Which way today? What shall I be? Are you the master of my destiny?"

The Moon Man replied, "Sew your seed, reap your crop, whatever it may be. You float on waves of stormy sea. Become calm and look up to regal tree. The leaves ablaze, fire light in their eyes. Look with joy and let the leaves fill your ears with their whispers. With autumn frogs chirp, for white will surely come. Just pause in darkness, pause in darkness, and hear the crickets hum."

The Moon Man shot up into the stars. "I'm right above you now, Mars at my side, and Sirius, Betelgeuse is my gentle guide. I'll be down soon to look around and see what you have done. And where I walk, I'll tread upon corn just to have some fun," the Moon Man finished. His thin body of undulating willow branches with birch tree arms transformed into a four pointed star the color of deep-blue ocean depths and darted about in the sky. Then down, down again to stand before the child-boy's eyes. Around him in the primeval dimness Tim noticed other things moving, undulating, gyrating. A shadowy sloth giant with blue glowing torch eyes. Red-eyed fruit bats the size of condors. Deep-orange centipedes twelve feet long. A pinkish barrel thing with tentacles groping, lashing out from its center. A crawling chaos of obsidian black with purple glowing brain fissure gorges and yellow ichor eyes.

The wind traveled in current tunnels through the gloom maples above. Branches swaying, saying a hushed "October, October, October." The air was scented with dead things and Sasquatch and giant sloth bears. In the distance a leaf conch fog horn called luminous dinosaurs forth. Violet, glowing pale green, indigo shadows moved slowly, swaying and whirling around. A circle of fire orange pumpkins appeared above and began to swirl. The misplaced youth looked to the sky, that endless world up above, to get his bearings, for he knew his stars. He found the Little Dipper, which he called the spearhead. *It's pointing north, or it should be where I'm from. There's the red planet, Mars. It should be to the west of the Moon. The Moon should be a half-moon. And there's silver-white Venus. Gee, I've never seen her so bright, so bold, so big. And there's Rigel, and Cepheus, and Draco, Andromeda, Ganymede, Cassiopeia, Hydra, and Triangulum. The stars, planets, and galaxies all seem in the right positions to me. Yet brighter somehow. Not obscured by greenhouse methane fog. The stars how they would have been, should have been in a Precambrian, Mississippian, Devonian world. The Moon is not there, having stepped down. A world a bit off-kilter, a bit arabesque from the one that I once knew,* thought Tim.

The wind picked up now, becoming a shivering torrent. Giant scarab beetle, dimetrodon, and undulating serpent clouds hurried through the sky. Tim heard a shuffling of footfalls as tar black ankylosaurs-sized crickets moved into circle the perimeter of the creature menagerie forming around him. In the center of the circle stood an ancient gray tree. As Mr. Moon suddenly reappeared and looked at a spot before the tree, a fire sprang up. A green fire. Deep melodic bone flute music floated on the wind as the black armored giant crickets began their symphony.

"Did you bring the key? Do you have it about? For you will need such a key to go in and come out," asked the saber-toothed, glowing-faced figure.

"The key?" Tim had forgotten all about any key. *Had the Marley spirit mentioned a key? Yes, now I remember. He had. Something about the color green. Something I can't quite remember,* thought Tim. Tim had other things on his mind. Things that travel by night in the shadows of endless time and space. Qui-quag rubbed Tim's leg with her body. She looked up at him quizzically and nudged one of his pockets with her nose.

"What's it got in its pocketsees?" asked a giant grizzly bear.

"Yes, boy, you must have the key or you're done. Surely you brought it. Let's not end our fun," said Mr. Moon.

Tim became frightened. *Do I need the key to get back? Will these things kill me or something if I don't have the stupid key?* he thought. In a last-ditch attempt, he reached deeply into the pockets of his blue jeans. In his right pocket, he felt his keys with the green rubber frog attached to the ring. In his left pocket, he could feel peanuts, which he always carried for his loyal friend. Three small dog-bone biscuits were there also and something else. Something round. *What the heck is that?* thought Tim. He drew the object out. It glowed with an orange sheen. It was the green pumpkin he had picked up when the pumpkin piñata had broken ages ago. It winked at him. Suddenly, there was a great tumult. Dinosaurs and the rest grumbled and made sounds of great awe as three hundred multicolored eyes glowed in the green firelight.

"Ah, then you do have it after all. Good lad! Then you'll soon be off. Just tell me now, my boy, where is it you're wishing to go?" asked the Moon Man. A purple luminous man-of-war, very large, floated up near Tim. An eight-foot-long salamander, shiny, oily black with light-blue circles running down its ribs, crawled up near the boy and looked at him with questioning glowing red eyes.

"To go? Where would I like to go?" said Tim aloud. He thought, *Should I go home? Home to the shrew? Home to dolts who pick on me? What would Qui-quag like to do?* He looked at his dog. Her golden-brown eyes just looked back. "Well, I don't know if you can. I don't know if it's possible. But yes, I think so. Yes. I'd—we'd like to go to Jupiter," he said.

"My dear lad, if there's one thing you should know, one shining beacon to see through all eternity, it is this: nothing is impossible. Jupiter it is!" the Moon Man said all aglow.

"But how will we get there? How will we go on such a perilous journey 601 million miles away?" Tim asked.

"We? There is no we. "You and your companion can get there with ease. Just use your key. I'll show you now. It's simple. Here's how. Just walk to the tree. The tree over there." the Moon Man pointed to the mammoth-gray tree towering in flickering green light. "Place your key in its center and you're on your way, as well as your friend," said the grinning orb.

They walked to the ancient tree. Tim looked at his dog. She looked back at him as if to say "If that's what you want." He reached out and placed the pumpkin key into a small circle of beetle tracks in the shape of a face. A face the same as the one that appeared on the pumpkin candy key. Blue night haze poured forth from the lifeless branches. Glowing bright-green pumpkins sprang from the reviving limbs. A leaf tornado whirled the pumpkins into dark air. They formed a large circle, their faces aglare. Faces of beast alien creatures from the steps of the ages. All floating in air.

"Good-bye," echoed upon the mystical wind.

"But wait, wait please, who are you?" cried Tim.

"I am the gatekeeper of lost souls," a windy voice answered.

Tim and Qui-quag were alone. Alone in a deep forest. As the night fog lifted, a twilight house appeared. Gray driftwood. A tower room. Window eyes of eerie green. Rustling inky curtains. A large smoking stone chimney. They walked up creaking wooden steps and opened the rust-hinged door. The pair of travelers entered. As they stepped inside, the door creaked closed. A shaking, a rumble, and the great rocket house moved. Before he could blink, there out a window was the gas giant, Jupiter. The pair could see blue and green, in light shades, moving at varied speeds in bands around the gigantic sphere. The eternal-swirling red tornado storm rushed chaotically among the tranquil bands of color. The haunted gray house landed. Tim and Qui-quag walked to the door, the boy turned the Marley knob. It smiled and winked up at him.

They walked out into the Jupiterian night. They walked through a green fog. It parted revealing a Dickensonian street of the nineteenth century. A man with a stovepipe hat on approached the two newcomers. Tim noticed that he was well dressed. He had on a deep-blue velvet coat with blue spruce-green trimmings. He looked more familiar to Tim as he came closer.

"Timmy, is that you?" Tim's father asked.

"Dad, Dad, but how? Are you real or part of a dream I'm having?" Tim said, amazed. Qui-quag sauntered over to the man and sniffed first his shoes and then his hand. She turned to Tim and wagged her tail. This was a signal that she used to tell him that this person is okay. She then jumped up, putting her paws on the man's stomach. He petted her gently on the head and rubbed behind her ears, just as Tim's father used to do. The boy moved closer.

"But, Dad, how can this be? I don't understand," asked Tim, miffed.

"Listen, Timmy. We don't have a lot of time. I will try to explain what I can. However, much of what I say may, for now, be difficult for you to grasp. First, how are your mom and April?"

"Well, Mom's okay. She seems happy sometimes. Mostly when we do well in school. She gets sad when she looks at your picture and sometimes when we talk about you. April, well, she's just April. She is a teenage girl, and like her friends, she falls in love with singers, actors, and some boys at school. I try hard to be nice to her. And well, I guess that's it. Except we live in a nice house in a woodsy area, and Mom works very hard teaching English," finished Tim.

"Listen carefully, Tim, as you will be going back soon. You're the man of the family now. You will find a way to get along with your sister. It may take time. Help your mom by doing as she asks, please. Keep up with your Tae Kwon Do. Are you using three motions, like I showed you?"

"Yes, Dad."

"What belt level are you now?"

"Blue belt with a red stripe" Tim replied.

The street had become more crowded with people, dogs, and horse carriages now. Tim and his father moved into the entrance of a large house.

"Good, Tim. Why and how I am here, well, hang on, partner. It's as Charles Dickens said in his short story *A Christmas Carol*. I know it's one of your favorites. Remember the line 'If you hope to escape the path I tread, you must face this reclamation'? It is very important to the cosmic scheme of things. Contemplate it later. Ask yourself, escape to where? To what? Remember how people in the 1800s claimed to see spirits leaving the body, sometimes as specters and other times as orbs. We really do! Maybe we do something humans call dying. Maybe we simply evolve or undergo metamorphosis into our next form. As caterpillars shed their cocoons to emerge butterflies, we shed our bodies. It may be like reincarnation. We go through changes to other life-forms to help us grow and develop. For some, it takes more time and more lives spent as humans or different life-forms to develop. Some must tread the same path, even fettered, or worse, until they have been corrected, elevated. What I do know is one becomes truly free, free to roam the universe, or just to rest as a star and gaze about. I have traveled about the earth as a radiating orb. I have looked in on you guys. You're okay. The Myan calendars end on January the fourteenth. Sappho, the greek poet and oracle, foretold 'the ending of things as they are.' The Ancient Egyptians, Empedocles, Nostradamas, and others have predicted that some cataclysmic event will occur. There will be a catastrophe in January of the year twenty-thirty-six. You will have to prepare a survival boat to get through the great flood. Plan to live on water for several years. There will be small islands, then gradually new lands will emerge. Canine survivors and wolves will become hybrids as well as the raining species. That is all I have time to say. I wouldn't mention this to Mom, but I'm not going to tell you what to do, Tim." Tim's Dad paused.

"Dad, are their other places than this to go on planets?" asked Tim.

"Billions, Tim, billions. Planets of Earth time periods. The knights in armor days, the wild West, cave man days, you name it. There's planets with humans, plants, planets having alien life, and planets populated with amazing and dangerous beasts. I spend a lot of time on the carboniferous planets, but you know how much I love insects. You enter the house you arrived in and close the door to return home. Aim high and good-bye, Tim. Good-bye dear friend, Qui-quag. I must be off," said Tim's Dad. He transformed into a sil-very-blue sphere. An Irish setter and several English springer spaniel dogs, that had been his faithful companions in life, appeared from nowhere and also transformed into colorful spheres. They followed the bright-blue orb that was Tim's father up into space.

Tim paused to look down the antiquated street for an instant. Qui-quag nudged his leg. Tim looked at his patient companion. They turned and walked to the haunted house spaceship. In they stepped. The door creaked shut. And then he awoke, the some-what-older youth awoke. In that time of bees, cold, seeking withered flower pollen. In that time of great insect dying. He awoke his head in the dream machine. His dog lay at his side.

What day is it? he thought.

Just then, he heard his sister say, "Hey, idiot, you better get ready for school."

Quickly Tim got up and put the October Dream Machine on the top shelf of his closet.

After school, I'll put this in the dusty wooden box in the attic, for which only I have a key, he thought.

"Get your books! Mom's mad! Where have you been?" April said, entering the room.

"With Qui-quag in a huge pile of leaves," said Tim with a light laugh.

"Come on, dorkweed, or you'll get it worse. Mom's mad 'cause we didn't see you at all yesterday. We figured you and your dog went for one of your all-day walks, got home after dark, had your usual popcorn dinner, and went to bed. We were gone shopping for me for new school clothes. Anyway, popcicle head, you better get movin'. I'm tellin' Mom you didn't brush your teeth and your homework's not done."

"Come on, April, please don't. You know Mom's got enough on her plate as it is. I'll fix your bike. Come on, please," Tim begged.

April was about to kick Tim when she froze. She saw something new in her brother's unique eyes that were sometimes light blue, and other times changed to a green that seemed to see into one's soul. Something strange and powerful. Something enchanting. Something otherworldly, something of malevolent All Hallow's Eve. Something not cruel but gentle yet very powerful, like the eyes of a gray wolf sitting majestically, immaculately, sitting and just watching, watching, watching. April paused and looked more deeply into the eyes of her brother. She saw a deep, distant, primal green glow. Very small, very faint, but there just the same. A blue-green crystal star in the center of each green pupil. Within them were two-thousand years of Egyptian wisdom, millions of years in a Permian swamp, ageless wisdom the color of time. Her face changed to fear then wonder.

"Okay, okay, I won't say anything. You've changed somehow, haven't you? What happened?" she asked.

"Yes, April, I have changed. But we gotta go now. I just heard the school bus. Come on." Tim grabbed his books, and followed by Qui-quag, he went down stairs.

"Tim, didn't you wear those clothes the other day?" asked his mother.

"Yes, Mom, I'll change them when I get home. Have a good day. You stay, Qui-quag. Be a good girl. I'll be back soon. Here are three peanuts." Tim flew out the old wooden door into October, followed by his sister.

Sherlock Holmes and the Mystery of Bigfoot

The Journal of Dr. John Watson

Friday November 7, 2014

Most of the Autumn leaves have fallen. Between the barren branches the winds blow often and strongly carrying mysterious whispers from the cold north west. The seamen who traveled the great lakes in the 1700s called these fierce winds the 'Witches of November'. Sherlock Holmes gazed toward the lake of swirling white caps, then up at the eggshell white textured ceiling of our new 221B Baker Street abode. The sun's morning rays illuminated the wood paneled wall across from where the sleuth reclined on our soft green couch.

"I heard one of them again last night Watson, or I should say Bunny. The creature emitted a short shrill screeching whistling sound. A wild animal like cry similar to the warning sounds coyotes and bobcats sometimes make. That makes it two nights in a row. I feel that we must both be on high alert my good and loyal friend,"

Holmes exhaled and gazed out the picture window of our gray up north country cottage on the largest inland lake in the state of Michigan.

I think a brief explanation of our present situation, and the circumstances surrounding it is needed. Holmes now calls me Bunny because on May 19, 2014 he transplanted my brain into the body of a splendid German Shepard. When I died after falling into a pit trap made by Professor Moriority's cutthroats at the culmination of solving the Mystery of the Green Lights and the Banshee at Duckett's Grove Castle, the brilliant Sherlock Holmes had my body frozen and kept on ice. This was the early beginning of the process now called Cryogenics. My faithful companion had to wait until he had perfected the surgical procedure, and for the right technological tools to be developed before he could proceed. This is why Holmes was so long in bringing me back to life.

Unfortunately, or fortunately, my body, which was old and somewhat war torn, was not savable after I was thawed out. This is why Holmes placed my brain into the body of a magnificent two year old German Shepard. Incidentally the beautiful Bunny was scheduled to be put to sleep as she had a rare genetic brain disorder.

We now live in this 21st century because Holmes discovered the true Fountain of Youth in 1918. By investigating the accounts of several Spanish priests written during the conquistadors conquest of the Mayans, Incas, and other native peoples Holmes discovered that the fountain was in Michigan and not Florida as Ponce De Leon thought. After investigating the legends of native Indians and examining stone carvings left by the Vikings, as well as ancient cave paintings, my friend was able to locate the true Fountain of Youth. It is in this area. We now both drink water from the fountain of eternal youth!

I say this brain transplant is fortunate as now my health is perfect! My senses are greatly improved. I can see incredibly well in the dark. I can smell things ten to thirty miles away, at least, depending on the wind. My sense of taste is incredible. Perhaps best of all Holmes and I can communicate telepathically as Holmes has revived the ancient link between prehistoric man and canines that proved so vital in elevating man to where he presently is. Sherlock Holmes has also made it easy for me to record my observations by linking my brain telepathically to our computer. And well there it is then, here we are in the 21st century, a pair of 19th century mystery solvers.

"Elementary my dear Watson, I mean Bunny, sorry my friend old habits are hard to break," Holmes began. "Some facts we know about the mysterious beast called bigfoot are that he is both secretive and elusive. If he is shot he vanishes in a flash of light. He is seen most often in remote regions of forest, swamplands, and other secluded places. Often strange lights are observed in his vicinity. And, I think, most importantly, although we have bone or fossil evidence for every creature known to man, past or present, we have nothing that proves such a creature exists," I nodded my head to agree.

"In addition we know that these creatures can be extremely violent and dangerous. Nine hikers were killed and horribly mangled and mutilated in the Daytlov Incident in Siberia in

1954. The autopsies clearly showed that the fractured ribs, crushed skulls, and the odd removal of some of the hikers' tongues could not have been done by humans. Many of the victims had deep scratches and punctures on their forearms which suggests to me that they were trying to fend off a bear, mountain lion, or perhaps a powerful bigfoot. This group of young college students must have been frightened to death to have run out of their tent into the twenty below zero winter night, some clad only in under garments. One of the last pictures taken by one of the unfortunate hikers was of a large, dark, hairy creature emerging from behind a tree. Oddly the last picture taken was of strange, unearthly lights in the night sky."

"These strange lights are, I think, very important to solving the mystery of these upright walking hair covered simian like things Holmes," I interjected.

"Yes my dear friend, that is a very astute observation indeed!" said Holmes.

"Two Pennsylvania encounters have served to shift my focus of solving the mystery of these 'Sasquatch'. The first incident occurred on July 30, 1966 at Presque Isle. Four young people were ending their day of swimming and frolicking at a beach on Lake Erie. Upon leaving their 1969 Ford Mustang became deeply stuck in the sand. While waiting for a tow truck, which one of the young men hiked to get, the two young women and their male friend saw a strange purple-white mushroom shaped object come down from the night sky and land behind some trees and brush. Witnesses in town also saw the strange object. A policeman arrived on the scene and the young man walked with him to find the landing sight of the unusual mushroom shaped flying object. The women remained in the car. Soon the women saw a light like a large flashlight beam coming toward them from the woods. As they watched a nine foot tall hairy beast walked in the direction of the Mustang. They panicked, rolled up the windows and screamed. The beast banged on the car denting and scratching it and then fled. Large bigfoot like foot prints were found at the scene. This event, which was a 'Project Blue Book' case at the time has just been recently released to the public."

"In the second incident," continued Holmes, "an elderly woman living in a remote wooded area heard noises on her front porch. Thinking it was a pack of feral dogs that were around before she loaded one barrel of her six-teen-gage shotgun. When she stepped out onto the front porch an eight-foot hairy beast came menacingly toward the old woman as it stared at her with glowing red eyes. She fired and it vanished in a flash of strange light. Hearing the commotion her son ran to her aide. He was sur-rounded by six of these unearthly creatures. He fired on them with his twenty-two caliber pistol and they vanished as well. Quite mysterious my dear friend, what does this all suggest to you?" Holmes relaxed, and leaned back into the green sofa gazing over at me, then he looked out to the white capped lake.

"In a word Holmes, extraterrestrial that is what I think," I replied.

"Lastly I mention the Montana rancher who while out hunting saw a hovering craft that shot a weird beam of light to the ground. He reported to a sheriff that a bigfoot creature descended in the beam. As the eight foot tall creature approached him the rancher raised his rifle and just shot. Again as in many other occurrences of this type the hairy beast vanished in a flash."

"Curious Holmes, most curious indeed," I gave my companion a puzzled look cocking my Shepard ears to one side.

As darkness fell Holmes announced "The game is afoot Watson, I mean Bunny!"

"Of coarse Holmes," I replied.

I then followed the sleuth into the back bedroom. The room has a space-foam bed at floor level, a stackable washer dryer, a floor fan, and a small wooden chest of drawers with a green shaded lamp on it. The room is wood paneled with forest green curtains, like the rest of our new 221B cottage. Holmes took a corkscrew device with threads on it and inserted it into a small hole in the blue carpet. He turned it counter clockwise. Soon Holmes lifted a round section of carpeted floor up. He unscrewed the handle and replaced it in the top drawer. After we both climbed into the opening the trap door was put back in place.

We both slid along the polished oak tunnel, which was illuminated by small green lights. The opening at the end of this secret tunnel appeared. We both flopped out onto a soft bed of moss one-hundred feet below the Dead Stream Swamp. We were now in the Green Grotto as my friend calls this secret subterranean swamp cave. A small waterfall runs soothingly down one mossy wall. A pond with cattails and dragonflies is at its base. In the center, immaculate and shimmering is the space craft Pegasus. She is sleek and the color of shiny blue armor. Her shape is somewhat like an Indian arrow head, yet with the smooth lines of the head of a dolphin. Her front or nose is a clear indestructible material that allows us magnificent views of our surroundings.

In an instant we hover up at an angle and out of a section of swamp that opened above us. Holmes activated the Bellrow shield telepathically, a transparent greenish sphere appeared around the craft.

"Not even an atomic bomb can harm us now, my friend," said Holmes.

"How big can you make this protective shield Holmes?" I asked as these new inventions and the technology of this age are unfamiliar to me as yet.

"It can be expanded to at least the size of the moon, and perhaps much farther. You see Bunny, Zek, our friend from the universe of yellow light and energy that floats just above our universe stated that in time one could develop their brain's power to enlarge the shield to be the size of most planets." Holmes chuckled and continued, "It is to bad that the piebald species, that upright walking ape, mankind has not yet advanced far enough to utilize such a device for peace and to better his condition," commented my companion.

"Now my dear friend it becomes a waiting game. We shall hover here, cloaked, and see what appears. If I am right we will soon detect the craft that the 'Bigfoot' use to get around on Earth, as well as to travel through outer space."

A smile briefly altered the eagle beaked face of Sherlock Holmes as he glanced at the Earth globe that hovered over the control panel of the

Pegasus. The seas on the globe are dark blue for deep water and lighter blue where the oceans and lakes are shallower. The land masses are browns and greens. This is a new invention of Holmes'. He calls it the 'Alien Finder'. The device, which is controlled telepathically, detects otherworldly space craft by identifying elements not found on Earth, and by the shapes of the objects.

Suddenly an eight sided mushroom shaped ship that emitted a purple glow appeared in miniature over the Alien Finder. The odd craft is right behind our new 221b abode!

"Look Bunny to the south," Holmes said in a soft voice.

As we hovered a mile north of our place the mushroom shaped craft emitted a pale, hazy conical shaped light beam. Amazingly a hairy creature, at least nine feet tall descended to the ground within the strange light beam. Holmes and I watched in astonishment on a screen as the alien being skulked around in the swamp-woods behind our cottage.

The clear glass like section slid silently back and clean swamp-woods air wafted in surrounding us. I smelled the stench of rotting fish and goat pen wafting on the southerly wind, the bigfoot smell I thought. The howl of this unearthly beast rose from below. Within seconds howls came from each side of the creature that had descended from the purple craft.

"It is as I suspected Bunny, there have been bigfoot aliens hidden in the cattails and woods behind our abode for some time! They seek, I think to do away with us or take us to their planet. I believe these beasts are highly telepathic. I also believe they have read our minds from afar and consider us a threat to them and their horrible business. For it is my contention that these bigfoot aliens have been, for at least thousands of years; taking humans to their planet to use as slave laborers, and possibly to eat."

"Shocking Holmes, quite shocking! I said aloud.

"We have learned much my friend. The alien finder indicates an ionic vapor trail that comes from an Earth like planet four light years away in the Alpha Centauri star system. The condition of the vapor trail also indicates the mushroom craft took four days to traverse the distance of twenty-four trillion miles, that's pretty fast. The Pegasus being much quicker can be there in the blink of an eye," Holmes explained. We watched the view screen as the three hairy intruders made their way below the mushroom shaped craft and were absorbed up into it by the beam of eerie light

"The game is afoot my good friend Bunny! We must be off."

The clear canopy slid into place around and above us. The alien ship shot off to the west in a blur of purple light. We followed. The craft came to a stop and hovered over the old Mickilson Ghost Town, a deteriorating lumber town and mill that was deserted in the nineteen thirties. The light beam descended down and engulfed one of the driftwood gray buildings. We watched, astonished, as within the beam twenty dark human forms were drawn up and into the mushroom ship.

Suddenly stars of red, blue, and green passed by. All at once they became streaks of color. "We will travel at their pace Bunny. This is a good time for you to enjoy the wonders of outer-space. Our destination, undoubtedly, is an Earth like planet located in the star system Alpha-Centauri, which is four point two light years from the Earth. I call this planet Voord. The word Voord was first used by Vidor Viking and refers to the giant, hairy, odious beasts that he and his men encountered in the new world. In 1005 A.D. the Vikings mined copper in Michigan's Upper Peninsula. The copper was a secret medal that helped to make Viking swords indestructible. Many of their runic accounts carved in large rocks tell of fierce battles with these giant beasts.

As we gazed out at the vast cosmos Holmes said "Bunny if I should doze off and the red craft, that on the screen represents the bigfoot ship should veer off coarse please wake me. There is plenty of food and drink in our galley. Would you like something now?"

"Some tea and biscuits would be nice Holmes," I replied.

These my friend got for me before closing his eyes. Beethoven's Sonata Number 14 in C sharp minor "Moonlight" played softly soothing us both. Of coarse I would not sleep while Holmes did.

The Journal of Dr. John Watson
Wednesday November 12, 2014

I had been sleeping when Holmes slowed the Pegasus near the planet Voord. In my dream I was running through an unending field of tall dry grass. Every once in a while I came across blue China plates with perfectly roasted chickens on them, which I ate. I awoke to the smell of honeyed bread, eggs, and ham coming from a silver bowl near me.

"Thank you for the ham and eggs Holmes. I must have dozed off, sorry. Where are we?"

"We are a bit more than 24 trillion miles from home my friend," said Holmes.

"Amazing Holmes, simply amazing, do you think we will have a great deal of trouble with these brutes Holmes?"

"Yes indeed my friend, I fear these waters run deep, deep and very, very dark. There is more to these bigfoot beings than I first imagined," said Holmes.

Before us is a Jupiter sized blue-green planet. It has three orbiting moons, one the size and coloration of the Earth's moon. Another is three times as big and a shimmering green color. The third moon is the size of the Earth and emits bright purple rays. Saturn like rings of light blue and pale orange surround this giant alien world.

"I have a plan Bunny," Holmes began, "we shall follow the decaying ion residue trail and descend, we shall become visible yet remain protected by the shield. We will see what we are up against and act accordingly."

I cocked my head to the left and my now brown eyes met his green eyes. Usually Holmes's eyes are a soft, serine blue-gray. I knew he was about serious business when they turned green.

"You know what they say about plans Holmes," I said.

On our coarse of descent I saw that the terrain was like that of Earth's Carboniferous Period 345 million years ago when reptiles and insects evolved, coal swamps formed, and shallow seas began to withdraw. The surface is a deciduous, conifer strewn swampland of very over sized trees and plants. Pine trees stand a mile high. Giant hundred foot tall cattails were everywhere. Brilliant, shimmering green and blue armored dragonflies ten feet long hover and fly between the immense cattails hunting their prey. Monarch like butterflies the size of pterodactyls flutter near us inspecting the Pegsus. I could see giant beetles and sixty foot long dark red centipedes weaving in and out of the ferns and plant life below.

We leveled off and hovered a mile away from a vast escarpment. The rock walls of this raised land are about three miles in height. We followed the ion vapor trail. In the center of the plateau sat a very large Mayan temple like structure. Brilliant blue rays glinted off the indigo colored stone the temple was made of.

Holmes guided the Pegasus to a hover near this seemingly ancient structure. We were greeted by an astonishing sight! In front of the Mayan like temple of indigo stone hundreds of bigfoot creatures walked about. Bigfoot children and adolescents played running and dodging about among their seven to eight foot tall parents. On the sandy ground large bright blue gourds, purple giant pumpkins, and other unearthly fruits and vegetables were laid out. Most of the creatures had brown fur just like the fur of grizzly bears, others had the same fur as black bears, which is often mixed with brown or gray. Some had reddish fur and averaged six feet in height. Holmes and I also spotted some immense beasts that had both the white fur and the twelve foot height of polar bears. We noticed that all of the other bigfoot quickly moved away from the white ones. These were the same kind of bigfoot aliens we had seen behind our cottage. Suddenly a group of twelve humans appeared at the end of this market square farthest from us. They were being whipped with some horrible cat-o-nine tail whips by three of the white beasts. Many had been bloodied on their backs and shoulders.

"This we cannot allow my loyal friend, I am planning on descending, are you with me?"

"Of coarse, look there Holmes, they have seen us." I said pointing off to our port side with my left paw to where several of the bigfoot creatures pointed up at us and jumped about in an agitated manner.

The bigfoot aliens scattered as we came lower for all to see. Holmes set us down to within twenty yards of the humans who we saw being beaten. There we sat as hundreds of angry red eyes stared at us in sheer astonishment.

Two of the white bigfoot began to approach us. They both hit the Bellrow shield at about the same time. One fell to the ground while the other was buffeted back as if it had run into a wall of quivering jelly. They both got up and began to flail away at the translucent green orb with their whips. After about ten minuets of this they both walked back to the humans they had been guarding. One of them approached the stone temple and began to ascend the steps.

Shortly after the white simian being disappeared into the top of the stone structure one of the mushroom shaped craft rose from an apparent opening at the top of the temple. It gave off a purple-white glow and made no sound. Holmes and I watched as the mushroom ship came to a stop directly above us.

First the craft fired red beams Holmes thought to be high intensity particle beams. After ten minuets they switched to what seemed to be a kind of sound pulse cannon. Finally the pale white beam came down around our craft. It may be, as my friend conjectured, a tractor beam that can raise or lower things. In any event none of these weapons had the least effect on the Bellrow shield. Frustrated by the failure of their weapons to harm us the occupants of the purple craft landed thirty yards from the Pegasus.

Three of the gigantic white furred beings came out of an opening and walked toward our shielded craft. We could see that one of the beasts stood at least two feet taller then the two monsters at either side of it. They stopped twenty feet from where the shield began. All three of the big-foot aliens grinned revealing grimy shark teeth.

"Why are you here?" This came to us both telepathically. We knew instantly that it was the tallest beast speaking.

Holmes addressed him, "We have come to free the humans and to make sure you will take no more people from our planet Earth," stated Holmes flatly as he looked directly into the eyes of the beast.

The tall one looked at each of the creatures
at his side. As he turned back I saw that his eyes
glowed as red as ambers in a fire. "We see that
you have great power," began the tallest bigfoot,
"therefore we will allow you to take your people.
We will no longer visit your world. Your technol-
ogy has made you so weak, human, that I know
you would not do the honorable thing and face
me in unarmed combat," he grinned wider show-
ing more of his filthy shark teeth.

"Oh no now the blighters done it," I
thought.

"Yes Bunny he has, be on guard please I am
going to meet his challenge!"

"Don't trust the brute Holmes," I said in
earnest, wishing I had my trustee Webley. Teeth
and claws will have to suffice.

Holmes walked through the transparent
green shield. I was at his side. As we expected
the three massive creatures lurched at us when
we got ten feet from them. Holmes jumped and
got in a good front kick to the leaders stomach.
I was able to jump and tear out the throats of
the other two beasts before they knew what had
happened. They both reeled back and away from
us. Holmes jumped up and between the arms
of the fourteen foot white monster. He landed
a fierce blow to the throat of the thing. It reeled
back and fell backward. As the white furred alien
bigfoot lay on the ground brown blood ran from
its mouth. As it breathed its last breath the fallen
giant saw that his two guards were dead.

Sherlock Holmes had gone a bit slower on
our return trip. We had several large green Belrow
shield orbs in tow with us. It had been exciting
and astounding to observe the cosmic sights.

As it turns out the bigfoot who lived on planet Voord were peaceful. They promised Holmes that there would be no more taking of humans from Earth. These creatures, who communicated telepathically; informed us that the largest white ape had ruled over them for two-thousand years. The white bigfoot came to Voord from some unknown planet. These native bigfoot were happy to remain on their planet and live in peace. They forced all of the remaining white bigfoot to leave in their space ships. Holmes gave them the secret of the Belrow shield that it may keep their planet safe from further invasion.

"Here is an interesting headline in the Resorter newspaper Holmes. It begins as follows: Authorities around the globe were both amazed and speechless as thousands of people who had been missing, having disappeared recently or years ago; have suddenly reappeared. Mysterious large green orbs have also been reported in the skies in the areas where these missing persons have shown up. Well there it is then Holmes all seems right in the shire again then."

"Yes my dear friend I quite agree, and I am also very glad you enjoyed your first real journey into the cosmos," My companion said as he settled in for a rest on our green couch.

About the Author

Tim is a native of Michigan. He graduated from the University of Texas at Dallas where he earned a Bachelor of Science degree in Generic Special Education, with a secondary teaching field of English. Tim holds belts in the martial arts of Chinese Seven Star Praying Mantis Kung-Fu, Tae-Kwon-Do, Isshinryu Karate, and Judo. Tim learned most of his Judo from the first woman Black Belt in America. While teaching on a Potawatomis Indian Reservation in Michigan's Upper Peninsula Tim got his Indian name, Wabi-Wagash or Little-White-Fox. He is a member of the Wolf Clan, and his warrior color is blue.

Tim's father Robert Veryzer designed the Sting-Ray Corvette as well as pioneering the Hover-Craft. He was also the head of the General Motors Styling Division. Mr. Veryzer taught Design at Perdue University before retiring.

Tim's cousin Tom Veryzer played Short-Stop for the Detroit Tigers, Cleveland Indians, White-Sox, and the Cubs.

Some of Tim's favorite authors are Rod Serling, Ray Bradbury, Edgar Allen Poe, H. P. Lovecraft, Charles Dickens, Jules Verne, H.G. Wells, Edgar Rice Burroughs, Sir Arthur Conan Doyle, and Mary Wolstonecroft Shelley.

Tim is a great lover of dogs. He grew up with English Springer Spaniels that his parents had flown over from England, and had a wonderful Irish Setter named Strider for a companion. He rescued a stray dog that looked like a coyote with zebra stripes on his way to school one morning and named her Watson. Watson helped Tim to create and compose short stories on their many walks back into the Dead-Stream Swamp.

Tim now walks with a magnificent German Shepard named Bunny. In Dutch the name Veryzer (Verijzer) means 'Teller of Truth'. Timothy, of coarse, means 'one who honors God'.

.

CPSIA information can be obtained
at www.ICGtesting.com
Printed in the USA
FSHW02n1912060618
48862FS